Pufnstuf
& Other
Stuff

Pufnstuf & Other Stuff

The Weird and Wonderful World of Sid & Marty Krofft

DAVID MARTINDALE

BOOKS

RENAISSANCE BOOKS
Los Angeles

For Sid, Marty, Puf, Joy & Siggy

Library of Congress Cataloging-in-Publicatlon Data

Martindale, David.
    Pufnstuf and other stuff : the weird and wonderful world of Sid & Marty Krofft / by David Martindale.
        p.   cm.
    Includes index.
    ISBN 1-58063-007-3 (pbk. : alk. paper)
    1. Krofft, Sid, 1929- . 2. Krofft, Marty, 1937-
3. Television producers and directors—United States—Biography.
I. Title.

PN1992.4.A2M37   1998
791.45'0232'092273—dc21
[B]   97-51752
                                                                          CIP

Printed and bound in the United States of America

DISTRIBUTED BY ST. MARTIN'S PRESS

Acknowledgments

It is one of my biggest pet peeves as a reader: picking up a book about a TV series, only to find the author did not speak with people who made the TV show he wrote about.

I want more than that. I want more than mere rehash of broadcast dates, character names, episode titles and plot summaries. I want more than rewrites of previously written magazine and newspaper stories. I want to learn something new and fun and provocative. I want to get inside the heads of the people who created, produced and performed the work that is so special it merits having an author write its story.

And because, as a reader, I want all of this, I would never dream of offering other readers anything less. That is why I am so indebted to the people who assisted me in the writing of this book.

It obviously is possible to write a book about the lives and work of Sid and Marty Krofft without their assistance. But it wouldn't be this book. Sid and Marty are two of the kindest and most generous men I have ever met. They literally opened their doors to me. Whenever I needed their help, they graciously and patiently made time for me. They shared countless stories. They answered any question, no matter how trivial. They made archival photos and material from their files available to me for publication in these pages. They introduced me to other people who played vital roles in their story. They became my friends. So I mean this literally:

Without their assistance, this book would not be.

I also wish to thank the many members of the Krofft television family whose insights and anecdotes breathed life into the telling of this story: Jean Anderson, Sharon Baird, Billy Barty, Ruth Buzzi, Joy Campbell McKenzie, Tony Charmoli, Robin Dearden, Bob Denver, Louise DuArt, Caroline Ellis, Wesley Eure, Allan Foshko, Ron Harper, Billie Hayes, David Levy, Patty Maloney, Barbara Mandrell, Chuck McCann, Maureen McCormick, John McIndoe, Jim Nabors, Susan Olsen, Donny Osmond, Butch Patrick, Jay Robinson, Si Rose, Van Snowden, Lennie Weinrib, John Whitaker, Jack Wild, Fred Willard and Ray Young.

Thanks also to Joseph Barbera, Michael Blodgett, Cassandra Peterson, Alan Rachins and Amy Yasbeck, who shared their stories about Krofft TV.

Thanks to everyone at Sid & Marty Krofft Pictures, Tracy Anderson, Dina Boyington, Todd Messegee, Randy Pope and Bill Tracy, who put up with my breaking the rhythm of their daily routines, and to Deanna Krofft Pope, Kristina Krofft, and Kendra Krofft, Marty's daughters, who are incapable of telling boring stories about the family.

Thanks to Bill Morgan, co-author of *Collector's Guide to TV Memorabilia: 1960s & 1970s* (Collector Books), perhaps the foremost expert on collecting Krofft memorabilia, for sharing his thoughts and photographs. Thanks to Jonathan Rosenthal of the Research Services Department of the Museum of Television & Radio in New York.

Thanks to Ann Abraham and Ginger Adams of the Family Channel, Deborah Diamond of Nickelodeon, and Ed Backes, Caroline Mendoza and Karen Reynolds of the Sci-Fi Channel.

Thanks to Brenda Scott Royce, my editor and a valued colleague, who championed this book all the way from proposal stage to print, Deborah Daly, who was responsible for this book's spectacular cover, and Susan Shankin, who designed the interior.

And, for her patience, thanks to Celeste, who need not read this book, having heard me tell every notable anecdote contained in these pages.

To all of you, as well as to anyone I have inadvertently omitted, I offer my sincerest and most heartfelt thanks.

Contents

Marty Gets the First Word

I would like to first thank David Martindale for his passion, talent and the many months he spent writing this book.

My brother Sid is probably the most special and talented person in my life. After reading this book I know why I'm exhausted, but hopefully this is just another beginning for us. It is very rewarding and also painful to be an independent company in the entertainment industry, especially today.

I am reminded how many fabulous people helped us through the years. I know if I mention a few of my most favorite people in life, both personally and professionally, everyone will understand: Trudy Bennett, Christa Krofft, Deanna Pope, Kristina Krofft, Kendra Krofft, Randy Pope, Taylor Lee Pope, Karson Krofft Pope, Van Snowden, Paddy Blackwood, Pat Davis, Al Tenzer, Rolf Roediger, Bill Tracy, Cynthia Asherson, Joseph P. King, Shelly Schultz, Lennie Weinrib, Si Rose, Allan Foshko, Billie Hayes, Jack Wild, Johnny Whitaker, Billy Barty, Tony Martin, Cyd Charisse, Mario Casilli, Joe Cassini, Fred Silverman, Bernie Brillstein, Michael Eisner, Dr. Stanley Josephs, Dr. Myrion Shapiro, Greg Carmock, Dina Boyington, and especially Ma and Pa.

MARTY KROFFT

H.R. Pufnstuf: The Krofft brothers' answer to Mickey Mouse.
SID & MARTY KROFFT PICTURES.

Can't Get Enough Pufnstuf
...or the Return of
Sid and Marty Mania

They never won an Emmy. There is no star bearing their names on the Hollywood Walk of Fame. They don't even rate a listing in *Who's Who in America*. But there is a generation of thirtysomething adults for whom no introduction is required.

If the names Sid and Marty Krofft don't ring a bell, it's likely you didn't spend your childhood watching Saturday morning kids shows during the height of the Krofft television era in the 1970s.

For the multitude who did, though, *H.R. Pufnstuf* (1969–71), *The Bugaloos* (1970–72), *Lidsville* (1971–73), *Sigmund and the Sea Monsters* (1973–75), *Land of the Lost* (1974–76), *Far Out Space Nuts* (1975–76) and *The Lost Saucer* (1975–76) now endure as cherished childhood memories.

They grew up watching the Kroffts' trippy Saturday morning shows, programs that blended flesh-and-blood actors with life-size puppets, catchy musical numbers and psychedelic color schemes, resulting in a unique brand of eye and ear candy never before presented in the form of children's television.

Yet compared to such pop-culture icons as Walt Disney, Jim Henson, Hanna-Barbera and Chuck Jones, the anonymity of the Krofft brothers still is largely intact. Indeed, at least on one level, Sid and Marty Krofft would have made ideal spokesmen for the American Express "Don't leave home without it" commercials. "You may not know me but . . . " they could say, flanked by Pufnstuf, Sigmund Ooze and a menagerie of other far-out characters they created.

"Most people I know don't even know what I do for a living," says Sid, the duo's colorful creative force. "When I meet new people, they say, 'What do you do?' 'Oh, just hang out.' I mean, I don't want to freak anybody out. So they have to find out on their own. Even at the gym where I work out, there are people who don't know what I do, who I am, and I've been there for thirty-some-odd years."

Most people may not know their faces, but as far as their names are concerned, that's another matter—at least for that still-loyal audience of former youngsters who the brothers originally catered to. Virtually any show bearing the "Sid & Marty Krofft Television Productions" logo inspires fierce devotion from these fans, even though they know next to nothing about Sid and Marty, the men.

It's also worth noting that closing any of these programs with the logo—the one with the funky rainbow-hued sunbeams—is grossly redundant. So distinctive were the look and the feel of these programs that the so-called "Krofft Look" is still as readily identifiable on TV as a Jack Webb drama or an MTM comedy.

"What's amazing to me still is the impact that our kids shows have had on all these young people who have grown up," says Marty, the younger of the two brothers by nearly eight years. "It's like we've somehow become a brand name today. It's been pretty exciting in recent years to discover just how many fans we still have across this land."

Says Sid: "It seems so strange that I can hand somebody my credit card in some faraway place and, wherever I go, people just totally freak out when they see my name on the card. It's pretty wild that it's continued all these years. It's fantastic, the feeling of people reacting that way."

Truth be told, that precious relationship between artists and audience dates back many years, to a time long before the brothers were first approached in 1969 by NBC executives about creating wholesome original programming for their younger viewers. In fact, the story of Sid and Marty Krofft goes back five generations and across the Atlantic—to the first Krofft puppeteer, living in Greece, who began to work wonders with sticks and strings.

Yet *H.R. Pufnstuf* is the work that became Sid and Marty's signature piece and it therefore qualifies as a logical focal point when telling their story.

It was the first of their many distinctive TV shows and, as is the case for many of their viewers, *Pufnstuf* has the most cherished place in the hearts of Sid and Marty Krofft.

As Marty puts it, "Like I always say, 'He's our Mickey Mouse.'"

If comparing Pufnstuf to Mickey Mouse—one of the most widely known cartoon characters in the world—seems a tad conceited, well, so be it. After all, it's undeniable that *H.R. Pufnstuf* did for the Kroffts' careers what Mickey did for Walt Disney's. "*Pufnstuf* was our first show that we put on TV," Marty says, "and I guess we hit a bull's-eye with it."

Did they ever! The show's title character, an enormous dragon-like puppet character with a monstrous yet endearing appearance, was the mayor of a fantasy land called Living Island, where everything (trees, houses, even the forces of weather) was alive. The show's ongoing story involved a youngster named Jimmy (Jack Wild). He had been lured out to sea by a whacked-out witch (Billie Hayes) who aimed to get her hands on Jimmy's golden flute, a magical instrument named Freddy that could actually talk.

That's when Pufnstuf ("who's your friend when things get rough?") and the other inhabitants of Living Island stepped in. They befriended Jimmy and countered Witchiepoo's sinister schemes by protecting him until they could find a way to send him back home safely.

"All the other shows that we did," Sid admits, "were in a way just variations on *Pufnstuf,* stylistically."

Other Krofft shows were often similarly themed as well: kids getting lost in some fantastic, at times even frightening, otherworld.

"That's the classic story, isn't it?" Sid says. "I mean, you're going on the adventure, as a kid, and all of a sudden something happens and now it's, 'God, when's he going to get home?' That became the great concern. It could be a little scary and I think that was part of the attraction. I mean, look at *The Wizard of Oz*. Look at all the movies Disney put out. They would scare kids, but kids loved them.

"Grownups today, when they approach me, they say, 'My God, you used to scare the shit out of me with the Sleestaks [bipedal lizard people in *Land of the Lost*].'

Jack Wild, Marty Krofft, Billie Hayes and Pufnstuf at Planet Hollywood in October 1996.
PHOTO BY BILL MORGAN.

"And even Witchiepoo. Witchiepoo, as silly as she was, she scared kids. Because they loved that little boy so much—and even the flute was their friend, Freddy the Flute."

Many of the Kroffts' subsequent shows also showcased the same psychedelic, almost hallucinogenic sense of color that had been established on *H.R. Pufnstuf*.

"I just love color," Sid says. "And my art director, Nicky Nadeau—who was with us for so many years, all through the successes that we had with all the television shows—he loved color too. I was just crazy about Technicolor in the '50s and '60s. Those great musicals. So that's where all that color came from. Color makes people happy. Color makes you smile."

Marty puts it a different way: "I like to think of our shows as being living cartoons."

Indeed, in a way, these weird yet wonderful shows were like adolescent acid trips, which in part explains why they were so enormously popular on college campuses. It was an era of drug-culture experimentation and, as far as many college-age viewers were concerned, tuning in was synonymous with turning on.

"We used to get more mail from college kids than we did from little kids," Sid recalls. "In a lot of the dorms, it was like the thing to do on Saturday mornings: get up, get stoned, probably, and watch *Pufnstuf*."

Even though Sid and Marty maintain they are anti-drugs, there still is no question that they created some of Saturday morning TV's strangest brew—particularly the trippy trilogy of *Pufnstuf, The Bugaloos* and *Lidsville,* their earliest three series.

The Bugaloos and *Lidsville* were just as far out as *Pufnstuf,* at times even more so. *The Bugaloos* was a peace lover's paradise, relating the story of a teenage band of rock-'n'-roll insects ("flying high, flying loose, flying free as a summer breeze"), while *Lidsville* chronicled a boy's wiggy adventures in a magical land of living hats ("everyone who comes to Lidsville really flips his lid").

As Billy Barty, a frequent Krofft series costar, puts it: "I don't know whether Sid and Marty belong in *Who's Who* or not...but somebody ought to put them in *What's What.*"

Good point. Because it's almost as if the Krofft brothers went out of their way to make Saturday morning TV the weird place to be.

"Well, you know," Sid says, "weird's not such a bad thing."

Nevertheless, after those first three shows, the Kroffts' creations underwent some subtle yet significant changes. Although still a little warped, their programs began to display less of that dreamlike sense of psychedelia.

That's due largely to changing times, as the hippie days of the '60s had begun to fall out of fashion. "I try to stay with the times constantly," Sid says. "You know, you can't just look back and say, 'Oh, my God, the '40s and the '50s and the '60s. *Those* were the best times.' I mean, it was great in the '40s and the '50s and the '60s. But that's not where we are any more. You've got to stay hip."

'And i Will Take You on a Trip'

Not unlike the way rock-'n'-roll fans have been known to hunt relentlessly for hidden messages in the lyrics of Beatles tunes—some of which were genuine, while countless more were "discovered" by listeners with overactive imaginations—episodes of *H.R. Pufnstuf*, *The Bugaloos* and *Lidsville* have also been known to be misinterpreted.

Even the names *Pufnstuf* and *Lidsville* were culprits. Weren't they not-so-subtle references to smoking marijuana?

No way, Sid and Marty emphatically say... and then they start to hedge a little.

Truth be told, Sid and Marty tend to get a little evasive whenever the subject comes up. Like savvy showmen, they see no reason to eliminate part of the mystique that surrounds these early programs: If some viewers choose to interpret the programs as drug symbology, well, so be it.

Says Marty: "There might have been some double meanings there, but that's for the audience to figure out. But some people, they hear the name *Pufnstuf* and they're immediately thinking about pot. In a way, I think that's what *they* wanted it to be about."

It's the same way with *Lidsville.*

"When that came out," Sid says, "there were people who just automatically assumed, well, a lid of grass. But a lid also means a hat, a top. So who knows where we were at that time, where our minds were? We were just trying to be hip. That was a very hip period, you know."

The Krofft brothers aren't so playfully vague, however, when asked if drug use was an ingredient in their creative process.

"A lot of people ask us if we were on drugs when we made these shows," Sid says. "Sometimes I tell them we *were* high—high on life—because life is the greatest drug there is. But we never, ever, did anything like that. These shows didn't just come from smoking a little pot."

Adds Marty: "I can guarantee you I wasn't on drugs. I don't believe in that. But our shows were so psychedelic, people thought we were. You really can't create anything like that on drugs. That's kind of a fallacy."

Jack Wild vividly remembers being somewhat mystified by college-age fans who took *Punfstuf*'s seeming drug-culture symbolism to heart. Whether such symbolism really had been planted in the episodes or was merely misinterpreted by viewers, he says, that's for Sid and Marty to answer, not him. But as far as he was concerned, "H.R." did not stand for "hidden references."

"I didn't know a great deal about the drug culture then," Wild says, "and I would hear from these guys who were saying, 'Hey, man, I really dig your show. I talk to the trees and the mushrooms too.' And my reaction to that was, 'What the hell are they talking about?'"

Marty is quick to note that, even though the reputation endures to this day, not once did anyone at the networks question the material. "We might have had some other thoughts in the thing, but at the time the networks definitely didn't pick up on anything and nobody ever objected. As a matter of fact, I think they liked it that our shows were so unusual."

But if drugs weren't a factor in inspiring the Kroffts to create such far-out fantasy worlds, what was?

"Well, I guess we have a few nightmares and then we wake up the next morning," Marty says with a laugh. "Actually, the truth might seem a little boring, but, well, we wanted to do something that would stand out and be unique. But trust me on this: You can't create this stuff stoned."

Maybe so, but the theories abound. And "evidence" like the fact that Sid was adamant for so many years about not revealing what the letters H.R. stood for merely served to feed those theories. "People are always wanting to look under the rugs," says Sid, who now claims that H.R. is "Royal Highness" turned around. "I mean, man's pretty curious."

At least one thing is certain: If a druggy subtext was encrypted into the episodes of *Pufnstuf*, *The Bugaloos* and *Lidsville*, it was done without the knowledge of the writers and directors.

Says Lennie Weinrib, who wrote all seventeen *Pufnstuf* episodes: "I used to have a couple of drinks with the guys, but I wasn't into drugs at all. It just wasn't my thing. It wasn't my generation. And the two guys I wrote with: Bob Ridolfi on occasion may have done a little grass and Paul Harrison was older than me and he wasn't into anything of that nature.

"So as far as I know about the writing, we weren't told to—nor did we—put in any secret things that people should look for. If anybody found anything, it may have been something that Sid suggested that had some double meaning and he didn't tell us what it meant. But there's nothing that I know of. 'Hand-Rolled Pufnstuf' is the best description of what 'H.R.' means that I ever heard. But Sid always said he's never going to tell anybody. He used to always say he was going to keep that a secret till his grave."

Adds Tony Charmoli, director of the *Bugaloos* and *Lidsville* episodes: "I had no idea that message was coming across and I never saw it in the scripts. The man writing the scripts was so unlike that, I don't think he would even know what it meant. So I have no knowledge of such references ever being deliberately put in. If I had been aware of it, I would have certainly offered to help."

The last word on the subject comes from Weinrib: "One day Sid and I were talking and he said, 'You know what everyone says the name Pufnstuf is, don't you?' And I said, 'Just a funny name of a character, right?' And Sid said, 'Oh, Lennie, you're so square.'"

That's why, although they still weren't conventionally grounded in reality, the bulk of Sid and Marty's subsequent shows weren't quite so brazenly *un*conventional.

The rest of the Krofft canon:

Sigmund and the Sea Monsters explored the friendship between two adolescent boys and a lovable sea monster who had been cast out by his own kind because he didn't want to scare people.

Land of the Lost related the story of a father and his two kids, a modern-times family that had become trapped in a *Jurassic Park*-like land before time.

Far Out Space Nuts and *The Lost Saucer* were both on the spacey side, literally—the former chronicling the adventures of a couple of reluctant astronauts, the latter involving a pair of extraterrestrial robots named Fi and Fum.

And yet another Krofft program, *The Krofft Supershow* (1976–78), introduced young viewers to an array of exciting serials that included *ElectraWoman and DynaGirl* (women reporters turned superheroes), *Wonderbug* (a talking dune buggy), *Dr. Shrinker* (an evil scientist who turns kids into miniatures), *Magic Mongo* (a bungling genie) and *Bigfoot and Wildboy* (a boy and his Sasquatch as environmental crime fighters).

Given the wide range of material, the fact that the Krofft name has become synonymous with drugs, at least in the minds of some viewers, is somewhat unfortunate and very unfair. After all, the most important common element of all—far more significant than the druggy overtones of the early shows—was that, for all their weirdness, there was an inordinate amount of intelligence in them as well.

Sid and Marty Krofft have never believed in talking down to their audience.

"I always felt that you don't put the child down," Sid notes. "Children don't want to be treated like children. They want to be treated like adults. And you want the adult to watch it with the child. That was the idea of those shows, that kids could enjoy it on one level, but Mom and Dad got a laugh out of it too because there were all these crazy things in there. We had funny writing, with clever jokes and double meanings. It wasn't ring around the rosey all the time.

"It's not hard to entertain a child. It's very difficult entertaining an adult."

Adds Marty: "There's a big spin coming out of Washington these days about making shows for kids that are educational. But I find it, personally, very difficult to believe a purely educational show is going to get the audience they want. When a kid is at home wanting to watch television, the educational show isn't going to be what he chooses.

"That's why I think the shows we did are of more value. We wanted to be entertaining totally, but we wanted to be responsible. So what we did was we made shows that were not purely educational—they were definitely *not* educational—but the values of who we are seeped into the shows. So I think our shows, with what's going on today, are a positive addition to what they're all talking about."

Simply put, Sid and Marty never intended for *Pufnstuf* to serve as video babysitter. They were far more ambitious than that and, as a result, many fans have never really outgrown Krofft TV.

By the same standard, can you imagine kids of the '90s having the same passion when they become thirty-year-olds that they have now about *Barney & Friends?*

Sid certainly can't. "Not that or anything else out there today," he says. "They're not going to remember anything. What's out there that has made such an incredible impact? *The Power Rangers?* That was all about kicking somebody in the groin. I think it was so weird that little kids were subjected to something like that."

Pufnstuf and company made such a lasting impression because there was something of genuine substance involved. But *Pufnstuf* was also important for another reason, one that viewers probably rarely take into account. Thanks largely to the success that began with that first series, a mini Disney-like studio was born and flourished.

The Kroffts' production company—which ultimately employed more than one hundred sculptors, artists, cartoonists, animation engineers and creative talent—branched out in numerous directions. Not only did they create a spate of other popular Saturday morning kiddie fare, but the brothers also crafted a feature film follow-up to *Pufnstuf* and produced a number of prime-time variety shows, including such hits as *Donny & Marie* (1976–79) and *Barbara Mandrell & the Mandrell Sisters* (1980–82) and such flops as *The Brady Bunch Hour* (1977) and *Pink Lady and Jeff* (1980). They tried their hand at producing movies: *Side Show* (a 1978 TV movie), *Middle Age Crazy* (1980) and *Harry Tracy, The Last Desperado* (1982).

And the Kroffts, who had designed attractions for the Six Flags theme parks, even had their own Disneyland for a brief time. Billed as the world's first indoor, high-rise amusement park, the World of Sid & Marty Krofft opened for business in 1976 in Atlanta's Omni International magnastructure, the site of what is now CNN headquarters. It closed less than a year later, hardly what one might consider a successful business venture. But true to Krofft form, few who attended could call their visit ordinary or commonplace.

This all occurred during a fabulously fertile period in their lives, a decade that practically belonged to the Kroffts. But one can't always stay on top and, in the '80s, their star power began to fade.

The Kroffts never were completely out of the picture, thanks to series like *Pryor's Place* (1984–85), *D.C. Follies* (1987–89) and a reprised

What a Bunch of Characters!

When it comes to office security, people often rely on alarm systems or guard dogs. Marty Krofft merely put a Sleestak on duty. So when people visit the offices of Sid & Marty Krofft Pictures, they first have to get past the Sleestak, a giant lizard man from *Land of the Lost,* that stands guard outside. Also out front are Tasha, the baby dinosaur from the 1990s version of *Land of the Lost,* and the heads of Cling and Clang of *H.R. Pufnstuf*'s rescue racer crew.

Some fans are astonished to learn that these character costumes—items that would be put in glass cases anyplace else—have merely been propped up in the room outside the Kroffts' offices, unprotected from damage or theft.

"Let me tell you something," says Deanna Krofft Pope, the oldest of Marty's three daughters, who works in the company. "We live life on the edge every day. Pufnstuf is in the accounting office. But he's not standing. It's just his head is over here. It's laying on top of our filing cabinets.

"One day, one of my dad's dogs ate Pufnstuf. The dogs come into the office and they work with us and one of them ate the extra Pufnstuf suit that was made. It was very sad. Pufnstuf was in pieces. It was repairable, but we were all in a little bit of trouble for a minute. I guess because we didn't have Pufnstuf up high enough. This dog can get into anything."

By the way, the dog, an Australian Shepherd mix that Marty rescued from the pound, is named Tasha.

Land of the Lost (1991–92), but their reputation as industry heavy hitters was no more. Their glory days, it seemed, were behind them.

But then a curious thing happened. More than a quarter of a century after *Pufnstuf*'s premiere, Sid and Marty mania began to make a major comeback.

"It's amazing," Marty says. "It just goes to show that if you live long enough, all this stuff comes back."

Indeed, the dry spell was over because all of the kids who were so captivated by Krofft TV in the 1970s—the same crowd that had transformed *The Brady Bunch* and *The Partridge Family* into pop-culture icons—still wanted their Krofft TV.

Sid and Marty Spend a Day in the Park

"It was ahead of its time."

Oftentimes that phrase serves as rationalization for a flop, but Sid Krofft might be on to something when he eulogizes the short life of the World of Sid & Marty Krofft, a spectacular indoor amusement park.

Located in an Atlanta high rise, the Omni International magnastructure, the park opened for business in 1976 and literally was one of a kind.

Says *Far Out Space Nuts* star Bob Denver, who attended the gala opening: "The best thing was this enormous pinball machine where you could ride around inside the ball. It was amazing. I mean, they had stuff that nobody else would ever dream up."

Like Delta's Flight of Fantasy. A highfalutin name for the escalator that carried parkgoers to the entrance, right? Well, not once you consider that this one-span escalator—which took people nine stories up until, as Sid puts it, "they ended up in the clouds"—was verified by the *Guiness Book of World Records* as the world's longest escalator.

Or like the Crystal Carousel, a three-tiered mythological carousel, made entirely out of crystal. "It was so beautiful," Sid says. "And you wouldn't believe what people did. They would want to take their clothes off and ride on it."

The park cost about $16 million to build. Remarkably, it didn't seem to hamper the Krofft TV empire in any way, with *Land of the Lost* in its third year of production, *Donny & Marie* in its second year and *The Krofft Supershow* about to launch.

"It was a crazy time," Sid says. "I remember I used to just drop in on the set of one of the shows and, boom, I'd have to go over to the next one or

One of the earliest indications of a Sid and Marty renaissance was in February 1995, when American Cinematheque paid tribute to the brothers with a gala retrospective of their work called "Can't Get Enough Pufnstuf: The Return of Sid & Marty Krofft." The event, held in Los Angeles, was a standing-room-only sellout, as was a follow-up show in July.

tend to something that had to do with our park. But we had great crews and, once a show starts running, it's like a Broadway show. You don't have to be there every minute of every day. It runs itself."

Some who visited the World of Sid & Marty Krofft complained that there weren't enough thrill rides, but it's safe to say that no one would call the place boring.

"There was entertainment everywhere," Sid says. "It was like a renaissance fair. And there was the Pufnstuf ride, dark rides and shows everywhere. We had a little Lilliput show. That's where little Patty Maloney had her own show. It was called 'The Lilliput Follies.' And there was a puppet theater where we had one of our puppet shows. It was awesome. It was the most awesome, innovative place ever."

And it also was a colossal money loser that closed its doors before a year had passed.

"Do you know why it didn't last?" Sid says. "The city had promised us to clean up downtown. We were right in the bottom of downtown, which was not the best part of town at that time, and people were afraid to go there. It was very dangerous. The Omni, which is now CNN, and the Omni Forum, where they have concerts and stuff, it's at the bottom of downtown. And it was just being developed at that time. And the city just didn't clean it up and we couldn't hold out.

"We weren't doing the business. We had a hotel in the building. We had an ice-skating rink at the bottom and shops and restaurants. Restaurants weren't even making it down there. Beautiful, beautiful restaurants. People were scared.

"Now it's a smash. Well, now it's CNN. That's where their headquarters are. But we couldn't hold out. It was like it was too soon. It was before its time."

"But you know what?" Sid remembers. "I was afraid to go, because I thought, 'Who the hell is going to show up to see this?' It was in that big theater and it would be so embarrassing if nobody showed up to see it. But people did come. In fact, they turned away thousands of people.

"I was sitting in the back while they showed many of our

shows, before this discussion thing that followed the screening. And I remember when *ElectraWoman and DynaGirl* came on and the people were so hysterical. I said to my brother, 'You know, we ought to bring that back.' And then *The Bugaloos* came on and people went crazy, just went crazy at that screening, and so I said to my brother, 'Oh, my God, let's bring it *all* back.'"

Practically no sooner said than done.

In September 1995, nostalgia giant Nick at Nite, a cable network that celebrates everything "old" on TV, brought many of the brothers' shows out of mothballs by presenting a sampler package of the Krofft canon in a Lollapalooza-style moonlight marathon. In tribute to *H.R. Pufnstuf,* they dubbed it "Pufapalooza."

Not only did this flashback festival score the cable network's highest ratings of the year, but a merchandising tie-in also cleaned up, selling more than ten thousand T-shirts to viewers by phone during a nine-hour period. Bear in mind that these weren't kids glued to their sets at three and four in the morning for the marathon's final hours and these weren't kids ponying up sixteen dollars for the shirts. These were grownups attempting to recapture their youth.

The Krofft comeback was beginning to build steam.

Later in 1995, MCA Records released a CD tribute to classic kiddie-show theme songs, *Saturday Morning Cartoons' Greatest Hits,* with prominent "alternative/new rock" bands covering tunes from their '60s and '70s childhoods. Krofft shows, which typically had memorable theme songs to begin with, were well-represented, with three of the nineteen tracks: Collective Soul performing "The Bugaloos"; Tripping Daisy tackling both *Sigmund* intro numbers ("Friends" and "Sigmund and the Sea Monsters"); and the Murmurs re-inventing "H.R. Pufnstuf."

A year later, in October 1996, the Family Channel revived five Krofft programs for a six-month run on its Saturday and Sunday morning schedules: *H.R. Pufnstuf, The Bugaloos, Lidsville, Sigmund and the Sea Monsters* and *Far Out Space Nuts.* The lineup brought in record ratings.

Also in October '96, Sid and Marty received the Lifetime Achievement Award from the SciFi Universe Awards.

A family reunion: John Whitaker, Marty Krofft, Sid Krofft and Wesley Eure in February 1995.
PHOTO BY TIM NEELEY.

In November '96, Pufnstuf made a surprise guest appearance on *The Drew Carey Show* during the show's memorable "What Is Hip?" musical number and, in early '97, Puf turned up as guest announcer on *The Rosie O'Donnell Show,* the hippest daytime talk show of the 1996–97 season.

At about this time, beginning in October, old Krofft programs—airing on Australia's Fox cable and Nickelodeon—became the rage once again down under, an intense wave of popularity perhaps even eclipsing what was happening in the United States.

Demand for all things Krofft, in fact, motivated Marty to visit Australia twice in a six-month period. "We've become pretty big there," he says. "The characters are all popular again. They've got another retro thing going down there. I think we might be more popular there now than we were the first time our shows were on."

But that's only the tip of the iceberg. Big-budget feature film versions of vintage Krofft shows are on the drawing board, beginning with a $40 million version of *Land of the Lost.*

"It's exciting for me and Sid, because this is practically our life's work," Marty says. "We're in the planning stages to do movies for those projects. We're in development at Disney with *Land of the Lost* right now. After that, we're doing *Pufnstuf.*"

Kollecting Krofft

Among many fans who collect Krofft memorabilia, the crown jewel of any collection is a Witchiepoo doll.

So imagine the added value—if not monetary, certainly sentimental—of a Witchiepoo that came directly from Marty Krofft.

Bill Morgan, one of the foremost collectors of Krofft memorabilia, has one. It cost $350. But as far as he is concerned, it's a priceless keepsake.

"Marty Krofft was at a comic book convention and I got there early, sat in one of the first rows and was attentive to everything he said, especially when he announced that he had brought three dolls with him," Morgan recalls. "There was a crowd of maybe five hundred people and they were all pretty much hard-core fans, so I thought my chances of getting that doll were going to be very slim.

"But when it came time to stand up for questions, where we actually walked up to a microphone, I really didn't have a question. I had a statement, where I thanked him for all the wonderful shows and good memories that I had growing up and I ended that with, if he would allow me, I would like to be first in line to buy one of the Witchiepoo dolls. And he said, 'You got it. You got it.' And I'm so glad I said that, because I asked the last question and then everyone got up and swarmed him at the table, because they were doing autographs too. It was supposed to be a line, but it was just a mob up there.

"And I saw him hand a doll to somebody and I saw him pick up a second box. And I thought, 'Well, I guess I'm not going to get one.' But he kind of parted the way between the crowd and made eye contact with me, pointed at me and I could see him mouth, 'You wanted one, right?' And then he waved for me to come up to him. I thought that was really great. Because he remembered me. I wrote a check that had a wobbly signature on it because I was so excited."

When it comes to collecting toys, comic books, lunch boxes and other memorabilia relating to Krofft TV shows, Witchiepoo dolls, produced in 1970 by My-Toy Company Inc., are among the hardest to get. But Morgan says it isn't that difficult to build a decent collection.

"The number of people who collect Krofft shows is somewhat small on a certain level," he says. "It's very, very small compared to something like *Star Trek*. But for anyone who grew up in that time and is a fan of classic TV and collecting memorabilia, the Kroffts are on the top. It's one of the hottest things to collect right now."

At the same time, a great Krofft collection won't come cheap.

"There wasn't a whole lot of diversity or quantity, like with *Star Trek*," he says. "So because of that and because the popularity is increasing, there's not too many items that are under twenty dollars."

Morgan, co-author of *Collector's Guide to TV Memorabilia: 1960s & 1970s* (Collector Books), suggests lunch boxes as a good starting point. "Paper items were made to be used and thrown away, so they can be a little harder to find, whereas a lunch box, after you were done using it, if it made it through the school year without being too banged up, it got put away in a cupboard.

"So I think they're easier to find, but because of the desirability, they're actually some of the higher-priced memorabilia. The lunch boxes seem to appeal to everyone, even people who don't collect the memorabilia. Just because they're colorful and neat items to have. Very dimensional and easy to display, whereas items like paper dolls or coloring books aren't as easy to display."

That may be, but Robin Dearden, costar of *Magic Mongo*, swears by the comic books she has saved. "My sister's a school teacher and a couple of years after the show had finished, she said, 'You'll never believe this. You're a comic book character.' Her kids brought in some comic books to school and she confiscated them. I still have them. And I show my daughter. She is four-and-a-half years old. I only have one episode of *Magic Mongo*. I'd love to have more to show her, to show her the fun stuff that mom did when she was younger, but all I have is the one episode and the comic books."

Similarly, David Levy, costar of *Wonderbug*, treasures his *Krofft Supershow* lunch box: "*Wonderbug* fulfilled a childhood dream of mine, which is to have my picture on a lunch box. I have a Ph.D. in psychology. But to my two-year-old son, I'm sure he's going to be much more impressed by the picture on the lunchbox than the Ph.D."

A Witchiepoo doll
can sell for as
much as $1,000
to collectors today.
PHOTO BY BILL MORGAN.

A variety of *Pufnstuf*
memorabilia was
produced from the
TV series and the
movie.
PHOTO BY BILL MORGAN.

Sid also has dreams of doing movie versions of *Lidsville* and *Sigmund* (with Pauly Shore involved). It isn't hard to imagine such projects being wildly popular with, as the saying goes, children of all ages.

Maybe even the Krofft brothers didn't realize it until recently, not until this second wave of popularity swirled around them, but childhood memories have the power to change people. It's undeniable that such memories can reacquaint grownups with the forgotten kid within and bring them back to a time when life was less complicated.

Pufnstuf and the other stuff enable that to happen.

"But I must tell you," Marty says, "the thought process when we did these shows, we weren't thinking, 'Will they hold up in twenty years?' We just wanted to be entertaining. We just wanted our shows to be fun for the audience of the day. It's strictly a bonus that they're definitely holding up."

Two decades ago, Sid and Marty Krofft kept young people entertained and sparked their imaginations. Today, these same shows have demonstrated the power to touch these lives once more, which is perhaps even more precious a gift.

Sid and Marty, circa 1974.
SID & MARTY KROFFT PICTURES.

ıt Takes Two
...or Sid and Marty and Sometimes Harry

They are total opposites and, at the same time, perfect complements to one another.

Virtually anyone who works with Sid and Marty Krofft comes away from the experience with that impression.

"The two of them were always hilarious together," says Bob Denver, the former *Gilligan's Island* star who did *Far Out Space Nuts* (1975–76) with the Kroffts. "They're so different. Sid's like this eccentric creative guy. Marty's a businessman and kind of show biz. One is like 6'2" or something [Marty]. The other's like 5'9".

"And they don't even look very much alike. I'd ask them from time to time, 'Are you guys really brothers or are you just putting me on?'"

Denver is joking, mind you, but he isn't very far off the mark.

Sid has the soul and the sensibilities of a true artist. He is colorful to the hilt, a master storyteller, and, at times, downright childlike in the way he views life, a quality that not only proves invaluable in the business of creating entertainment for children but which also allows him to touch the child in each of us, young or old.

Marty, albeit a talented puppeteer in his own right, is far more pragmatic than his older brother. He is the one who treks into the office every morning, the one who "networks" and keeps a watchful eye over the Krofft empire. Simply put, his art includes the art of the deal.

Billie Hayes, who worked with the Kroffts on *H.R. Pufnstuf* and *Lidsville,* says the two are "as different as night and day—but I love them both dearly."

Wesley Eure, star of *Land of the Lost,* makes a good point when he offers a slightly different comparison: "They're like salt and pepper." After all, one missing ingredient, a sprinkle of one without a dash of the other, makes the dish incomplete.

Ask any of the people with whom the Krofft brothers have worked and you get variations of the same story.

Donny Osmond, who collaborated with them on *Donny & Marie,* remembers them this way: "Sid was the eccentric one, but they're both that way in their own respective elements. I mean, Sid, when you talk to him, he's kind of like in space. Sometimes you don't really know if it's going in. You're talking to him and you don't know if he's really listening because his mind is creating, always creating, constantly. And Sid is a very soft-spoken kind of person, like, 'Yeah, cool, far out.' Head in the clouds, creating while you're speaking.

"Whereas Marty is like, 'Hey, Donny, howya doin'?' Show biz. He takes care of the political aspect. They're both very creative obviously, don't get me wrong. But they complement each other. They're complete opposites, but that's why they complement each other."

Ruth Buzzi, costar of *The Lost Saucer* and a frequent guest star on *Donny & Marie,* puts it this way: "Sid and Marty were a perfect match, because Sid was really the one with the tremendous imagination. The numbers that we did on the *Donny & Marie* show, it was just great. And they were Sid's ideas. Marty's so smart and he's a lot of fun, but Sid's like fifteen times more imaginative—or at least he knows how to express his imagination.

"So that makes them a terrific couple. And I'm sure it kept them a lot of times from arguing too. I never saw those two men argue. I'm sure they did, behind the scenes. But I never saw them argue. It was a very good balance. They are a great combination. The two of them are just wonderful, wonderful men and I would love to be working for them now."

Patty Maloney, who costarred in *Far Out Space Nuts,* sees them this way: "Each one allows the other one to be who they are. There's no conflict between them in that way, because Marty allows Sid to be the extremely creative end of the business. And Marty is definitely the businessman and Sid would be the first to admit that he wouldn't even want to touch that part of it. But that's what makes them so unique and that's what makes them so different and yet connected."

And Butch Patrick, star of *Lidsville,* remembers them like this: "Marty's great. Marty's the one who hired me basically. Marty was the businessman, but he also was a pretty neat guy. Sid was the one who ate all the drugs and came up with these strange concepts. It's funny. I remember Marty was the one who had kids, whereas Sid was kind of *like* a kid. They each had their own distinct personalities and their own little areas of expertise."

And their extreme differences aren't merely confined to work or personal style, either. It's also evident in the way they live their daily lives.

Says Jay Robinson, who played Dr. Shrinker: "You couldn't have two people more dissimilar than those two brothers. You wouldn't even believe they were brothers. Sid goes down to the beach every day and runs nine miles, every day, along the Santa Monica Beach. He's quite the health enthusiast, very disciplined about exercise and his diet. He won't eat anything but organic vegetables. Loves nature. There's a removable roof on his house and plants everywhere.

"And Marty is totally the opposite. He doesn't give a damn about the athletic side of anything, smokes cigars, drinks martinis. He drives a big Rolls-Royce. Marty's always been a great showboater, like P. T. Barnum. And Sid is a gentle, lovely soul. They both have their ways."

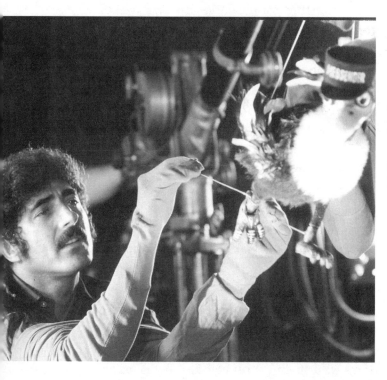

Sid Krofft takes a hands-on approach with the puppetry effects in *The Bugaloos*.
SID & MARTY KROFFT PICTURES.

But how did such a distinct division of duties develop? Sid, the creator; Marty, Mr. Business?

"I guess," Marty quips, "because I was too stupid to know any better."

Perhaps the best explanation for the dichotomy is this: Sid literally was born to work with puppets, trained in the art since childhood, whereas Marty was clever enough and pragmatic enough to pick up art and business along the way.

"We are fifth-generation puppeteers," Sid says. "We worked with marionettes. That's the family that I come from, a marionette family."

Cydus Yolas Krofft—a.k.a. Sid—was born on July 30, 1929, in Montreal (although it has often been reported he was born in Athens, Greece). He was the third in a family of four boys.

Brothers Hy and Harry were older than Sid, but Sid was the one selected to carry on the Krofft legacy for another generation. Why Sid and neither of his older brothers? "Oh, who the hell knows? I don't know. Because I was better looking?"

It's All Greek to Them

To find the first Krofft puppeteer, the man who started a family legacy, you have to go back two centuries and cross the Atlantic Ocean.

In Athens, Greece, sometime during the late 1700s, a man named Peter Krofft took up a trade that, five generations later, would have an impact on children's television of the 1970s.

But if you want to know anything more about the man, or anything substantial about the storied Krofft Theatre, Sid and Marty Krofft are sorry to have to disappoint. The brothers may be gifted entertainers, but in the art of digging up one's roots, Alex Haley-style, they leave a lot to be desired.

"At the old Krofft Theatre, which was my father's, they did ballet and opera with puppets, in a stage with a symphony orchestra," Sid says. "And he learned from my father's father and all the way back. My grandfather played all over the world with the Krofft Puppets, but eventually my father had to shut down the theater because he began to see too many empty seats."

Beyond that, the facts about the family history start to get a little fuzzy.

"It was my father who moved the family from Europe to Canada and then later to the United States," Marty says. "And my father died when we were kids. I was twelve years old when he died. So I don't have a lot of background on the Krofft Theatre other than I was told there was a Krofft Theatre that dated back to Athens.

"You see, the European community never, ever documented anything the way we do here and so I have trouble documenting that. We have nothing in writing. No posters, no anything.

"My father wasn't a puppeteer, but he ran the puppet shows. And going back beyond my father, I have trouble telling you anything that I absolutely know to be factual."

More likely, the truth is that Sid was the one with the temperament of an artist. It was evident even at a tender age.

"When I was seven years old, I was the son chosen. Basically, my dad just said, 'You're the one.' I don't know why. It was all through a spiritual feeling of some sort, I guess, that my dad had about me. Then he started training me and pretty soon I started professionally touring the whole world. My dad had me travel with circuses and carnivals. I was in vaudeville, right near the end of it, and burlesque and in nightclubs, doing my puppet act."

Often performing his shows in nightclubs that had policies against letting minors pass through their doors, Sid quickly gained fame as "the world's youngest puppeteer."

"God, I was so young," he says. "I remember this one great story that happened in New Jersey. I showed up at the club on opening day with my dad and we were rehearsing with the music. And the owner came in and said, 'Who the hell's this kid?' And my father said, 'Well, that's the act.' He said, 'No way. I'm going to lose my license.'

"I forget the name of the club. The guy who owned it was like with the mafia. I was nine. Nine years old, playing in a place that I couldn't even get in. You had to be twenty-one and they were really strict. And it looked like I wasn't going to get to go on, the owner was so against it, but my dad talked him into it. It was like a week before Halloween, I think, and my dad talked him into putting a mask on me and hiding me down in the kitchen and telling everybody that I was a midget. And I had to work with this mask. And the waiters and the waitresses, they told everybody that I was disfigured and they had to hide me coming in and out.

"So the boss said, 'Okay, just for tonight.' But I went over so big that he wanted me to play there for two weeks."

By the early 1950s, Sid became a headliner at the Lido, the world famous Paris nightclub, and at the Follies-Bergere.

"I opened at the Lido in Paris in 1951 and I was in that show for two years. Everybody from all over the world comes to see that show. Man, that was a trip. The show at the Lido didn't start until 11:30 and I used to go on at 1:00 at night. I worked there seven days a week and I was like the star of the show, but I was told by the owner, 'The only reason you're here is for the girls to change their costumes. So don't ask us for anything.'

"I remember during the week in the summers, I'd fly down to the south of France. It would take three-and-a-half hours to fly it in those days. And I'd fly down just to go to the beach. Because I didn't go on until 1:00 in the morning, so I could fly back at five. And boy, I guess if I didn't show up, then the girls couldn't change their costumes."

The owner of the club may have pretended that Sid was nothing special, but everyone clearly knew otherwise. Over a period of nine years, Sid proceeded to take his act to the four corners of the world.

"My agent in Europe said, 'Where do you want to go? Because every major club in the world wants your act.' They just gave me a map and I put little Xs down. And I played everywhere. I wanted to go to countries that didn't have tourists. I played all through Egypt, Damascus, Beirut—all strange, exotic places—for the people.

"I think now that probably was the most successful part of my career, moreso than any of the successes we had with our television shows. Because, in the Arabic countries, they never saw anything like my act and I was like a god to them."

A gross overstatement, you say? Hardly. With apologies to John Lennon, who once claimed the Beatles were bigger than Christ, there was a time when, in the Middle East, Sid Krofft was even bigger than the Beatles.

"Yeah, I was the biggest. They loved me there. That was the height of my entire career. I mean it. In all of the Arabic countries. I'll never, ever forget it."

The people there literally were in awe of Sid's seeming ability to turn his marionettes into living, breathing entities. Many feared him and his peculiar power—yet they were intrigued even more.

"They wouldn't even come near me. They didn't understand what I did. They thought I was like a magician. And honestly, hundreds of people would wait for me outside of my hotel just to look at me, every night, when I'd go backstage. That went on for about seven months, in all of the Arabic countries that I visited.

"Word got around and I became like the biggest star in the Arabic countries. Every night when I'd come to work, there'd be flowers and silk and all kinds of things that I would donate to the hospitals, because I couldn't take them with me from club to club."

All because, with sticks and strings, he was able to make an inanimate doll come to life.

"There's a great, great story. The first place I played was a club in Alexandria. It looked like something out of a George Raft movie. It was like they were all smoking their water pipes. And it was so big. It sat about eight hundred people. And they had all these belly dancers and it was so strange it was frightening. And this dusty old curtain closes and you couldn't hear yourself speak. You couldn't see anything because there was so much smoke and it was like a real, authentic Arabic club. There were no white people there. As a matter of fact, I needed permission to go down into that part of the city.

"Anyway, I set up my act behind this curtain. And we hit the tape and my act began. The Paris Symphony Orchestra, when I was at the Lido, had recorded the music for my whole act. I had given the conductor two hundred bucks and he had the symphony orchestra put it on tape. And there was a space after the introduction, a little overture, and they would introduce me in Arabic and my act would start. You couldn't hear the music or anything. It was so noisy in there. And when the curtain opened up, it was like somebody stuck a knife in their backs. I mean, all of a sudden there was total silence. They never saw anything like it.

"Now, I used to work right on the floor, not in a puppet stage, and my act is like, well, it was weird. It was like an acid trip. And the music was written by Henry Mancini when no one knew who he was. And it was all musical. It was like a concert. So anyway, I finished my first number. Nothing happened. Silence—no reaction from the audience. Okay, that was all right. I just go into my whole act. I mean, I'm on the stage for a good twenty-five minutes. And there is total, total silence. And after a while I'm shaking. I can't find the strings and every time I pass my assistant, he says, 'Just keep going. Keep going.' Although sometimes he'd say, 'They must really hate you.'

"It was a horrible experience because I was bombing, totally bombing. Big time. So now my act is almost over and I do the big finish. It was this big black number. I had, oh, I would call it almost an automatronic, big prop, with a big black jazz band on it that all worked electrically. And it was a hot, hot finish. Usually I'd stop the show cold.

"But this time, the lights come up and I step forward with my two puppets. Nothing. Just silence. And then, all of a sudden, like somebody pulled a knife out of their backs, they stood up and they screamed, smashing the tables with their fists and shouting something that sounded like 'Beast!' I see these strange faces and they're grinding their teeth and waving their fists at me. And so my assistant pulled me back under the back curtain and we go. My dressing room—I'll never forget it—was like in the kitchen. And my assistant shuts the door. And they're screaming louder and louder. And the owner of the club, he spoke French, he came running back and he's screaming, 'Where is he? Where is he?' And my assistant said, 'They're going to kill him.'

"And the owner said, 'No, no, they want him to do it all over again.' They were saying 'bis.' Well, I know what 'bis' means. It's a French word. 'Bis' means do it again, all over, start from the beginning. So I went back and did it again."

That was 1953, when Sid was a mere twenty-three years old. By the late 1950s, Sid and his puppets were opening for Judy Garland in her Las Vegas show and on tour.

In fact, *H.R. Pufnstuf* wasn't even his introduction to the world of television. "I was on the very first color telecast in the United States," he says. "It was in New York. I think only 150 people had sets. It was *The Glass Hour,* because, with television, you were looking through glass. The Golden Gate Quartet sang, 'The kneebone's connected to the ankle bone.' They were real famous then. And then I did my big skeleton number."

The skeleton number was Sid's signature routine, the most famous part of his act. "It started with like Dracula flying around, like a bat, and he went into a coffin. And then the coffin blew up, like it had burned up, and out came the skeleton from the coffin and it all falls apart. Then all the bones fly all over the stage. It was an incredible number. It was a show stopper."

He also performed his one-man act—introduced by a few bars of "World on a String"—for larger TV audiences on *Shower of Stars* in 1957 and twice on *The Ed Sullivan Show* in 1959. So the move to television in the '60s wasn't as far a leap as one might initially imagine.

It's worth noting too that Harry Krofft also became part of the Krofft television team for many years, but only a very small part. He certainly was never as intrinsically involved a player as Sid or Marty. In a manner of speaking, in fact, he was like Zeppo, the fifth Marx brother, the one who never appeared in any of that comedy team's movies.

Butch Patrick jokes that Harry was his favorite Krofft brother because, "He was the one who signed my checks."

Adds Ray Young, who played Bigfoot in *Bigfoot and Wildboy*: "I never met Harry, but we called him the Shadow. Because, you know, here were the Krofft brothers, Sid and Marty and then Harry, but nobody ever met Harry."

The reason Harry was the mystery man of the group, Marty explains, is that he was never really a fully involved part of the business.

"Harry was never really interested in the puppets," Marty says. "I brought him out here to help with the office. For a number of years, he was the office manager. Then he went on to do something else. He was never really part of Sid & Marty Krofft. It just never worked out that way."

Says Sid: "Harry didn't know a thing about puppetry or show business. And he didn't care. He's a businessman all the way. As a matter of fact, he eventually quit because it was too much. Show business was, like, crazy. It wasn't a normal life. So he got into real estate."

Harry, now semi-retired, lives in the San Fernando Valley in California.

And what of oldest brother Hy? "We lost him in the war," Marty says. "He was killed during the invasion of Okinawa in World War II."

The family business functioned just fine without the older brothers, but it wouldn't be the same if Sid had to go it without Marty.

Marty Krofft—that's his full name: just Marty Krofft, with no middle name—was born in Montreal on April 9, 1937. By the time he was old enough to walk, Sid already had begun to tour professionally and was making a name for himself. Unlike the two oldest brothers, though, Marty soon found he had a knack for the family art of puppetry—and he did it entirely on his own.

"When I was in Europe," Sid says, "Marty took the puppets that I left behind and did his own act. He was never trained like I had been and his act wasn't as good as mine was. I mean, how could it be? He's a very good puppeteer, but I had all of the best puppets with me."

Says Marty: "Yeah, I was totally self-taught. I just decided, 'Yeah, I can do this.' You know, the puppets were always around. Sid had an extra set of puppets, so I borrowed them. And I basically just picked it up on my own."

Like Sid, Marty's successful solo career began before he reached his teens, although many of his early performances might be a little hard to document today. After all, on occasion, Marty performed using the name of his now-famous older brother.

"He would actually work around New York with my name," Sid recalls. "Because I was already sort of known as the world's youngest puppeteer. So he used my name, Sid Krofft. It's funny. I played just about every theater in New York, but I never played the Palace. But Marty did. And he played the Palace in my name."

Marty is quick to point out, however, that he didn't perform as Sid so often as Sid would have you believe.

"I think I performed under my own name most of the time," Marty says. "Maybe a couple of times I did it under his name. I don't remember, but I think he could be right."

Regardless of whose name was being used in those early days, Marty quickly made a name for himself as well.

"When I was real young—ten, eleven, twelve—I was doing a lot of television shows with the puppets," he recalls. "And I did it always on my own. I did Ted Mack's *Original Amateur Hour.* I was in a show called *Startime Kids,* where I was the teenager of the week. I did several shows like that. I did Paul Whiteman's show, the orchestra leader. He was famous at the time. I did Kate Smith's show once. I did a lot of shows. Mother Goose Shoes had a show for kids every week. I did that a number of times. I did my puppets at a lot of different places."

Life With Father

So what's it like having wheeler-dealer producer Marty Krofft as a father?

"It was a pretty trippy childhood," Kristina Krofft says. "I mean, there are so many wacky stories that don't even seem possible. It was pretty wild."

Marty and his wife Christa, a former Playboy Playmate of the Year, have been married since 1962. They have three grown daughters: Deanna, Kristina and Kendra. Sid has no children.

How wild, how unconventional could the kids' lives be?

Most children don't have a father who tools about town behind the wheel of a car that once belonged to a Beatle. Marty had Ringo Starr's Bentley.

Most children don't have a *Tiger Beat* cover boy living under their roof. Jack Wild stayed with the Kroffts during his *Pufnstuf* days.

Most children don't have members of the Osmond family as birthday party guests. But Donny and Marie helped celebrate the Krofft kids' special days every year.

"I was madly in love with Donny," Kristina says. "I was like wearing purple socks every single day. And Deanna and I, we used to dress up and perform for them, for the Osmonds. The Osmonds came to every single one of our birthday parties. Deanna always got to be Superchick or Marie. She was all the pretty girls because she was the younger sister. I had to dress up as Kaptain Kool and Donny Osmond. She was a little bit country and I was a little bit rock 'n' roll.

"And we made the costumes exactly like their costumes. We had Kaptain Kool and the Kongs costumes and Donny and Marie costumes and they used to come to our birthdays and we'd perform for them. Every birthday."

Deanna notes that there were times, of course, when it was embarrassing to have such a famous father. "We got teased a lot. Because all the kids knew all the words to the songs and they were making fun of us at school. Kids can be very cruel. If there's someone to pick on, they pick. And when-

In fact, Marty had as much, if not more, exposure to television in the early days than Sid had. Marty certainly was introduced to the airwaves at an earlier age. Perhaps that's why, Sid casually theorizes,

ever he would drive us to school in the Rolls, we would duck or make him drop us off a block away so that no one would see us get out of that car."

Says Kendra: "Make that three blocks away. I just hated having to ride to school in that car."

One of the most embarrassing moments, according to Kristina: "I remember we moved to a ranch in Santa Ynez, California, and I remember my mom coming to pick us up from school with our housekeeper Ernestine with Sleestak heads on. And Deanna and I ran and hid at the other end of the school. We were like, 'We don't know these people.' I mean, we were in the country and my mother comes to school with a Sleestak head on. Can you imagine what everyone in town was thinking?"

All things considered, though, any complaints seem to be greatly outnumbered by pleasant experiences.

Says Kendra: "It was definitely exciting. There's never really a dull moment. I was in *Pryor's Place.* I would jump rope and stuff. And I was in scenes with Richard Pryor. Had a talking part and everything. I have a picture of me with Mike Tyson, because he was on *D.C. Follies,* and I have one with Don King and Whoopi Goldberg. And I got to work wardrobing on the new *Land of the Lost.*

"You know another cool thing? Halloween was our holiday. Because we always had the big costume closet in our house and we could choose costumes for Halloween. There would be Bugaloos costumes and Donny and Marie outfits and characters from *H.R. Pufnstuf.* They made me my own personal Witchiepoo outfit. We always had the best costumes."

One of Deanna's favorite stories about her famous father, meanwhile, involves her son Karson's birthday party:

"I had the party for my son and I hired a guy to play a pirate for the party. And my dad comes to the party and the guy who's the pirate goes, 'Oh, my God. You're not going to believe this. I was just at the comic book convention standing in line to get your autograph.'"

that Marty seems to have a greater love for working in that medium.

Another reason, quite likely, is that Marty is better equipped to cope in the highly competitive industry.

It was during Marty's teenage years, long before teaming up officially with Sid, that he also became adept at another craft, the craft of doing business.

"Do you know that when Marty was seventeen years old, he was the number one car salesman for Ford?" Sid says. "He won the prize for the year. He worked at a car dealership in Long Island, New York. And Marty, at seventeen, was the number one salesman. He won a free trip to the Bahamas."

Marty claims his business acumen came to him as naturally as puppetry did...and, in this area, he also was entirely self-taught.

"I did sell cars when I was seventeen and eighteen years old—and I did it for about a year and a half and I was successful at it. I was kind of self-taught. I have more of a business mind probably than Sid would ever have. And I don't know whether I picked this up from anybody other than myself. You know, maybe I picked it up from living in New York for six years and surviving in New York. That's where that came from."

In short, Harry Krofft was pure businessman, with little or no interest in show business, and Sid was the artist for whom monetary matters had more or less no meaning. But Marty was the 'tweener who learned to master the nuances of both art and commerce.

Says Marty's daughter Kristina: "I have met so many people who tell me how my dad can go into a meeting and sell a show without even having anything to sell. He's just such a good salesperson. He can make you believe that he's got the greatest idea on this earth and at the end you realize, 'What the hell's the idea? Oh, well, doesn't matter. It sounds great. Let's buy it.' He's just a genius at that. That's what he's a genius at."

Says Marty: "Sid was always 'the artist.' He never did have a business sense. So I came in and filled that vacuum."

That's why Sid and Marty, who joined forces in 1959, work so well together. That's why, today, one man cannot be the topic of conversation without the other's name coming up. They are connected by a bond that is stronger than a mere ampersand.

"Actually, they really have only one thing in common," Lennie Weinrib says. "It's the fact that they are both fearless. Sid is fearless about ideas. He doesn't waste anything. He doesn't throw anything away. No dreams and no ideas that come to Sid are ever thrown away. They end up somewhere, in a park, in a show, in a rubber suit, in a marionette. He doesn't throw away any of that. A lot of us, we throw away so many wonderful ideas. But Sid goes right to work and has somebody build it or he builds it or they sketch it out. He uses his dreams. He uses his fantasies. It's kind of wonderful.

"And then Marty, he will make deals with anybody. I think he would meet with God to discuss financing. He is totally unafraid. Marty will meet with anyone to talk about how fantastic the show is going to be and what the structure will be and make the deal, talk to lawyers, the dealmakers, business managers, stars. He'll meet with anybody and say, 'I want you to be on my show. What do you want?' He'll talk to their agent. He's absolutely fearless in the area of dealmaking the way that Sid is fearless in the area of ideas. And that combination is absolutely incredible."

The Brothers Krofft are more than mere brothers, more than just partners. They are the true definition of teamwork.

They've Got the Music

How many kids have music companies named after them? Two of Marty Krofft's daughters do.

The rights to the theme songs to *H.R. Pufnstuf*, *The Bugaloos*, *Sigmund and the Sea Monsters* and other Krofft shows all belong to the girls' music companies: Kristina Music and Kendra Music.

"My company's worth nothing, but I have a music company named after myself," Kristina says. "It's probably got two dollars. But it's exciting. Of course, I've never seen a cut from anything involving Kristina Music. But that's okay. My cut was Boston University."

Kendra, the youngest daughter, born while *Land of the Lost* was in production, takes pride in the fact that her music company is the more successful. "Mine does better than Kristina's," she says. "I think it has more money in the account."

Marionettes from *Les Poupees de Paris* had style and grace.
SID & MARTY KROFFT PICTURES.

One Banana, Two Banana, Three Banana, Four! ...or The Birth of a Notion

In a manner of speaking, Sid and Marty Krofft are partly to blame for Barney.

No, the Kroffts have nothing to do with the big purple guy, a dinosaur who is a favorite with pre-schoolers and an irritant to adults. But if it weren't for an innovation adopted decades earlier by the Krofft brothers, Barney the dinosaur might be singing songs not of friendship, but of extinction.

Simply put, Sid and Marty helped popularize the practice of putting a person inside the costume of an animated or puppet-like character.

Today, it hardly seems like much of an innovation at all because it has become so commonplace. It is done all the time at theme parks, in stage shows and on television.

Mickey Mouse has been greeting visitors to the Magic

Kingdom ever since Disneyland opened its doors on July 17, 1955. And Jim Henson, whose first network TV appearance on *The Tonight Show* dates back to 1957, introduced oversized Muppets into his act, most notably with *Sesame Street*'s Big Bird, very early along the way.

But Sid and Marty took this simple idea of putting people in puppet costumes and used it to create an entire world unlike any before it.

"There were people in walk-around suits before *Pufnstuf,* before we got on, but I don't think anybody had done a whole show like that ever before," Marty says. "We were the first ones who took a live-action show and made like a living cartoon of it. That's what we did first."

And had *H.R. Pufnstuf* not been such an enormous hit, would there be so many lookalikes today? Would McDonaldland characters be hawking hamburgers in TV commercials? Would programs like *Pee-wee's Playhouse, The Huggabug Club* and *Barney & Friends* pepper the airwaves? Would mascots such as the San Diego Chicken and Phillie Fanatic be entertaining sports fans from the sidelines?

"Don't get too carried away," Sid protests. "I don't think you can say that if we hadn't done it first, nobody would have thought of putting people in suits. Who knows? You can have an idea and there are three people at that very moment with the same idea.

"Everything's been done before. It's just in the way you package it. All over the world. Nothing is original. I don't know. Maybe there was somebody way ahead of us who did crazy things like that. But I didn't know about them."

Neither did the McDonald's Corporation. Otherwise, it might not have lost its multi-million-dollar copyright infringement case to the Kroffts, who sued the fast-food chain after it introduced McDonaldland, a distinctly *Pufnstuf*-like place, in youth-skewed advertising campaigns.

Of course, there's no need here to belabor the evidence regarding who gets credit for the innovation. The important part, in this context, is that the notion of putting people in puppet suits harks way back to the Kroffts' pre-TV days, back when their claim to fame was strictly as puppeteers, while their celebrated stage careers were flourishing.

Says Sid: "In our puppet shows, we would have little people—they were called midgets then—and we would put them inside a suit with strings on them and mix them on stage with our marionettes. The critics always said the Krofft puppets were so lifelike, but we never revealed to anybody that there were little people mixed with our marionettes.

"We did a show that played to a million people at the New York World's Fair. It was called *Les Poupees de Paris* and it basically was a puppet show for adults only. You had to be twenty-one years old to see it. And the reason for that, it was like a takeoff on the Lido or a Las Vegas show: Tits and ass, only with puppets. And we used every trick in the book, everything that had been passed down to us and everything we had picked up over the course of our careers. I mean, here was a stage that had waterfalls and swimming pools and the puppets would actually be swimming and stuff like that."

In other words, this puppet show was a far cry from *Howdy Doody* and *Punch and Judy*.

But back to the person in the puppet suit.

"In that show, we had a little person who was like a marionette," Sid says. "And everybody thought it was a radio-controlled marionette, because it pulled its strings down and broke out of the stage and went right into the audience, right up the aisle, and then disappeared.

"It was in a big horror number that we'd do. It started with like a Frankenstein, with the laboratory and all that stuff. And up above, in a puppet stage—because *Les Poupees de Paris* was in a massive puppet stage—we threw the controls down and the puppet kept going. And an elevator would take it down to the first row, right at the lip of the stage, and it would keep walking with all the strings trailing behind him. And then we would black out. We'd drop it in a trap door. Or if we didn't have a trap door, we would black out and somebody would come and pick it up in the dark.

Generation Next

Even when Sid and Marty Krofft have absolutely no direct involvement in a film, television or stage production, it's often possible to find their fingerprints.

That's true not only in terms of their influence on other artists, but also in the fact that two of the top puppeteers in the business—Van Snowden and Tony Urbano—started their careers with the Kroffts.

Snowden—the man behind the Cryptkeeper on *Tales from the Crypt* and who did special effects puppetry in such films as *Alien Resurrection* (1997) and *Starship Troopers* (1997)—worked with the Kroffts for more than two decades.

"Van Snowden did everything for us," Sid says. "He right now is the greatest puppeteer on the planet."

Says Snowden: "I started with them in 1962. The first thing I did with them was *Les Poupees de Paris* at the York Theater in New York. I directed a lot of their live shows in the Six Flags parks, and I have been in almost all their TV shows."

He was Pufnstuf in many of the roadshow versions of the show and played such TV characters as Tweeter on *The Bugaloos* and Sweet Mama on *Sigmund and the Sea Monsters*.

Snowden theorizes that the Krofft shows remain popular with their original audiences, even though they no longer are children, because the kids shows were never really kids shows.

"And that was the sensation of *Les Poupees de Paris,* the marionette that kept going without anyone at the controls."

Sid says the idea of mixing little people with his puppets was a natural follow-up to a mind-blowing trick he had pulled off for years in his solo act.

"My encore was me working a puppet of me that worked a puppet. I used to work my act dressed all in black and I was on stage, not in a puppet stage. I was on stage and I worked my marionettes down on the floor. The spotlight would hit the marionette, but you could see the reflection of me operating the puppet.

"Anyway, in my encore, I had a puppet that looked just like me in black that worked a puppet, a juggler, that didn't work too well. And

"We never did shows for kids," he says. "We geared it toward the family, with an adult slant. Because the Kroffts' start was with adults. So we never went really all straight kiddie stuff, the way *Barney* is."

Snowden says he can't single out any of the Krofft shows as his favorite. "Because it was another lifetime ago. I've done so much stuff since those shows. It was like somebody else did it."

Another longtime Krofft alumnus who made good is Tony Urbano, who oversaw the spectacular alien puppet effects in *Men in Black*, the 1997 blockbuster movie.

Says Sid: "Every one of those puppeteers who did *Men in Black*, because it's all puppetry, every one of them started with us and was with us for so many years. Tony Urbano, who was in charge of all the puppeteers, well, Tony started with us. He built all the puppets for the first *Les Poupees de Paris* and was with us all through the '60s and the '70s, including *The Barbara Mandrell Show.*

"He opened up a puppet school for us. That's where all the puppeteers came from. And he used every one of them for the movie."

So the Krofft puppeteer tradition will live on...just not necessarily with the Krofft name attached.

"Oh, definitely," Sid says. "There's so many of them and they all started with us. Then they went on to *The Muppets* or branched off into movies and became big, important puppeteers. Every one of them, every single one of them."

the orchestra would stop and then it would start up again because the juggler kept dropping the pins. So the puppet of me threw the controls down on the ground. And what happened? The juggler puppet falls to the ground if you drop the controls. And then I take the controls of the puppet of me and I throw them on the ground.

"But this puppet, instead of falling to the ground like the juggler, it picks up the little puppet and walks offstage. It was the very first radio-controlled puppet. And I'm talking about more than forty years ago."

Years later, when the Kroffts were crafting *Les Poupees de Paris*, the notion of having little people masquerade as marionettes was essentially a variation of the same idea.

And like magicians employing misdirection to pull off their illusions, the Kroffts went to elaborate extremes to keep people in the dark.

"We never told the press we had little people in the show," Sid says. "We used to tell them they were radio-controlled puppets. We always invited people backstage after the show and they always would ask about that puppet. 'Where's that puppet?' I guess they thought if they could see it close up that maybe they could figure out how it was done.

"But we had a fake one backstage. We'd have a puppet, one we didn't use in the act, lying in a box. And we hid the midget in the dressing room. It's funny. They used to say, 'Oh, the Krofft puppets are so lifelike.' Well, that's because they were. And I don't think anyone ever figured it out."

Sid and Marty officially teamed up as a duo in 1959. At the time, Sid and his marionettes were the opening act for Judy Garland in her Las Vegas and roadshows.

But it was *Les Poupees de Paris* that was the true eye opener, the show that propelled Sid and Marty to a new level in the entertainment industry.

The extravaganza, which cost $300,000 to mount, requiring twelve puppeteers to work the 240 marionettes, began in a San Fernando Valley theater-restaurant in 1960, then moved to P.J.'s in Hollywood for a one-year engagement, then to Las Vegas and the Seattle World's Fair before arriving in the Big Apple (where twenty-four puppeteers were used). Once there, it proved to be the only entertainment show that lasted the entire two years of the New York World's Fair and the only theatrical attraction there to turn a profit, averaging three thousand customers a day.

In retrospect, there's a tremendous irony in the fact that the Kroffts, so revered today for their wholesome family programming, had earlier made such an impact with a musical comedy revue that children weren't allowed to attend because of its risqué adult content.

"When everyone else was doing family entertainment, we were into nudity," Marty notes. "And when everyone got into nudity, we started doing family entertainment."

Among the main attractions in *Les Poupees* were chorus lines of sexy marionette showgirls, their semi-nude and perfectly proportioned four-foot-tall bodies draped in expensive silks, satin, mink and real jewels.

Sid can't help laughing when he recalls how, during the show's initial performances in New York, the brothers were instructed by the fair's powers-that-be to show substantially less skin, even if that skin belonged to marionettes.

"You wouldn't have that problem there today," he says, "but I guess at the time they had a problem with undraped feminine charms."

The Kroffts later took *Les Poupees* around the globe, entertaining audiences in Japan and Australia.

But it was while doing that show in New York that the Kroffts caught the eye of Angus Wynne, owner of the Six Flags theme park chain. Wynne's own spectacular show, a colossal money loser called *Broadway to Love,* was next door to the Kroffts' show and Wynne was thoroughly dazzled by the multitude of carney-style tricks they had used to generate word-of-mouth buzz and smash-hit business. After all, this was a mere puppet show—a nudie puppet show, that's true, but a puppet show nonetheless.

"He approached us," Sid recalls, "and said, 'I'm so amazed. I cannot believe what is going on here. You're like the Barnums of this era.' And he said, 'I'm building a new park in Atlanta and I would like to build a theater there for you.' We said, Yes, of course, we'd love to do it. We would have been fools to pass that up."

The brothers shut down *Les Poupees* in 1967 and created a $150,000 show called *Circus* for their new 1,200-seat Six Flags theater, which became the park's number one attraction—more popular, even, than the many enticing thrill rides that filled the park.

"It was very psychedelic," Sid says. "We used to play nine times a day and kids would stand in line for four and five hours, waiting to see it. Forget about the rides. This became the biggest part of their trip.

"It was because no one ever saw anything like this before. Ever. Puppet shows were *Pinocchio* and *Snow White and the Seven Dwarfs.* Puppet shows were for little kids. This blew their minds. And here we were competing with ninety thrill rides and we were the number one attraction."

Les Poupees, Part Deux

Has our look back at the Kroffts' famous topless puppet show whetted your curiosity about *Les Poupees de Paris?*

Given that the long-running show shut down three decades ago, there literally is a generation of Krofft fans that has never had the chance to see it—or anything remotely like it, for that matter.

But that may change, Marty says, because the desire to revive the show is very strong.

"Yes, it's a very good possibility," he says. "As a matter of fact, we tried to revive it in 1995 at the Mirage in Las Vegas, but it hasn't happened yet. But it's still something that may happen."

The reason for the delay?

"Well, it hasn't gotten off the ground properly because it's going to cost so much to mount it. It could cost anywhere upwards of four million dollars. They're so elaborate, the puppets. That's probably the one thing holding it back.

"If we ever get rich again, we'll do it ourselves. It's not something that's dead. It's something we would like to do again when the time is right."

It was hardly a stretch, therefore, that the Kroffts soon had puppet shows in the four Six Flags theme parks and that they became creative consultants for the parks as well. The Kroffts set up shop in the Los Angeles area in what formerly had been an airplane hangar. Their shop became known as the Factory.

"They set us up in Sun Valley and we were like a mini-Disney," Sid says, "where we built rides and we built all the stuff for the Six Flags parks. And when the season was over, we opened our doors to everybody. Ringling Bros. came to us and Ice Capades and all the television shows. We were building stuff for the Jackson Five tour and for other big rock-'n'-roll shows."

In less than a year, the brothers were grossing one million dollars combined from their shows at the Six Flags parks, and more was being generated through those other jobs, which included attractions on San Francisco's Fisherman's Wharf and at the Queen

Mary, the famous British ship that became a tourist attraction in Long Beach, California.

Business was booming and Sid and Marty were continually making a bigger name for themselves.

As a matter of fact, even though *Pufnstuf* is correctly credited as being the Krofft brothers' first TV series, their first recurring gig on series television came a few years earlier on *The Dean Martin Show*. Sid and Marty were hired to create a puppet chorus line—different style characters than the *Les Poupees* chorus line, mind you—and then they were fired because the act generated *too much* fan mail.

"We developed the dressing room puppets, the chorus line for the show," Sid says. "They were like Topo Gigio-operated puppets. It took five people in black who got crushed out on the screen to do them. And there were these chorus girls in the dressing room and they did little numbers. There was a dumb girl. There was a very sophisticated girl. There were four or five characters and a stage manager. And Dean Martin would come into their dressing room and he'd talk to them. And they did a number each week."

The act quickly became a viewer favorite. Then Liberace unintentionally ruined it for Sid and Marty.

"Liberace had a huge fan club, maybe a quarter of a million people. And in his newsletter, he said, 'As you know, Sid Krofft, who I discovered...' He really didn't discover me, but always used to say that. I toured with him for a couple of years, so they all knew who I was, all the Liberace fans. And he said in his newsletter—he did this on his own—he said, 'I'm sure you're all watching him on *The Dean Martin Show*. Isn't it wonderful that he has a series? Would you write a letter to NBC and Dean Martin and tell them how much you love the puppets.'

"A huge amount of mail came, because Liberace's fans did whatever he wanted them to do. And it backfired. We were fired because we got too much mail and Dean Martin didn't like that. In a lot of the letters, people called him a drunk and he freaked out. So they fired us. We were signed for twenty-six shows, but we did like maybe only eight of them."

Even as burgeoning stars on a hit TV variety show, however, the

Kroffts still weren't exactly household names—not until a series of events that would dramatically change the course of their careers.

It all started with the Banana Splits.

Hanna-Barbera Studios approached the Kroffts in 1968 about designing costumes for characters to appear in *The Banana Splits Adventure Hour* (1968–70), a Saturday morning program that mixed cartoon clips with live-action sequences.

Dean Martin chats with the ladies in a marionette chorus line, regulars on *The Dean Martin Show* until they were replaced by the Golddiggers.
SID & MARTY KROFFT PICTURES.

Compared to such Hanna-Barbera classics as *The Flintstones, The Jetsons, Yogi Bear* and *Scooby-Doo*, *The Banana Splits* rate little more than a footnote in the careers of animation giants William Hanna and Joe Barbera.

In fact, Barbera can recall some of the most minuscule details about his earliest cartoons, but he says that *The Banana Splits* are barely more than a blip in his memory. But for Sid and Marty, the show proved to be monumental.

The show's live characters were the Banana Splits themselves, a mod rock band comprised of four cartoon-like animals (Fleegle, Bingo, Drooper and Snorky—a dog, gorilla, lion and elephant) who would perform short comedy sketches and musical numbers before introducing Hanna-Barbera cartoons.

The Kroffts were brought preliminary drawings of these four characters and were asked to design "walk-around suits" that would transform them into three-dimensional beings.

"They came in with the idea and a rough sketch," Sid recalls. "We had to redesign them. And after it was all said and done, when the Hanna-Barbera guys walked out the door, I looked at my brother and I said, 'My God, because of us, they're going to make millions.'"

The seed of an idea had taken root. Now all it needed was a little nurturing to grow and bloom.

Enter NBC, the network that aired *The Banana Splits*.

"They were so leery about the whole thing, the people at NBC, that they used to come and watch us build these things and they thought that our place was amazing," Sid says. "It was the head of daytime programming who, after seeing all of this, said to my brother and myself, 'Why don't you guys come up with your own television show?'

"And that's how *Pufnstuf* was born. They said, 'Why don't you create your own show?' And I said, 'Well, why not? Why should they be the only ones who make millions?'"

Sid quickly developed the concept of what would be *H.R. Pufnstuf*. There was a good reason for Sid to work so quickly. Larry White, head of programming, was leaving town at the end of the week and the Kroffts wanted to have something prepared for him before his trip.

"We gave it to him on a Friday," Marty recalls. "Larry White didn't fly. This guy only took trains. So I met him at Union Station. And he had the treatment on the train with him for the weekend. And he called me on Monday and said, 'You have a deal.'"

After that, the pace never slowed. *H.R. Pufnstuf* was the first new show officially picked up by the network for the 1969–70 television season. It would be on the air by the following fall, premiering Saturday, September 6, 1969, in a 10 A.M. time slot.

And to paraphrase Neil Armstrong, who had walked on the moon only a few weeks earlier in July, Sid and Marty's first show would prove to be one small step for a man in a puppet suit…one giant leap for the Kroffts' careers.

What a Sport!

Sports mascots such as the San Diego Chicken and the Phillie Fanatic owe a debt of thanks to Sid and Marty Krofft's creations, if only as an indirect influence.

But one member of the sideline mascot family can call the Kroffts his parents.

Sid and Marty designed the '70s sideline mascot for the NFL's Atlanta Falcons.

"It was called No. ½," Marty says. "That's what was on his uniform. After a while, when the team kept losing, they fired him. It wasn't his fault that the team was losing, but I guess someone had to take the fall."

Marty says that was the brothers' only foray onto the sports playing field—and that opportunity arose because of their ties at the time to Atlanta, where their indoor amusement park, the World of Sid & Marty Krofft, was based.

You can see the Krofft influence in other unlikely areas as well. They also designed the walk-around suit of the giant glass pitcher of Kool-Aid, used for many years in that company's television commercials.

"Rolf Roediger, who did all our puppet making, would have been involved in that," says Sid, who says he would rather drink poison than the sugary soft drink. "It was designed by our company and built by us. But I didn't have anything to do with that."

Dr. Blinky the owl, Pufnstuf, Jimmy, Cling and Clang huddle up.
SID & MARTY KROFFT PICTURES.

Can't Spend a Little 'Cuz He Can't Spend Enough ...or How Pufnstuf Nearly Ruined the Kroffts

They leaped before they looked.

When Sid and Marty Krofft committed to producing their first kids show, *H.R. Pufnstuf,* for NBC, they literally had no idea what this foray into the world of television would bring.

The show ultimately proved to be the crown jewel in their celebrated careers and its success opened doors to countless other possibilities. In hindsight, the Krofft brothers say they were lucky. As Marty puts it, "I guess you can say that *Pufnstuf* was just a charmed show."

But what if *Pufnstuf* had turned out to be a flop? That certainly was a possibility, for the simple reason that Sid and Marty were wet-behind-the-ears rookies in this exciting, different medium. This inexperience could prove particularly damning if they were unable to recognize and avoid production pitfalls until hopelessly mired in them.

Sid and Marty both remember, for example, that the greatest obstacle when it came to making their first TV show was putting *Pufnstuf* together without breaking the bank.

"We never did a show before that," Sid says. "That was our first one. And the hardest thing to pull off was the budget. We went a million dollars over. That doesn't sound like that much money today, but we almost lost our company. We really didn't know what to do, how to do it, and we did it on film, which made it even more expensive."

Add to that the fact that Sid refused to compromise his vision in any way, even though compromise is a way of life when it comes to making television.

Even George Lucas cut his Jabba the Hut scenes out of *Star Wars* in 1976 once he realized he couldn't afford the expensive special effects required to depict what he had in mind. Had it been Sid Krofft instead of Lucas at the helm, the Jabba scenes wouldn't have been abandoned, but the film's finances would have been thrown into hopeless disarray.

"I would not allow anything to be cut out: ideas, characters, sets, music, everything. I mean, visually I saw the whole thing and I didn't want any of it disturbed. It was our first show. So how could I? And they always tell me that I go over budget because I don't like cutting anything.

"As a matter of fact, the last episode of *Pufnstuf* is a 'dream' show because we were out of money. So we just did a little tiny opening and closing and used clips from all the shows. That was the only way we could afford to do it."

Marty confirms that the economic situation during the *Puf*-in-production days became extremely dicey.

"We were way over budget because the network didn't pay us enough to make it," he says. "That was the problem. We only got $52,000 a half-hour for *Pufnstuf*. And if you look at what's on the screen, you know why we almost went broke. Every dollar that we got is up there on the screen, every dollar and then some.

"That was because of our inexperience in budgeting the show. My brother said, 'Don't worry. I've got it covered.' But we didn't know. It wasn't his fault. It's just that it was an ambitious undertaking and we were in way over our heads. We were in love. This was exciting to get our first series. It was ours. And so we went the full nine yards."

Again, what if *Pufnstuf* hadn't been a ratings success?

Marty shudders to think what might have become of the Kroffts and their company. "We were in major trouble. Major, major trouble. And it took us quite a while to get out of that hole. This is the tough part of being independent. You don't have Big Brother supporting you. Everything we had went into this. At the time, we were doing puppet shows at the four Six Flags parks. And we were taking all that money and putting it into *Pufnstuf*.

"I don't know what we would have done had the show failed. It would have wiped us out financially. What would we have done after that? I don't know. I would have probably gone back to school to become a dentist."

Fortunately for the Kroffts, the program proved to be so popular it thrived for two years on NBC (even though it amounted to only seventeen episodes), followed by a year on ABC and then another two-and-a-half years in widespread syndication.

"That's what pulled us out of the hole," Marty says, "the fact that it was a big hit. General Mills came in as a sponsor and we wound up with a five-and-a-half-year run with those seventeen episodes."

Simply put, the charm and the quality of the work itself proved to be the Kroffts' financial salvation.

Of course, given that almost every nuance of the show harked back in some way to the Kroffts' stellar careers in puppetry, was there ever any real danger of failure? Not on an artistic level, at least. Unfortunately, art isn't always the primary concern in the TV business.

"Did you know that the network turned down the title, *Pufnstuf*?" Sid says. "They said I couldn't use it and I said, 'Why?' And they said, 'Well, it sounds too feminine. It sounds like a powder puff.' So I said, 'Well, I'm not changing it.' So that shows where their heads were at.

"Also, another story is that they definitely wanted to see the rough cut of the first episode and we didn't want to show it to them. There was no music and no sound effects yet, but they insisted. And they rejected the show. They said that it was just awful and they wanted us to go back to reshoot. Then we put down the effects and music in it and we sent it back. We didn't do anything else, didn't change anything, didn't reshoot anything. And they said, 'That's great.'"

From where did the idea of *Pufnstuf* come?

Even though it's certainly possible to stumble across an idea for a children's show and develop it in a matter of days (that's what happened with *Sigmund and the Sea Monsters,* for example), Sid says the various elements that comprised *H.R. Pufnstuf* were the culmination of a lengthy career and a lifetime of experiences.

Says Sid: "The Pufnstuf character came from a show in the San Antonio Fair [Hemisfair '68]. We had a show called *Kaleidoscope* that we did in the Coca-Cola Pavilion and there was a character in it called Luther. The show was all about a superhero who was changed into a dragon by a witch and the only way he could be changed back was to be kissed by someone. But who wants to kiss a monster? So that was the theme of the whole show. It was his search. It was a big musical.

"And that character became so popular at the fair that that's where that whole idea came from. When I created *Pufnstuf,* I started with the idea of this great character from the San Antonio Fair."

Like Luther, a lovable monster, Puf turned out to be a dragon: eight feet tall, bright green, with white Western-style boots, a four-foot tail and a head as big as a satellite dish that was topped by a shock of bright orange hair. He wasn't exactly the same, mind you, and refinements were made. Luther, for example, didn't have arms.

As for Pufnstuf's name, the Kroffts got some help from an outside source.

Says screenwriter Michael Blodgett, a longtime friend of Marty's: "Marty called me one time in those days and he said, 'We have got a network deal. I've pitched it and we've brought Luther in and they basically are buying it and they love the concept. But it's called "Luther Land." And the network has come back to me and said it sounds too much like "Lutheran Land."' And he said, 'We've been ordered to change it ASAP. Do you have any ideas?'

"I hadn't done any writing. I was an actor at that time. But I just sat down and thought about it. And it occurred to me that the most popular dragon was Puff the Magic Dragon. So this should be Puff and all of his stuff. And then I wrote it on a page and I changed it around, figuring it's going to be much more eye-catching if you just jam the letters together like that. And I called him back maybe an hour later. I said, 'Hey, try this. Sit down, open up the squawk box so Sid can hear it. I want to tell you your title: *Pufnstuf.*' And they went, *'Pufnstuf?'* 'Yeah, Puff and all of his stuff. You know, like Puff the Magic Dragon.' And they went, 'Wow!'

"Then Marty called me back about a half hour later and he says, 'Sid wants to put 'H.R.' on the front of it.' I never heard what the letters 'H.R.' stood for."

Says Sid: "The letters 'H.R.' are just 'royal highness' turned around."

Living Island, meanwhile, comes directly from Sid's love for nature and beautiful places. "I lived in Maui for eight years and I'm the biggest ad for that island. I've been all over the planet and it's the most beautiful place in the world to me."

Given the many parallels, it's also undeniable that *The Wizard of Oz* was a major source of inspiration for Sid.

For starters, like Oz, Living Island was an enchanted place populated by an eclectic assortment of eccentric and unusual characters, a place where even dancing trees and Judy Garland-like singing frogs had personalities.

As was the case with Dorothy in Oz, Jimmy, the lad who was shipwrecked on Living Island, was constantly searching for a means of returning home, even though doing so would mean having to leave his many new friends behind.

Dorothy and Jimmy were each menaced by a wicked witch, although it's worth noting that Living Island's Witchiepoo was as inept as she was evil. The motivation for each witch's sinister deeds was similar as well: the Wicked Witch of the West angling to get her hands on Dorothy's ruby slippers, Witchiepoo conspiring to take Jimmy's diamond-freckled golden flute.

And while Dorothy traveled along a Yellow Brick Road, Jimmy almost got to make his way home in the first episode along a Magic Path.

Clearly, *The Wizard of Oz* made a big impact on Sid. In fact, he remembers the theater and the city in which he first saw it.

"I was nine years old and we lived in Providence, Rhode Island. I saw it there, in the same theater where I saw *Gone With the Wind*. My God, I'll never forget that because it made a big impression on me, an enormous impression. I mean, it was the perfect movie. The next perfect movie that I ever saw in my life after that was *Star Wars*."

But it's important to note that the Kroffts weren't merely cannibalizing Frank L. Baum and a classic Judy Garland movie musical. Thematically the show might have resembled Oz, but visually it was all Krofft.

"We call it the 'Krofft Look,'" Marty says.

Indeed, the late Nicky Nadeau, who had worked with Sid and Marty for many years and was credited in *Pufnstuf* for "creative design," actually received credit in later series as being in charge of "the Krofft Look."

If the term sounds a tad pretentious and self-important, well, so be it. Besides, television critics coined the phrase in print before Sid and Marty appropriated it.

"The Krofft Look is basically the same look, the same feel, the same visual style, the same sense of color that we have had and refined over the course of many years," Marty says. "We just put a label on it. It was just a natural follow-up to what we had been doing in our stage shows."

Incidentally, another major source of inspiration for Pufnstuf isn't so plainly obvious as the *Oz* influence.

Lennie Weinrib—who wrote all seventeen episodes of the series, first teaming with writing partner Bob Ridolfi, later with Paul Harrison—remembers it this way: "Sid and Marty and I were sitting in the office, as we had many times, only we had a different kind of a conversation this day. Sid and Marty said to me, 'Listen, we want to go on television. We have a couple of characters that

Freddy's Flight

Some people never learn.

Witchiepoo constantly tried and failed to take Freddy the Flute from Jimmy in *H.R. Pufnstuf.* She even briefly had Freddy in her possession from time to time, only to lose him once again. But twenty-five years later, on September 8, 1995, real life imitated art when it was discovered that Freddy the Flute had been stolen from the Kroffts' warehouse.

"Oh, it was hideous," Sid Krofft says. "They went into our warehouse. By the time the alarm system went off and the police came, they were gone. And they didn't take anything else, which was so weird. Only Freddy. That was all we could find that was missing. Out of all of that stuff."

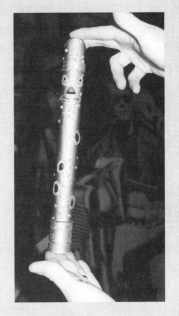

There was a happy ending, however. Two months after Marty offered a $10,000 reward for Freddy's safe return, the flute was turned in anonymously to a Los Angeles TV station.

"We never did find out who took him," Marty says. "All I did was, we got some publicity on it and then we put out a reward and then it was returned to us with a letter that they were just returning the thing. They didn't want the reward. They wanted nothing."

Marty likens it to the school teacher who, dealing with a classroom theft, turns out the lights and says if the stolen item is returned, there will be no questions asked.

The original Freddy the Flute went on display at Planet Hollywood in Hollywood in October 1996.
PHOTO BY BILL MORGAN.

Besides, Marty says, what would have been the point of vigorously pursuing the culprit?

"What am I going to do? There was nothing for me to do. I mean, with all the crime in L.A., the police weren't going to put all those major cases aside and start searching for the guy who stole Freddy the Flute."

Triumph and Tragedy

Just when you start to think you have life figured out, fate has a way of playing cruelly ironic jokes.

It happened to Lennie Weinrib while he was busy crafting the scripts for *H.R. Pufnstuf:* He tragically lost his first writing partner, Bob Ridolfi, because of a car accident. Then, almost comically, he found a new partner, Paul Harrison, because of a dispute over a parking space.

Ridolfi died in an auto accident on New Year's Eve 1968.

"Poor Bob Ridolfi always had a fear of cars," Weinrib remembers. "He would walk to work. Whenever I asked him to let me drive him home, he would usually make an excuse. Once in a great while, in the pouring rain, he'd let me drive him home. He lived like fifty blocks away from the office. I think he always had this premonition that something bad would happen to him in a car. And he was right.

"It was New Year's Eve. I drove him home and we drove past an accident at 6:00 at night. There was like a five-car accident on Sunset Boulevard. I said, 'Well, you see that? That's what happens when people start drinking early New Year's Eve. I hope to hell whoever you're going to be with tonight, you're going to be careful.' He said, 'Oh, we're going to four or five parties.' And I said, 'Oh, Bob, come on, man. You're afraid of cars. Why don't you go to one party and stay there?' And he said, 'Well, maybe you're right. Maybe we'll just go to one or two. It *is* dangerous.' So I drove him home and that was the last time I ever saw him.

"I got a call the next day. 'Do you know a Bob Ridolfi?' I said, 'Yes, he's a friend. He's my writing partner. What is it?' 'Oh, he was killed.' *'He was what? What are you talking about?'* 'Oh, he was in a head-on collision.' What had happened was they went from one party to the other. He didn't listen to me. He was in the back seat with his new wife—six weeks before, I had been the best man at his wedding—and somebody ran a red light and smashed into them head on. Everybody in the car was injured. He and his wife in the back were injured the worst. They had to use the jaws of life to cut him out of the car. He never made it to the hospital. He died en route."

Only a short time later, the happy news that *Pufnstuf* had been greenlighted by the network was tainted by the loss of Weinrib's dear friend.

"Sid and Marty called me to tell me the show sold. Bob never lived to know that he sold his first script. I'm sure he knew from up in heaven that his show sold, but it was a very sad thing. Of course, I made sure that he got credit on the show and that the money was given to his widow, Jan. I made quite sure that nobody ever forgot the residuals that were due to him that were to go to his estate. But it was such a shock, in the middle of such joy and happiness, for this to have happened."

Making matters worse, Weinrib says, was the network's insistence that he get cracking on additional scripts, preferably with a new partner.

"Right away, the network said, 'Well, who's going to work with Lennie?' I was really like in a trauma, but they wanted to get going and do scripts very quickly. And I thought, 'Jesus, what am I going to do?' It was like I could sit down with Bob and we were inside each other's head. We absolutely knew these characters cold. And now one half of the team was gone and the network is saying, 'Start turning out scripts. Let's go.'"

Then fate interceded once more.

"I had a special parking place for my Rolls-Royce and every damn day this old farty car started parking in my space," Weinrib says. "I purposely paid a lot of money so I could have my car specially parked there so nobody would scratch it. And almost every day, this car was in my space.

"So I asked the parking attendants about the car and I was told, 'Well, there's this guy. What can we do? He comes in certain days of the week and, for some reason, he grabs your space.' So I said, 'Well, who is he? I'll ask him please not to do it.' 'Don't get in a fight with him.' I said, 'I'm not going to fight him. But I'm going to set him straight.'

"So I go upstairs, go to an office, walk in. And this guy, an older man, he says, 'Can I help you?' And I say, 'Yeah, you can help me. You can stop parking in my space.' He said, 'Who the hell are you?' I said, 'My name is Lennie Weinrib. I've had an office in this building for a long time. And I'm in a very bad mood because my partner just got killed in a car accident and I really am not going to put up with you, whoever the hell you are. I have a Rolls-Royce, which I worked very hard to buy, and I'm paying for a space and you're in it every day.'

"He said, 'Calm down, calm down, I won't park in your space. Sit down a minute. Have a cup of coffee.' Anyway, bottom line is, that was Paul Harrison. We met that way."

Harrison, who had been a producer on such shows as *The Eddie Fisher Show* and *The Untouchables,* was down on his luck. A friend was letting Harrison use his office space so he could bang out scripts that he then was having a hard time selling.

"Life hadn't been treating him too good. So he said to me, 'I feel bad to ask you this, but you said you might be looking for a writer. Do you think that I might work with you?' So anyway I read his stuff and I liked it. We sat and talked a lot. I brought him out to the Kroffts. They liked him. I liked him. Everybody liked him. And the rest is history. He and I wrote the rest of the series.

"But it's funny, this guy and I immediately squared off and then we settled down and, from then on, we were good friends to the very end."

we used in our live show. We've got Pufnstuf, this big character with the cowboy hat and the boots, and we've got this crazy witch. And basically we have them running around. She's chasing him, he's chasing her, whatever. But where do we go from there? Do you have any ideas?'

"Well, the night before, I had seen a show that I watched every week religiously, *The Prisoner,* with Patrick McGoohan. And I always loved the idea that they caught this secret agent, put him on this island in a strange, sort of futuristic setting, and every week the idea was that he tried to escape and he never could get off the island. It was a great show. I really enjoyed it. Everybody did. So I said to Sid, 'You know, I watched a show last night with Patrick McGoohan, which I adore, and wouldn't it be fun if we do something like *The Prisoner?* We have a kid who is trapped on an island. The kid keeps trying to escape. The witch is chasing him. Maybe Pufnstuf is helping him. I don't know how it plays out. But the idea is that he can't get back home. He can't get off the damn island, just like on *The Prisoner.*' And they said, 'Hey, that sounds pretty good. Go with that.' And so I went back and started to write."

Pufnstuf was beginning to take shape. And while Weinrib and Ridolfi were toiling away with the script, the Kroffts were searching for the talent to make their unique vision come to life.

In addition to their already-assembled team of skilled puppeteers and little people, the brothers had to cast two human parts, Jimmy and Witchiepoo, and they hit the jackpot with Jack Wild and Billie Hayes. But even in casting these two, neither of whom the Kroffts had met before *Pufnstuf,* there was a huge element of pure luck.

Says Wild, a British-born former child star who was sixteen years old when he did *Pufnstuf:* "They had seen me in *Oliver!* and apparently it was Sid Krofft who said to Marty, 'Look, that is our Jimmy. He is the one we've got to have. And we've got to do whatever's necessary to get the guy.' And that's what they did. They called my business manager and did the deal."

That's all true. But there is another part of the story that Wild is unaware of: Had Sid not been privy to an advance copy of the Oscar-winning musical in 1968, he might not have known to pursue Wild until the casting process was already well under way.

It seems that Lionel Bart, the composer who put Charles Dickens' *Oliver Twist* to music, was a friend of Sid's. "And Lionel Bart was in L.A. with a rough copy of *Oliver!,*" Sid remembers. "It didn't have any music or sound effects yet, but he wanted me to see it, a rough cut of it, because he was so worried about it.

"And I saw this kid and I couldn't believe this little kid, the Artful Dodger. We had just gotten the order for *Pufnstuf* and I had said to my brother, 'We've got to find a real unusual kid.' I didn't want a brat because, to me, most kids try to be adult. And I wanted a kid who the little girls are going to love as well as the boys. And I wanted somebody they can relate to. I didn't know what the hell we were looking for, who that might be. We hadn't even auditioned anyone at that point.

"And then Lionel Bart shows me *Oliver!* and my search is over. I told my brother about this kid and he saw a little piece of film on him and he agreed. We had to have this kid. So we flew him in. I seem to remember that we couldn't even find him at first, that it took some searching. But we did it, whatever it took, because we *had* to have that kid."

Jack Wild as Jimmy.
SID & MARTY KROFFT PICTURES.

'Come and Play With Me, Jimmy'

They don't make shows like *H.R. Pufnstuf* any more.

So says Jack Wild, who starred as Jimmy in the series and the big-screen follow-up of the same title, an acting credit that still rates prominently on his resumé even though he has been through much, personally and professionally, in the past quarter of a century.

"I know it's a cliché to say they don't make shows like that any more," he says, "but it's a cliché that happens to be true. And I know I'm biased, but they just don't do it.

"And I think that's very sad, because most of today's kid stuff has far too much violence. It all seems to be negative, as opposed to positive and fun. It will go full circle eventually, because it can't continue this way, all this rubbish on TV."

On that day when there is a return to more wholesome children's programming, Wild adds, *Pufnstuf* would serve as a worthy standard for producers to try to match.

"I've yet to meet or hear about anybody who didn't like *Pufnstuf*," he says. "Without sounding flash, that is a fact."

Unlike many of the young actors who starred in Krofft programs, Wild never left show business as he grew to adulthood. His career still flourishes, particularly on the British stage.

Born in England in 1953, Wild first turned heads and achieved stardom as the Artful Dodger in *Oliver!,* a movie role for which the then fifteen-year-old earned widespread praise. (The *Hollywood Citizen-News,* for example, heralded him as "the most precocious film discovery of 1968.")

The kid could do it all and had charisma to burn, as was further evidenced by his performance in *Pufnstuf.*

"Jack could do anything we asked of him," Marty Krofft says. "I mean, not only could he sing and dance, but he was a good actor too. That kind of combination, that's not a common thing to find in a kid."

Adds costar Billie Hayes: "The Kroffts could have hired a different kid and maybe it would have worked just as well. But I wouldn't count on it."

Not surprisingly, Wild—who says one of his cherished souvenirs long after the show wrapped was one of the original Freddy the Flutes—is equally generous with praise for the Kroffts. The mere fact, for example, that he and the Krofft brothers remain close, decades later, speaks volumes.

While *Pufnstuf* was in production, in fact, Wild actually lived with Marty, his wife and three daughters. That time together, he notes, established a bond that is much stronger than a mere employer-employee relationship. And when Marty called Wild in 1995, asking him to help promote the Nick at Nite Pufapalooza marathon, Wild hopped on a plane and came to New York.

"I had an absolute ball doing the show," he says. "I've got nothing but great—not merely good, great—memories of it. I was in paradise, to put it mildly."

That's why he has so enjoyed the resurgence of *Pufnstuf* in recent years. "I find it a little bit hard to take on board, actually, how over the years people have sort of held that in their memories and look back on it now with lots of happiness."

In late 1996, Wild started putting together a "mini-album" that would team him once again with *Pufnstuf* characters while also writing his autobiography. The book frankly reveals a rather traumatic period in his life, when a drinking problem became so severe it jeopardized his health and his life, as well as the triumph of overcoming alcoholism after he became a Christian in 1989.

"We've found that there has been a lot of interest in this," he says, "and a lot of it is because of the resurgence of the series. I'm hoping that there will be a lot of positive results from it."

Clearly, this is an entertainer who has no qualms with being so strongly identified with a past role from his teens.

As he sees it, "Without the public, actors would sort of get nowhere fast. The bottom line is it's the fans indirectly paying our wages for the work that we do. We should be thankful that people are actually remembering what we've done. Because nowadays, people do have so much to choose from. In every scenario, the public is spoiled for choice.

"So I feel lucky that someone has chosen to give me their time to say, 'I thought that was really good'—or even 'I didn't think that was as good as when you did this.' As far as I'm concerned, that is the only way to look at it."

What's more, Wild says if he ever uttered a disparaging word about *Pufnstuf* in the past, he really didn't mean it.

Pufnstuf and Jack Wild, reunited at a Los Angeles comic book convention in 1996.
PHOTO BY GREG DAVIS.

"Oh, there might have been a time when I would say I was tired of it, but only in a joking fashion. It was only to make someone laugh. But the honesty of the situation is I still love it and it still stands up, even today. And how can anything like that be negative?

"Considering the amount of happiness it has given people, I am just lucky to have been involved."

Wild's theory on why the show has endured?

"Because of the actual story line, it's timeless, and because it's so color-ful. And even the characters. Their voices, they sounded very much like John Wayne or Mae West or W. C. Fields or somebody who was already a big star in their own right. And therefore, not only would you have the youngsters loving visually what they were seeing, you'd also get their parents looking at the characters and saying, 'Yeah, that one's Mae West. That one's W. C. Fields. That one is Groucho Marx.'

"In other words, what Sid and Marty had created was a thing that was fun for the youngsters as well as for their parents. Which was a good thing in the long term. Because now that the youngsters have grown up, there's still something there in the show for them to be entertained by."

Billie Hayes is also quick to sing Wild's praises.

"Everything fell into place when they got Jack," she says. "That's my personal opinion. You had to have the right kid, a kid who was extremely talented, musically as well as as an actor. And that's what they got when they found Jack. He was skilled. He was professional. He wasn't precocious. He wasn't full of himself. I could sense no ego trip or anything.

"The only problem that Jack and I ever had was in the very beginning: I couldn't understand one damn thing he said. I said, 'I don't know what you're talking about!' I said, 'Speak English!' He said, 'I am speaking English!' And I said, 'No, you're not! You're speaking Cockney! I can't understand you!'

"We just really fell in love with each other. And me being so typically Midwestern and he being so British, I figured, 'Well, I hope this works.' And it did. It really did. To this day, we're still great friends. I was lucky to get this kind of a kid to work with and I think that he feels that he was lucky to have gotten me."

Similarly, Sid, Marty and Wild speak just as highly of Hayes. In fact, Sid is so devoted to her that he says he can't imagine casting any other actress to play Witchiepoo in the on-the-drawing-board *Pufnstuf* movie. "I don't care if I could have any of the biggest names in the movies for that part," he says. "I want Witchiepoo to play Witchiepoo."

Says Wild: "Billie Hayes was so good as Witchiepoo, I always thought she should have won an Emmy."

Hayes, who later played Weenie the Genie in *Lidsville,* is quick to note that, had an element of pure chance not come into play, she possibly never would have met the Kroffts or landed these two terrific roles.

"I was in Las Vegas doing *Hello, Dolly!* with Betty Grable," she recalls. "And there was a fellow in the show, the fellow playing Cornelius, by the name of Peter Walker. And when the show was over, even though I had been living in New York up to that point, I moved out to L.A. And one day I got a phone call from the Kroffts' office.

"And what had happened is that Peter Walker was in a restaurant in Hollywood and he knew Sid and some of Sid's friends. And Sid told him what they were up to. And Sid said, 'But we're having a hard time finding someone to play Witchiepoo, because we want

Billie Hayes as Witchiepoo and Martha Raye as Boss Witch in the movie, *Pufnstuf*.

Which is Witch and Who is Who?

Whenever someone dismisses Billie Hayes's portrayal of Witchiepoo as being nothing more than a Margaret Hamilton wannabe, she can't help being a bit bewildered by the comment.

After all, she insists, her character and Hamilton's Wicked Witch of the West (made immortal in *The Wizard of Oz*) have virtually nothing in common.

"I don't know how anybody could have thought that we were copying her," Hayes says. "These two witches are totally different. Margaret's character was a pure villain, whereas I never really look at Witchiepoo as a villain. And they don't even look alike. Witchiepoo, with the red hair and the warts, and Witchiepoo doesn't even have the classical witch's nose.

"The only thing that I can thank Margaret for: She's from Ohio originally and I'm from southern Illinois. So we're really like neighbors. And people from that part of the Midwest, we all have a very similar sound, similar rhythms to our voices. There's a monotone, a flatness to the voice. At least I have found that in the Midwesterners I have met. Margaret had it and I've got it. Anyway, I've got to tell you the truth: I got a record of *The Wizard of Oz* when I knew I was going to do Witchiepoo. And I listened to it and I paid close attention to her voice. The voice is the only thing we've got in common."

It so happens, incidentally, that long after Hayes and Hamilton had become known for their respective bewitching roles, the two met, became friends and even compared notes on the nuances of one another's portrayals.

"Paul Lynde and I were close friends for years in New York," Hayes recalls. "He came out here first and I came out after. And he was going to do a Halloween special. And he asked me if I would do it as Witchiepoo. And I said, sure, of course. And so he said, 'I'm going to get Margaret to do it too. The two of you can be like sisters.'

"Margaret was staying at the Holiday Inn up on Hollywood Boulevard and we were filming over at ABC on Prospect. And so I said to her, 'I live over in Laurel Canyon and so why don't I just pick you up every morning?' And we became really nice friends, really good friends. And I'd never dreamed that she'd ever watched *Pufnstuf*, but she told me, 'I love your character because, unlike mine, you're funny.' She said, 'I wasn't allowed to be funny.' And she said, 'You poor thing, you never pull anything off but, boy, you sure try.'

"I've got a picture of Margaret [who died in 1985] and myself together. It's only a small Polaroid, but I really cherish it."

Hamilton wasn't the only person who thought Hayes made a lovable wicked witch. Hayes vividly remembers an incident during the filming of Pufnstuf that gave her insight into how children viewed her character.

"They had had a group of these people on the set one day and they were there while we were filming a segment where Witchiepoo's broom catches fire. And so Witchiepoo is trying to put this fire out and I'm yelling my head off and I'm mad and, oh, I'm really nuts. And it's really fire. I mean, this was not a fake fire. It was a controlled fire, sure, but it's fire. And while I was wandering around and acting like a wild lady, I notice out of the corner of my eye, there's this little blond boy, about three or four years old, sitting on the shoulders of this man. I don't know why I noticed him. Humans are funny. I'm in the middle of this scene, this fiery scene, and my eye catches this cute little kid.

"So it's later the same day. The group that visited our set had lunch in the commissary and Sid or Marty, I can't remember which, came to me in my dressing and said, 'Billie, I know it's lunch hour, but would you mind just going over for a split second to the commissary, just to wave to everybody in the room and then you can go back and have your lunch? Would you mind doing that?' And I said, no, I don't mind. So I put the wig back on and the hat, the whole thing, I went over there and waved to the kids and walked amongst the tables, this and that, and they wanted to touch me, all that stuff. And now I'm getting ready to leave. And there was a lady with this little blond boy. And I recognized this boy. It was the same little kid.

"And I thought, my God, I must have scared the living hell out of him, the way I was carrying on like crazy. And so I went to walk by him because I was getting ready to leave. And the woman said, 'Excuse me, Witchiepoo?' And I said, 'Yes?' And she looked at this little boy and she said to him, 'Well, go ahead, ask her.' And I thought, this little boy, if I bend down and get too close to him, he watched that scene, he's just going to be scared to death. And he's just staring at me like he's mesmerized. And so she says, 'Go ahead, ask her.' And he shakes his head, no.

"So I bend down so that I'm level to him. I don't touch him, though, because I'm sure he's afraid of me. So I just get like level to him. And I said, 'Do you want to say something to me?' And he shook his head again. And she said, 'Now go ahead, you wanted to ask her.'

"And so he looked at me and said, 'Will you hug me?'

"When I told Margaret that story, she said, 'Never in a million years would a kid ask me to hug them.' She said, 'That's just it. You endeared your-self to these kids. Even though some of them were frightened of you, at the same time, they want-ed to touch you, they wanted to be near you.'

"This little boy said, 'Will you hug me?' And I wrapped my arms around him and just hugged him and I held him so tight. And it was a lesson to me, because these children real-ly take what you're doing seriously. You are a real per-son to them. And so you really have to take what you do seriously. I find a lot of people who do children's shows, they don't think that way.

"It's like I tell people, I never once did that show thinking that I was 'mere-ly' doing it for children."

Billie Hayes.
PHOTO BY TIM NEELEY.

her to sing and dance and have a lot of energy.' And so Peter said, 'Wait a minute. I was in *Hello, Dolly!* with somebody. You've got to take a look at her. This is the person to do that role.'

"So anyway, through Peter discussing it with Sid, that led to Sid discussing it with Marty and their director, Hollingsworth Morse, and they called me out to the Factory and I read for them. I did a musical number with no music, a number that I have done for years that I do so well I didn't even need a piano. And that was it. They called me a day or two later and told me that they had decided on me. That was it.

"But if Peter Walker hadn't been friends with Sid and if he had not happened to have mentioned me, I probably never would have been brought into the lives of Marty and Sid."

Having the right talent in place was a major step in the right direction, but there still were other land mines that had to be sidestepped, hurdles that had to be cleared.

First and foremost, as mentioned already, was the fact that Sid and Marty were novices when it came to producing a television show. But the Kroffts succeeded because they managed to adapt their years of experience to fit a different medium while assembling the right crew of technical support.

Says Weinrib: "Producing a television show is like being a fireman who's always on duty. You never know when the next fire's going to break out and in what department it will happen. The costume people are having a problem. Or the puppeteer in the suit can't get up to that certain crevice, so we can't do that joke that certain way because they can't physically do it. Or the director says, 'How the hell am I going to shoot that? I don't have a big enough set and we don't have a stunt man to do that gag.'

"In other words, it's a constantly evolving situation, producing a show. And if you lose control at any moment, you might not be able to make the show in the time and for the money that you've accounted for. So it means that everybody—the artists, the writers, the musicians, the puppeteers, the cameramen—everybody has to be working together with one single purpose in mind, and that is to make the best damn show that you can."

Says Hayes: "The Kroffts were smart. They hired the right people and they listened to them. Like Si Rose, who was one of the producers. He had done many shows, many prime-time shows, and the Kroffts really listened to Si.

"If you don't know what you're doing, you can hire a bunch of duds and totally wreck the thing. But we lucked out because everybody came into that show as professionals with good backgrounds. I have done shows since then where I couldn't believe what I was dealing with. I couldn't believe that people could get that far in show business and not know what they were doing. It would have been easy for the Kroffts to have made major mistakes, but they didn't. And Si Rose was one of the guiding factors for that."

Says Sid: "Si Rose is an incredible friend of ours. He produced *McHale's Navy* and he came in because we didn't know that much about television in the beginning and he was already an established producer-writer. And he's the coolest. He's just the coolest man. He came in just to help us a little and he got so involved and loved it so much that he hung with us for years."

Rose—who served as executive producer on *Pufnstuf* as well as *The Bugaloos, Lidsville, Sigmund and the Sea Monsters* and *The Lost Saucer*—confirms that he had no intention of joining the team in the beginning, but then he got hooked.

"We were old friends and I was at Universal Studios producing *McHale's Navy* at the time," Rose recalls. "We were just friendly then. You know, we would talk and I would give them some ideas here and there. Nothing more than that really. I finished my deal at Universal and I was just doing some pilots. Sid and Marty had just sold *Pufnstuf,* and they had been in production with it.

"They had this great idea, a grand idea, and they like to do everything in this terrific style that they have. And money's no object. And they suddenly realized that they had a monster going because the cost was really rising tremendously. So they asked me, could I help them out? And I said, 'Okay, I'll come over and see what's going on.' I looked over the scripts and stuff like that."

Rose was merely going to offer more advice and move on. That was his plan anyway.

"I was working on these pilots, so they asked me to come in on a deal, like half a day or something. And Saturday morning television, I didn't know too much about it. But I started learning. And being with them, it got so interesting and exciting that, after doing it for a while, I grew to love it. They made me an offer to come and join the company. And so, after a lot of thought—I had been in prime time all these years, but I thought they had something really good going—I came aboard and joined them."

Had Rose not come aboard, the financial hole that the Kroffts had dug for themselves might have gotten even bigger.

"They were very successful with their puppet shows, *Les Poupees de Paris* and all that, and they really knew how to put on first-rate entertainment," Rose says. "But dealing with the tight form of a half-hour television show, that was a new experience for them. As the years went by, they picked up all the knowledge of how to put on a television show. But in the early year or two, it was difficult.

"The toughest thing was to get them to cut down. Sid would want the world and Marty would try to get him down a little, because he used to watch the money. And then it would come to me and I would have to say, 'Let's see if we can get a budget where we can do it every week and not lose a ton of money.' Because they did lose quite a bit of money on *Pufnstuf*.

"But in the long run, I guess you could say it was well worth losing, because it launched them into Saturday morning television and later into many, many things."

One element of the show that was all Rose, Sid adds, was the canned laughter. "That was Si Rose's idea. Because he was the king of sitcoms at that time. He said that was how a sitcom was done and these shows really were like sitcoms.

"He felt that it needed a laugh track, that it was just too dry without it. And I could be wrong on this, but I don't think there were any shows on Saturdays before us that had canned laughter."

Sid says that Nadeau, his longtime art director, also was responsible for bringing in countless fresh ideas and talented personnel.

"Nicky Nadeau was with us right from the beginning. I knew

him from way back, when I did my live act. He was with the New York Ballet Company and he was the most incredible artist. And I said, 'Some day, that's what you're going to be doing for a living, not dancing.' I approached him when I had the idea to do *Les Poupees de Paris,* the adult puppet show, and Nicky not only designed the whole show but he also designed the theater and built it. I mean, he was fantastic.

The Case of the Purloined 'Puf' Stuff

No wonder they dubbed him the hamburglar.

Have you ever noticed the striking similarity between McDonaldland, the fast-food fantasy land created in the early 1970s to sell McDonald's hamburgers, and *H.R. Pufnstuf*'s Living Island?

If so, you aren't alone.

When McDonald's introduced an advertising campaign featuring McDonaldland—a place populated by *Pufnstuf*-like characters such as Mayor McCheese, the Purple Grimace and the Hamburglar—Sid and Marty Krofft felt they had been violated, that the advertising agency behind McDonaldland's creation had plundered through the Kroffts' intellectual property and pilfered their ideas.

This was a case in which imitation wasn't accepted as sincere flattery. Sid and Marty decided to sue.

"It's the leading case in copyright law today," Marty says. *"Sid & Marty Krofft v. McDonald's.* We took them to court in 1971 and it got resolved in 1983. It took more than ten years. We went to the appellate court in the United States and they reversed the judge, the federal judge who ruled against us, and it's now the leading case in copyright law."

Perhaps the creation of McDonaldland wouldn't have been so galling had representatives of the ad agency not consulted Sid and Marty, tapping their brains for ideas before developing their own version.

"The agency came to us, to create McDonaldland, a la *Pufnstuf*," Marty says. "And the next thing I knew, they did it all on their own after they had

"When we got into television, he was the head art director. He brought all these very odd people who weren't just Hollywood artists. They were people he had found and people he knew. I mean, we had the most creative bunch of people and they were all fresh. It wasn't like digging into the Hollywood bag of the ordinary, same kind of look. That's why our look became so distinctive. Because no one ever saw anything like that. So he gave us the Krofft Look.

access to our work. And what they really did was copy a lot of our characters and push them around a little bit."

A clear case of copyright infringement, it would seem, but establishing the indiscretion in court was easier said than done.

The legal strategy Team Krofft pursued was reminiscent of a climactic scene in *Working Girl* (1988), the movie that starred Melanie Griffith as a wannabe executive with a great idea and a credit-grabbing superior (Sigourney Weaver). At the end, when asked to recount the genesis of an innovative idea, Griffith's character concisely but definitively reconstructed the thought process while Weaver's hemmed and hawed, saying only that she would have to "check my notes."

"That's exactly what happened in this case," Marty says. "The guy from the agency said he had a dream about it."

Says Sid: "When they went on the stand, their side, our lawyer asked the president of the agency, 'Well, where did you get the idea?' And he said, 'Oh, I just woke up one morning and got the idea.' And our lawyer said, 'Well, what kind of a background do you have?'

"And that's really all he had to do, because when I got on the stand, I was on for two days. I'd never even been to court before that. And they just wanted to ask me to tell the whole story of my life, where my background came from and how I created the show.

"We came in with one lawyer. They came in with a whole team. God, they had like ten lawyers. But that shows you, in America, that the jury knows. They were totally on our side. Because they could relate to these two little guys who didn't have the largest company in the world. But we were honest in what we said. I think that's why we won."

"I worked with him so many years that we could just be in a room and he knew exactly what I was thinking. I'd come up with a crazy idea and he would just draw it and then he'd give it to his artists and they would go further with it. That's why *Pufnstuf* was so out there."

Says Billie Hayes: "What happened was the Kroffts lucked out. This particular show had everything in place. Everything was in place with the right people at the right time. We had the perfect director in Holly Morse, who was a really fun, skilled director: no play-acting at being a director, no ego trips. We had a really experienced choreographer, Hal Belfer. We had great camera people. The best voice people in the business, Lennie Weinrib, Walker Edmiston and Joan Gerber. And writers who understood what the Kroffts were going for."

Clearly, Weinrib was a particularly important member of the Krofft team, given that he performed double duty as writer and voice specialist.

"Lennie was with us for years," Sid says. "Lennie did the voices for Pufnstuf and Ludicrous Lion and Dr. Blinky. In fact, he did three or four voices, maybe five. I'll bet that any voice you ask him to do, he can do."

Writing and doing vocals weren't really separate jobs for Weinrib, though, because he has long felt that once he knows a character's voice, he knows the character. As he sees it, creating the voice is part of the writing.

"Take the case of, say, Ludicrous Lion," Weinrib says. "And you'll find that this scenario projects into all the other characters. As we were writing him, we thought, well, what is he like? Well, he's a con man. He's trying to fool everybody. He's putting one over on them. And as we were creating him and writing him, I said to myself, 'Wait a minute. He's sort of a W. C. Fields kind of guy.' So I started looking at some of my old W. C. Fields tapes and said, 'That's it. That's Ludicrous Lion.' So I said to Sid, 'How do you like the idea of W. C. Fields.' And he goes, 'That's great, Lennie. I love it.' And once we decide on the voice, the lines come easier.

"The same thing goes for Dr. Blinky. As soon as we decided that

Ludicrous Lion, played by Johnny Silver, was a feline con artist.
SID & MARTY KROFFT PICTURES.

Blinky was going to be an Ed Wynn-type of character, as soon as we knew how this character would talk, we also knew how he'd act in any given situation. And it becomes easy. It works even down to the little characters, like the candle or the skull in Witchiepoo's castle. If they're going to be scary, I say, 'Gee, I wonder how that will sound as Boris Karloff.' And then we know that every time we write the skull a line, he's got to be like Karloff.

"So the way I always approached the writing: How do the characters sound? Once you know that, you've got the whole thing licked."

Pufnstuf was different, mind you, because his voice was an original, not an imitation of a famous personality.

"The voice I gave to Pufnstuf, Marty always thought it was Jim Nabors, but it has nothing to do with Jim. I wanted to create a very soft kind of 'Hi, boys and girls. My name's H.R. Pufnstuf. Well, I'll be wangdoodled. Look at ol' Witchiepoo.' I tried to make it very soft and very careful. So it has nothing to do with Jim Nabors, which is more of a screaming, hillbilly voice.

"And another thing I did was I started looking up words in old slang dictionaries. That's where I got 'wangdoodled' and 'hornswaggled.' 'Well, I'll be wangdoodled.' 'Well, I'll be hornswaggled.' Those were early American words and I thought it kind of fit, since he was an Americana kind of figure, with the boots and the hat, to give him a language all his own."

And, of course, whenever the Kroffts express gratitude to the "little people," without whom they never could have accomplished such an ambitious undertaking as *Pufnstuf*, they aren't merely uttering the standard Hollywood cliché. In the weird and wonderful world of Sid and Marty Krofft, little people are valued performers.

"We employed more little people than anyone," Sid says. "No one employed that many since *The Wizard of Oz*."

"I really have to say this," Hayes says emphatically. "I feel that it's very important that some of the little people be given credit for this show, because these people were absolutely brilliant at what they did in these costumes, people like Angelo Rossitto and Joy Campbell and Felix Silla.

"It wasn't their faces that you saw or their voices that you heard, but the work and the beauty of what they did is theirs. Everything that you see on that screen, physically, that's the little person, performing. And I feel that they're unsung heroes."

Wild agrees wholeheartedly, although he remembers that acting alongside little people in character costumes wasn't always the easiest thing to do. "It does become awkward, because you have to learn the voices for the different characters," he says. "You have to know the script inside out. Because when we were filming it, the people inside the costumes were not the people doing the voices. It would be one lady, the dialog director, sitting by the camera, who would do all of the voices. And occasionally, instead of looking at the right character, I would look at the lady by the camera and say, 'What are you saying?' For a sixteen-year-old, it was a little bit confusing."

Not only did he grow accustomed to that practice, though, but by series' end he had even learned all the nuances of movement of his costume-clad costars.

Say, for example, that one day Roberto Gamonet, who wore the Pufnstuf costume throughout the series and in the movie that followed, might have had to call in sick and a different puppeteer would take his place for a day of shooting. If so, Wild says, he would have immediately recognized that a different person was in the suit, strictly based on the person's body movement.

"They were all lovely puppeteers and each had his own way of moving, as everyone does, whether you're in show biz or not," Wild says. "For the whole of the TV series, there would be the same people as the same characters and the majority of them actually did the movie as well.

"And as far as I'm concerned, Roberto, the guy who was in Pufnstuf, he was Pufnstuf. It was in his attitude. When he was in that costume, his body movement was his language."

The crew that Sid assembled to perform inside the costumes was a colorful assortment of characters as well, ranging from show business veterans such as Sharon Baird, a former *Mickey Mouse Club* Mouseketeer, to industry novices such as eighteen-year-old Joy Campbell.

Who's Puf's Friend When Things Get Rough?

Did you hear the one about H.R. Pufnstuf and Elvira, Mistress of the Dark? The two are old friends.

Cassandra Peterson, widely known for her bosomy Valley Girl-as-vampire, horror-movie hostess persona, once spent the day on Puf's arm.

Says Peterson: "I worked for Sid and Marty a zillion years ago, before I was Elvira, as a hostess in this suite at one of these big conventions where they sell movies and TV shows for syndication. That's how I met them. I was working with them as they were trying to sell *H.R. Pufnstuf.* And I had to sit around with this giant Pufnstuf creature all day and walk the poor guy around so he didn't bash into things. You know, he could barely see to walk in that thing. It was so weird.

"Since then, I've known Sid and Marty through all kinds of different things, some wonderful projects. They're a crackup. They're a trip. A really, really interesting couple of guys. It's hard to believe they're really brothers. That's a really, really hard one to buy, but I guess they are."

Says Campbell, who played Orson the vulture and Cling, the taller of the two cops: "A lot of these guys were people who had worked with Sid and Marty for years, doing their puppet shows, and who had quite a few years of show business. Roberto, the guy who played Pufnstuf, had been a very famous puppeteer in his home country of British Honduras. He had done lots of stuff down there and then worked with Sid and Marty for years.

"Sharon Baird was my best friend on the set, probably because she, Billie Hayes and myself were the only women. Sharon was ten years older than me, but she looked after me and we're still good friends. Felix Silla had been in the business forever. He was Cousin Itt on *The Addams Family.* And whenever Orson and Cling were in the same scene, Felix usually was the one in the Cling costume.

"And then there was Andy Ratoucheff, this little Russian who must have been about eighty years old. A little, tiny old Russian man who always was toting his Bible and admonishing us about something we should be doing or shouldn't be doing. Every once in a while, the poor man would go into these convulsions because he had asthma. They had to have oxygen on the set and give him a timeout now and then."

It's an inexact science trying to identify the people in the costumes, incidentally, because the show's credits never specified who was who. What's more, given that each puppeteer had more than one role, it was not uncommon for a costumed character to be played from time to time by a backup.

But here is the way it usually worked out for the major roles: Gamonet played Puf. Because of her dancing skills, Baird had several "showcase" roles: Judy Frog, Lady Boyd and Shirley Pufnstuf. Johnny Silver played Dr. Blinky and Ludicrous Lion. Campbell played Orson the vulture and Cling, the red-suited cop. Angelo Rossitto played Seymour the Spider and Clang, the shorter, green-clad cop. Silla and Ratoucheff, the pinch hitters and bit players, usually were inside the Horsey get-up. And Jon Linton, Scutter McKay, Robin Roper and Jerry Landon were brought in specifically to play the tall trees.

Si Rose refers to the little people as unsung heroes, noting that the work they were called upon to do was far from easy and that their qualifications for the jobs involved much more than their diminutive size.

"One of the things I remember," he says, "is that it gets so hot in those costumes. It gets very, very hot and there's no way to get air in there. That would be one of the biggest concerns while we were shooting. Because when the lights go on and everybody's running around and you're on a tight schedule and somebody says, 'Do you think we ought to take a break for the "suits"?' And when you have to say, 'No, we're two scenes behind,' you feel just terrible."

Says Sharon Baird, who, though not a little person, is very short: "Every costume has its challenges. Some weigh a lot. Some are very tight-fitting. They get extremely warm. But the way I always looked at it was it's good for your skin: It's a built-in sauna."

Rose admits that, unlike Sid and Jack Wild, he didn't have so practiced an eye that he could identify the person inside the costume, based solely on body movement. "But I can tell if someone bad is inside. If they don't move around and do the right things, the whole thing falls flat. You can't just put anybody inside one of the suits and let them stumble around. It took work getting puppeteers who were good."

It's worth noting, incidentally, that the people in the costumes, albeit not practitioners of the brand of puppetry most commonly associated with the art, genuinely deserve the title of puppeteer.

"Getting the characters to lip-synch, getting them to move the mouths in a realistic and believable way so that you could then dub it and get the words in, that could be quite a challenge," Rose says. "There often would be a device inside the costume that would enable the puppeteer to work the mouth. Otherwise they'd work the mouth with their hands.

"I remember Pufnstuf evolved through the years. Roberto used to have to use one of his arms inside to work the mouth, so Pufnstuf would always have one arm swinging, like a dead arm. It used to drive us crazy. Then finally they worked out a way to control the mouth, so he could have the use of both arms."

Says Baird: "When you're in a costume and you have to move the character's jaw along with the words, sometimes you have to pull with your hands on a mouth, what they call animatronics, and sometimes you used your fingers to blink eyes and move mouths. With some costumes, you do it by moving your head. It's just how the costume is made."

What's more, the puppeteers had to do more than merely move the mouths for dialog. They had to act and emote. Before the cameras ever rolled, the puppeteer and the voice person often got together to make sure a character's mannerisms would match the voice and speech pattern.

"When you're in costume," Baird says, "you usually go along with what the voice people are doing and you go along with their moods from what you hear."

Weinrib describes how the process worked: "First we'd get on the set and we'd read for the cast how the lines will sound and what the pacing is. Then, on the actual set, during filming, the dialog director would read Pufnstuf's lines and Blinky's lines and so on and the puppeteers do their thing. Then, in post-production, the voice people, Walker Edmiston, Joanie Gerber and myself, we would get into the sound studio for ADR, which is automatic dialog replacement, and replace all of those lines with the actual lines that you would hear in the finished product."

If any single link in this elaborate chain snapped, the illusion that these puppet characters were speaking in these highly stylized voices would be shattered.

"Everybody had to be in synch with everybody else," Weinrib says.

In fact, just about the only puppet that was a puppet in the traditional, conventional sense was Freddy the Flute.

"Whenever you saw closeups of Freddy talking," Sid says, "I operated that. Every time there was a closeup. He worked with a rod down below, like a little squeeze rod."

In spite of all the elaborate work that was going on behind the scenes, Wild says that *Pufnstuf* was a happy set. Working on the show was so much fun, he says, it didn't even seem like work most of the time.

"To be honest, I didn't actually take it seriously as a job. My only concern was that I was pleasing the director and Sid and Marty and that was it. That was my only concern. I wasn't taking it any more seriously than that."

Yet in spite of all the talent involved, there still were more missteps that could have been made, particularly the aforementioned budgetary concerns.

Says Sid of having to work wonders with a budget that was minuscule even by 1969 standards: "I've never had the money to really do a show the way I wanted to do it, but I've been able to get a lot out of a little. Today people don't think twice about spending $100 million on a movie. It just makes me sick to see some of them. 'Oh, $100 million for a movie and it's no good?' That's a joke."

In fact, at one point Sid explored the possibility of taking *Pufnstuf* to prime time.

"*All in the Family* was based on a famous English show and it was an incredible hit over here," he says. "A lot of the hit shows here were taken from shows that were on in England. And when *Pufnstuf* started running at night in England and it was getting good ratings, I said to Fred Silverman, 'Hey, if people are watching it in England at night and it's a big hit, let's do a better version of it and put it on at 7:30, 8:00 at night here.' But he didn't listen. It could have been like a campy thing at night, maybe at 7:00 on Sunday. But he didn't listen. He didn't go for it."

A few years later, ABC passed on doing *The Muppet Show* as a prime-time series, out of concern that adults wouldn't watch it. The show became one of the most successful first-run syndicated shows in TV history, running from 1976 to 1981. The only difference: Sid never got the chance to prove whether he was right about Pufnstuf.

In retrospect, Sid says he is grateful that compromise wasn't part of his vocabulary when producing *Pufnstuf*. After all, each of the other Krofft series has troubling flaws, some great, some small, that nag at him to this day. Even the feature film version of *Pufnstuf* that followed the series in 1970 (with Martha Raye and Mama Cass added to the cast as witches) failed to meet Sid's ever-ambitious expectations.

"Kellogg's financed that whole movie and Universal distributed it. It was just that *Pufnstuf* was so big that they said, 'Hey, if you can make a movie for under a million dollars, let's do it.' And Kellogg's put up the money, because they were our sponsor. We rebuilt the entire set, because the one we had for the series wasn't big enough for the camera to capture. You know, TV is a little different from movies. You have that little tiny square there and we needed the stuff to be higher and wider.

"It looked beautiful, but it was done with such speed that I felt we could have done a lot better. I mean, it just happened and we did it, boom. I have a hard time with the movie myself, watching it. It makes me uncomfortable."

As for the series, though, Sid considers those seventeen episodes of *Pufnstuf* his finest work in television.

"You know, I don't watch my shows at all. I haven't seen many of them in so many years. I've even forgotten some of them. There's just so many of them, so many episodes. But *Pufnstuf*, when it was running again on the Family Channel, I did turn it on every Saturday. Now I've seen all seventeen again.

"I look at the other shows and I have to turn away every once in a while because I think, 'Oh, my God, how did I ever allow that?' But I look at *Pufnstuf* and they are gems. They are so good. I'm really proud of those."

Rose believes *Pufnstuf* was an important show, not just in terms of enabling Sid and Marty to gain a foothold in television, but also in that he sees its influence on non-Krofft programs that have come since.

"So many things that Sid and Marty had in *Pufnstuf*—like the talking trees and all the talking objects; everything was talking, all these inanimate objects—many other people have picked up on that. Sid and Marty created something to be copied by everybody."

But why limit themselves to only seventeen installments of what quickly proved to be a success and ultimately achieved cult status in the years that followed? For starters, the seventeen episodes, Marty points out, represented the standard one-year order for a Saturday morning show at that time. "And the only reason that we didn't do more," he reveals, "was we couldn't afford it."

That's right. *Pufnstuf* fans will find it disheartening to learn that the show actually had gotten a renewal notice from the network and that it was Sid and Marty themselves who opted against doing a second season.

"The way it happened was the new program director came in at NBC, George Heinemann, and this guy offered us 5 percent escalation over the $52,000-a-show arrangement of the first year," Marty says. "But he had no rooting interest in this thing. He had no emotional involvement. The last guys, Bud Grant and Larry White, are out at NBC. They're doing something else. And we just had to pass.

"They picked *Pufnstuf* up for another seventeen episodes. But we couldn't afford to lose another million dollars or another $700,000 or whatever it would have been. We had to say no."

Today, many adult fans find it hard to believe there were only seventeen episodes, because it must mean they watched the same shows over and over again. Although there are a number of valid explanations for repeat viewing (such as a child's stubborn belief that this one is sure to be the one where Jimmy finally manages to find his way home), Sid merely chalks it up to a youngster's fondness for things familiar.

"I didn't understand why they reran the stories on Saturday mornings so often. You know, you only made seventeen and you ran them for a year, over and over and over again. That's nearly four times a year the same show will run. But when they got hooked, they wanted to see it again.

"Kids love watching the same show over and over or hearing the same story. And what do parents do? They read the exact same story to them all the time. And they demand it. Why do they go see a Disney movie over and over again? And then they want their parents to buy the videotape and they sit through it one hundred times."

So why make more when viewership of the originals didn't seem to wane even after the third, fourth and fifth airings?

Even though it stung a little at the time to have to pass on making a second season of *Pufnstuf*, Marty believes today that it was for the best.

"In hindsight, I don't know if doing more shows would have been a good thing or not. Because these seventeen episodes, they're golden."

With so much love put into the making of them, how could they have been anything else?

What a Bunch of Characters!

Why does Pufnstuf wear white cowboy boots? Why was Freddy a flute and not, say, a violin? Sid Krofft recounts his thought process during *Pufnstuf*'s creation:

H.R. Pufnstuf: "Pufnstuf, that character, came from a show that we did for Coca-Cola. He was called Luther in that and he was a superhero who was changed into a dragon. And Luther was a cowboy, a superhero cowboy. And because he was a hero, the boots that he wore had to be white. Pufnstuf wore a little white cowboy hat too. That's why."

Freddy the Flute: "He had to be a flute because I like to use the same letters, alliteration. Freddy the Flute. It sounds good, doesn't it? It rolls off the tongue. And I remember when Jack Wild couldn't say 'Freddy,' because the way he says an 'R' becomes a 'W.' So it was 'Fweddy the Flute.' And I loved that. The minute I heard that, I knew that that was going to catch on with the kids."

Witchiepoo: "At first, we didn't know what kind of a name to give her. Miss Witch, I think, was the first thought. And then I thought, 'Not Miss Witch. That's too gentle.' We weren't happy with any of the names we came up with until we came up with Witchiepoo."

Cling and Clang: "That's their names because they drove that little fire truck with the bell on it. You'll notice that even their hats were shaped like bells."

Ludicrous Lion: "That's another alliteration name. 'L.L.' And he *was* ludicrous. That was his character. We drew him and I looked at him and said, 'God, that's a ludicrous lion.' And with a name like that, the rest just naturally follows."

Judy Frog: "She's Judy Garland. That's an inside joke because I always toured with her, but a lot of people didn't pick up on that until they were grownups. When they see it today, they pick up on it immediately because of the microphone and the voice. Joanie Gerber does the best Judy Garland. She used to do it for me for my puppet shows."

The Bugaloos in concert: John McIndoe as IQ, John Philpott as Courage,
Wayne Laryea as Harmony and Caroline Ellis as Joy.
SID & MARTY KROFFT PICTURES.

Flying Free as a Summer Breeze
...or The Story of the Bugaloos

So why are Sid and Marty Krofft's television shows so far-out, so psychedelic, so downright strange?

One obvious reason is that nobody sees the world in quite the same way Sid Krofft sees it.

The creative sparkplug of the Krofft team, Sid is a living, breathing Peter Pan who describes himself as "the original hippie." In fact, places like Living Island, Tranquility Forest (home of *The Bugaloos)* and Lidsville don't seem quite so fantastic once you have toured Sid's home in Los Angeles.

"I am probably one of the craziest, most-whacked-out people for living things and plants," he says. "My house, it has no walls. It's inside and outside. All these plants just grow into the house, so it's like you're really living in a forest. My whole house is built out of old barnwood and old bricks. So it's like the Hobbit lives here."

One "furnishing" that always attracts attention is an enormous eucalyptus tree that grows right through the middle of his home.

A beautiful treehouse, with ornately crafted doors and a removable stained-glass window in each wall, sits thirty feet up in the air, offering spectacular views of the city to the west and the San Gabriel Mountains to the east.

"I love living things. I love nature. This is how I got the idea for Living Island, where everything was alive."

Not surprisingly, Sid is also a strict vegetarian.

"I only eat living food and I have forever. I have for more than forty years. All raw food. I bake my bread in the sun. I was always concerned about my health and the fuel that I gave my body. It's

'Climbing High and Diving Low'

Taking flight like a Bugaloo might have seemed to be a summer breeze. But making it look easy certainly wasn't.

The show's flying sequences were accomplished by using Chroma-key technology, a special effect that allows the electronic superimposition of an object in front of a background. In this instance, the actors were strung up on wires and dangled in front of a huge blue screen, while footage of the backdrop—whether it be trees from the forest or merely clouds in the sky—would be shot without the actors.

Then, when the separately shot images were combined into one piece of film, the wires would magically disappear and the Bugaloos would appear to be flying through the forest solely under the power of their tiny wings.

"The bane of our existence was that very innocent line in the script," director Tony Charmoli says. "The line that says, 'And they fly from the forest.' Do you know what it means for them to fly? Do you have any idea how complicated it was to do the flying sequences?"

John McIndoe, for one, didn't seem to mind. "We were kind of pioneers in Chroma-key in those days. It was fun flying like that. Actually, it was a blast."

There were times when the effect got a little hazardous, mind you. "One time, it was like one funny scene, it took thirteen takes to land on a balcony," McIndoe recalls. "We kept having to do it over for one reason or other. And on the thirteenth take, I went *through* the balcony.

like a car. Give it bad gas and it doesn't work. I'm so happy to be alive and I want to feel good every single day, not three days or five days a week."

With an outlook like this, is it any wonder that shows such as *H.R. Pufnstuf* and *The Bugaloos* turned out the way they did? There's nothing Pollyanna about these programs, mind you. Sid just naturally sees the world in this light, no rose-colored glasses required.

What's more, almost every nuance of his early TV creations, Sid says, harks back in some way to something that happened in

Bang! Crash landing."

One of the first twelve takes would have to do.

And there was another aspect of flying that created constant technical headaches—the Bugaloos' motorized wings.

"I remember when we first fitted them with their wings and they discovered that the little motors in them made too much noise," Jean Anderson says. "We had to overdub on a lot of the shows because the microphones that they use for film and television are so sensitive and they picked up all these extraneous noises.

"I remember Sid saying, 'What's that noise?' And then, in Sid's own inimitable fashion, 'Oh, my God, it's the wings. Oh, Marty's going to be so mad.' Because it meant more expense, of course. It was awfully loud and the technicians were such purists."

So was Sid, which meant that not only must the wings stay as originally planned but also that, any time a Bugaloo was seen in flight, the wings must be in motion.

"I went through so much of a headache getting that done," Sid says. "And I hated when somebody, the director or sound people, would want to stop the wings. I would always say, 'No way. I went through torture trying to get this worked out. I want those wings working.'"

So the motors were padded and placed inside little cloth pockets on the Bugaloos' backs. But in any scene in which the wings were moving, noise-free dialog had to be dubbed in later.

his life, a life without a great deal of turmoil. Sid is a pacifist. So why should his shows be any different?

"We had an incredible staff of people working with us, including some of the most talented puppeteers in the world, so I don't want to get carried away and say that it's all me and only me," Sid says. "But shows like *Pufnstuf* and *The Bugaloos,* most of them are ideas that came from my experiences."

And perhaps more than any other show he created, *The Bugaloos,* the series the Kroffts introduced to Saturday mornings after closing the door on *Pufnstuf,* reflects Sid's peace-loving state of mind and desire to find tranquility.

"The Bugaloos were kids who wanted to escape all the problems of the world," Sid says, "so they sprouted wings and went to tranquility. That was what it was about. It was in the '70s. Every decade, we have problems. And the '70s were no different. And I just thought, 'Tranquility, yeah, wouldn't it be great if we could find a little tranquility?'

"It all came from that idea. It was just the times. We all live with the problems of life, don't we? We're all caught up in it. I don't care who you are and what you've got. You still have the same problems everybody has, maybe even more. And I just like to be peaceful. I don't want to be part of all that craziness out there. And so that's what that was really about.

"Everybody wants to split and go live in Hawaii or on an island or something. And that's tranquility. And wouldn't it be cool if you sprouted wings? And just fly around? We all want to be a bird or a bug. I mean, they have the best lives, until they get eaten up."

Stated in more concrete terms, *The Bugaloos* was the story of four musically gifted teenagers with shaggy hairstyles and mod clothes who happened also to have wings and antennae ("we're in the air and everywhere; flying high, flying loose, flying free like we all could be").

The foursome:

Joy (Caroline Ellis) was the only female member of the group, a fetching beauty with a lovely singing voice. Fittingly, she was a beautiful pink butterfly.

Harmony (Wayne Laryea) was black and, judging from his shirt's brown-and-yellow horizontal stripes, clearly a bumblebee. He played the keyboards.

IQ (John McIndoe) was tall, blond and handsome. His green shirt, yellow vest and bell-bottomed slacks (with green-and-white vertical stripes) put viewers in the mind of a grasshopper. He played guitar.

Courage (John Philpott) was short, dark and handsome, wearing white slacks and a red shirt with white spots on the back. A ladybug...that's right, a male ladybug. He was the band's drummer.

What a Bunch of Characters!

Leave it to Sid Krofft to create a kids show in which one of the characters had doubt about his sexual identity.

Consider the roster of insect leads. Joy was a butterfly, Harmony was a bumblebee, IQ was a grasshopper and Sparky, their sidekick, was a firefly.

But was Courage, the character played by John Philpott, really a male ladybug? Would the Kroffts really want to open that gender-bending can of worms?

Sid says he has heard this question from viewers for years. In response, he usually suggests that this line of analysis is overdoing it just a tad.

"I don't think I meant for any of the Bugaloos to have character traits based on which specific insects they were," he says. "I mean, Caroline Ellis was a beautiful girl, so why not make her a sweet little butterfly? And John McIndoe was so tall that he sort of looked like a grasshopper. But really, they're just these kids who wanted to split to tranquility and so they sprouted wings. We just gave them wings and an interesting mix of coloring for the costumes."

But McIndoe, who remembers gently ribbing Philpott about the male ladybug thing at the time, says he wouldn't put it past Sid to have slipped something in.

"You know how Sid is. I think it was just that seemed to make sense at the time."

Oh, yes, and in keeping with the Kroffts' little people-in-puppet-suits tradition, Billy Barty played Sparky the Firefly, a close friend of the Bugaloos.

They all lived in Tranquility Forest, a beautiful place where blades of grass were as big as mighty oak trees. But even in Tranquility, it seemed, not everything was perfect.

Sid describes it best: "The other side of tranquility was where everything was up and crazy. And that's where Benita Bizarre lived. She was the villain. She tried to get rid of tranquility. She couldn't deal with it. Because she lived in a jukebox and she liked everything loud. She lived with Woofer and Tweeter. Those were her sidekicks. For her, everything was uptown and hyper, horns and loudness. Everybody talked loud. It was the opposite of tranquility."

Flamboyant Benita Bizarre leaves Harmony and Courage speechless.
SID & MARTY KROFFT PICTURES.

The aptly named Benita Bizarre was played by comic actress Martha Raye, who earlier had worked with Sid and Marty in the *Pufnstuf* movie. Benita envied the Bugaloos' musical abilities and often sought to steal them for herself.

Not exactly the stuff of standard Saturday morning fare, is it? In fact, the dreamy, trancelike quality of all this makes it a little hard to believe *The Bugaloos* got on the air at all. After all, even *Pufnstuf,* as weird as it sometimes got, was about something far more tangible than the desire to achieve a peaceful state of mind.

"I didn't know at the time that it was so bizarre," Sid says in retrospect, although he must have had some clue, given Benita's "bizarre" name. "It definitely was a weird show. It's almost like we were making a music video, only nobody knew what a music video was at that time."

And it could have been even weirder had Sid and Marty not reined it in during production. "We didn't really do this, but the idea was that down below was where all the 'bummers' were, the police and all. We didn't do that. Then we also would have had a place where all the squares lived. It was going to be about all these different facets of life."

Weird, you bet. But a kids show with a sweeter nature you aren't likely to find anywhere.

"Sure, it was unusual, but *The Bugaloos* was a delightful musical show," executive producer Si Rose says. "And it's amazing. I saw it on cable recently and I couldn't believe this was a Saturday morning television show that had original music and a singing group.

"Every week, they had new music and songs that were completely original. I couldn't believe the quality that was going into Saturday morning at that time."

The tunes were written by Charles Fox (music) and Norman Gimbel (lyrics), a prolific duo whose best-remembered TV theme songs include "Happy Days," "Making Our Dreams Come True" (*Laverne & Shirley*) and "The First Years" (*The Paper Chase*).

As was the case with *H.R. Pufnstuf,* NBC placed an order for seventeen episodes of *The Bugaloos*. The show debuted on September 12, 1970, nearly a year to the day after *Pufnstuf* had premiered.

It wasn't anywhere near as big a hit as its predecessor—chalk that up to a sophomore slump, perhaps—but it ran for two seasons and enjoyed some measure of side success thanks to the quartet's record album, *Bugaloos,* released by Capitol Records in 1970.

"Who knows?" Rose says. "At another time, with a little more promotion, they might have caught on bigger."

Cast member John McIndoe seconds that emotion. "We were a bit ahead of our time. I mean, how many other shows at that time were concerning themselves about the environment?"

Given the premise and the stylish presentation, it's impossible to say whether the acting and musical skills of the four title players made any real impact on the success of the series, plus or minus. Yet Marty still went to extraordinary lengths when casting the four roles.

I went to London, put out a casting call," he recalls. "And about eight thousand kids showed up. We held the auditions at EMI in Manchester, at the EMI house. They let us use their facilities because they were involved and Capitol Records was involved with us at the time. And EMI, I think, owned Capitol Records. So we had thousands of kids show up and we auditioned them all. I went there alone, actually, and I got it down to like the last five or six people.

"As a matter of fact, one of the guys who we turned down was a guy by the name of John Reed, who wound up being Elton John's manager. Every time he sees me, he says, 'Thank God, you saved my life by not picking me.'"

It's worth noting that this curious twist of fate hasn't been lost on McIndoe either. "For the part of IQ Bugaloo," he says, "it was down to three guys...me, John Reed and Phil Collins."

That's right, *that* Phil Collins.

In fact, McIndoe adds, Collins' mother was the musical agent for the Bugaloos, even though Phil didn't get the part.

"The way I see it, if one of those guys had gotten it instead of me, rock 'n' roll history might have changed. And whenever I see them, I say, 'Hey, guys, you know, you're lucky you didn't get the part.'"

The casting process worked like this: The Kroffts hired Jean Anderson to put out a casting call and whittle down the candidates to about sixteen front-runners. "I was in London when I got the call to work for them," Anderson recalls. "It was Easter weekend and it was very difficult getting all the children there. So what we did was put an ad in two of the local papers. It talked about the show and a recording contract and children came from all over Britain, by train, hiking, any way they could get there."

The process of sifting through thousands of young people, by the way, was easier than it sounds, Anderson says.

"I didn't have to do anything. The right kids just jumped out. The Kroffts told me what they were looking for and I had the drawings that Sid and the art director, Nicky Nadeau, had done. And it so happened that each of them looked like the character that had been drawn for me. I couldn't believe it. The minute I saw Caroline, for example, I knew she was the one. This little girl walked in and it was obvious. It was magical from the beginning."

When Marty arrived, he narrowed the list of candidates even further.

Says Anderson: "One of the funniest things I ever saw was Marty, during the final auditions, and they had this song that they kept playing and playing: 'Give me a ticket to an airplane.' So we're up in this suite in the Dorchester Hotel and here's Marty Krofft, standing in front of these kids, directing them to do some movement. Caroline was always into it, but the others were too shy.

"And there was Marty, this big tall man, with his arms out, flying and singing, 'Give me a ticket to an airplane,' and the kids were all staring at him like he had lost his mind. 'What is he doing?' But he had to. He couldn't believe that they were so quiet. I mean, they looked the part. They had all the right physical characteristics, without the costumes. But they weren't naturally just leaping about being Bugaloos right away."

In fact, McIndoe remembers that, after relocating in America, the foursome weathered a bit of a shaky start before forming an abiding friendship.

"Actually, it took a while for us to become totally friendly," he says. "At first, you know, there's always that competition thing. Myself, I went around with musicians all the time. So I was okay with it. I was cool. And Little John was very cool, very naive, very humble, lovely kid. The other two, Caroline and Wayne, they came from that stage school upbringing and they were always in competition. But after a while, it was laughable and it just disappeared. The competition thing just totally disappeared."

Says Ellis: "We all got on very well together, but Wayne and I had both been acting, whereas the two Johns had been in the musical business. Besides, John McIndoe's star sign is Aquarius, so

The Joy of Being a Bugaloo

Today, Caroline Ellis leads a life very far removed from her days of teenage stardom on Saturday morning TV.

So far removed, in fact, she didn't have the foggiest notion anyone even remembered a quartet of musical insects called the Bugaloos.

Says Ellis, now a real estate agent and mother of one living in Spain: "I had no idea that *The Bugaloos* and the other Krofft shows were still so popular. It's only really because my brother Tony, who just by chance was playing around on the Internet and put in the words 'The Bugaloos' and all this stuff started showing up, which has been a bit mind-boggling. Of course, he phoned me up here and said, 'Did you realize?' I said, 'No, I had no idea.'"

Fittingly, Ellis, who played the character named Joy, has only happy memories of being a Bugaloo.

"It was a dream come true. It was a magical time that I'll never forget. Sid and Marty Krofft had come over to England after they had had their success with *Pufnstuf.* Of course, when they'd come over to cast for *The Bugaloos,* it was a hugely publicized thing in all the papers. People came from miles around to audition.

"So the fact that I actually got the part was a bit mind-boggling and breathtaking in itself. And then, to be whisked off to Hollywood was every actress's dream. That period for me was very exciting, very rewarding."

It also entailed long hours and a demanding workload.

"At the same time we were doing the television series, we were doing the album at night. We were all physically exhausted and we all had effects of that. It was hard work. You're up at 5:00 or 6:00 in the morning and to bed at 2:00 in the morning and having about three or four hours sleep every night. You can only go on so long working at that sort of schedule. But you're on a high. You're on a buzz. You're enjoying every moment and the body just seems to carry on.

"In fact, we were all prepared to carry on further with *The Bugaloos.* The idea was that we were going to go back and do a film with Columbia. But it was a time when the film studios were having a recession, I think, and the film was postponed. And I was offered another TV series in England and I thought, 'Well, I can't sit around waiting and waiting to be called back to America.' So I accepted this children's television series and the whole *Bugaloos* thing, unfortunately, died away."

Throughout the 1970s, after having done *The Bugaloos*, Ellis worked on British TV from time to time. But mostly she gravitated toward the stage.

"As much as I enjoy television, it was always the theater I had to go back to. Because that was my greatest love. I loved the live response that you get, the connection you have with the audience, which you don't get in television or in film."

In fact, perhaps the only thing that could pull her away from acting, she says, was motherhood.

"My daughter is nearly twelve. I stayed in the business right up until I got pregnant with Sasha. I was always very lucky. I always got work. It was always very good. But like most people, you eventually get married and you want to have children. And I decided, when the time comes, when I do eventually have children, I'll step away from the business and be a mother.

"Sasha was born and we came to live in Spain. I ended up liking Spain very, very much. My marriage broke up and I decided to stay here and now I'm involved in real estate. Which is quite funny because my family originally was in real estate and that was never something that I planned to be in.

"I obviously miss the theater. But my daughter is important to me and I'd like her to have a pretty normal, sane upbringing. And in that business, very often children in that business or the children of well-known people end up being precocious and having a few problems later on in life. I wanted her to have a normal sort of upbringing. As it happens, she's very extroverted and probably would be very good in television. But there's time for that in the future. If that's what she wants, that's up to her."

Ellis theorizes that the Kroffts' shows endure not only because of their unique trippy style but also because of their sweet nature.

"I don't think it was like sickly sweet, if you know what I mean. But it was so unusual. It was so different from anything else that was ever on television. I've never seen anything quite like it since then either."

he was always a bit up in the clouds, in the nicest possible way, and he would sort of disappear with his guitar now and then and get embedded into his music."

Anderson, who after casting watched over the Bugaloos during their stay in the States, says, "They were absolute innocents and it wasn't easy being in Los Angeles. They were mesmerized. Big John [McIndoe] is very gregarious. And I remember him from the beginning being right at my elbow, so excited about coming to America. Caroline very seldom had much to say. She was very much a private person...and very much like her character. She was neat and tidy and dainty and sort of remote in a fairytale way. The boys were full of life and mischief and interested in the new country. The rock and roll stuff was fascinating to them. Sunset Boulevard was hopping. But Caroline didn't have much interest in any of it."

Counters Ellis: "Oh, I don't know. I had my fair share of adventure as well. Three boys together with a girl. I suppose you can imagine some of the things we got into."

Sid and Marty's four young actors were pleasant enough, but none had true star power, as evidenced by the fact that their careers never really took off after *The Bugaloos*.

In fact, Rose concedes that this may be the show's only shortcoming, the fact that there was no Jack Wild, admittedly a very tough act to follow, in the mix.

"John McIndoe, he worked very hard, but I thought he sometimes looked a little lost," Rose says. "The girl was cute and the black young man, he was really good. He was very sharp. And the shorter, good-looking one, he was nice-looking and he worked hard.

"But they were just kids. I mean, Jack Wild had all this experience going in. But this show, they hadn't been doing anything. So to get them together and suddenly they're acting, that's tough. But it was such a pleasant show and I loved those kind of melodies that they were playing."

Says Tony Charmoli, who directed all of the episodes: "I would have liked a little more experience from them, but how could you do that? I think Benita kind of startled them too with how pre-

The Other 'Joy' of Sex

The birds and the bees do it, but not a naive group like the Bugaloos.

That's why, during the series' end-of-season wrap party, director Tony Charmoli plotted "to help those kids grow up."

He tells how: "Remember how Joy, the girl in the series, lived in the flower. They all lived in the forest and her home was the flower, like a big lily that would open up, and she would say, 'Good morning.' Well, for the wrap party, I hired a stripper, a nude dancer, and I got her in the studio and I sneaked her into the back of the flower, like our regular actor would get in, just before the entertainment.

"I had my cue with the lighting spot guy. I said, 'When I say something and direct attention over to the flower, all spots hit the flower.' So it was my turn to thank the cast and the company and the crew and everybody sitting there. And I said, 'And over here to Lotus Land, where Joy abides.' The flower opened and totally nude, except for two pasties, was standing our nude dancer, saying 'Good morning.'

"I tell you, the Bugaloos flew to the stage and they gathered around the flower in awe. They just were so shaken up. And the whole company, even Martha Raye, burst out in applause. And the girl performed her routine and then they closed the flower and I sneaked her out the back and we went on with the evening. Sid said, 'Oh, my God, Tony. What are you doing? This isn't permitted in the studio.' And I said, 'Well, permitted or not, we just did it.' And I said, 'Well, just consider it hygiene class, a sex-orientation class, for these kids.'"

pared she was. The Bugaloos would forget lines at times and it was a drain because there was so much to have to be done. And to pull up their energy often was difficult. But in the long run, it was a very wonderful experience."

Billy Barty says he also liked the foursome personally and enjoyed working with them. "They were cute. They were good performers and pleasant people to work with. I can't remember everything about them. I don't know whatever happened to them. But those kids worked hard."

As for the fact that Barty has no idea what became of his former costars, don't read anything into it that isn't there. After all, he was forty-five years old when *The Bugaloos* went into production and can hardly be expected to have bonded in any meaningful way with a quartet of young people less than half his age. "My son was born when I was working on *The Bugaloos,*" he notes.

As for Martha Raye's performance, no one involved in *The Bugaloos* offers anything short of rave reviews. She probably would have stolen the show regardless of who her costars were. As Charmoli puts it, "Benita was every drag queen's dream."

Sid, a longtime fan of Raye's, says she was his first and only choice and that he was able to sign her up in large part because of a friendship that went back many years.

"I loved Martha Raye. I always have. I knew her when she was a huge, huge star. But to me, she was always a star. She had a club in Miami that I always used to go to. And she was who I wanted from the very beginning. But at first, she could be a real pain in the ass. You had to send a car for her and she would arrive late. Things like that.

"God, she caused so many problems because, you know, we got very little money on those shows. And you couldn't be a star. You had to just work your ass off and get it over with. I mean, you couldn't do a million takes. You couldn't afford it. It wasn't a nighttime show. It was a little children's show. In those days, we used to get about $65,000 an episode.

"But it was at the point in her career where—oh, I don't know, she just wasn't a happy lady at the time. And not a huge star any more either."

Even if she was a turbulent presence on the set, it didn't show on screen in her hyperkinetic performance.

"Oh, she was great," Sid adds. "And after a while, she hooked into it. She finally did hook into it."

Says Charmoli, who is almost as big a Martha Raye fan as Sid: "Being the real pro that she was, she would never even need to look at the script before the next day. I remember I would go into the makeup room and she would say, 'Oh, good morning, Tony.

Martha Raye as Benita Bizarre, every drag queen's dream.
SID & MARTY KROFFT PICTURES.

What are we shooting?' And I would say, 'We're shooting pages one through eight.' And she would have a girl read the script to her while she was having her makeup and hair done and she would memorize her lines in the makeup chair. By the time she got to the set and we were ready to do it, she had all of her lines. She knew everything."

Says Si Rose: "She really expanded on the character and she turned it into a much broader, funnier character. She really let loose as Benita Bizarre. I look at some of the old shows and that was some of the best stuff she's ever done."

The Bugaloos and Sparky take to the road in psychedelic style.
SID & MARTY KROFFT PICTURES.

Ellis recalls, "She was so over the top. She was a lovely lady, an absolutely super lady. I only have very fond, very good memories of her."

Joy Campbell, who played Woofer, one of Benita's sidekicks, remembers Raye this way: "She was generous. She was kind. She was a hoot. She never had any star arrogance. Very professional. She wanted to do everything right the first time.

"My first exposure to her was on the *Pufnstuf* movie. And Holly Morse, who directed the movie, being the professional that he was, he told all of us, who had never met her, 'I want all of you to call her Miss Raye. She's from the era where she expects that sort of thing.' He was very, very high on protocol. He didn't want anyone to breach anything. 'Don't call her Martha. Don't call her Maggie.' Her real name was Maggie O'Reed. And then Holly said, 'If she tells you that you can call her Maggie, I would like you to feel comfortable doing that. But please, in the meantime, call her Miss Raye.' Well, when somebody gives you that kind of a warning, you figure, God, she's going to be inflexible. She's going to be absolutely no fun at all. You've got to call her Miss Raye. You've got to walk around on eggshells. But that probably lasted about a day before she announced to everyone, 'By the way, my friends call me Maggie. So you can choose where you want to be.'

"By the time that they had her in *The Bugaloos,* she knew all of us and she was right at home and she had no pretentious attitude about her at all. She stepped right up and one of the first things she said was, 'Dinner is at my house tomorrow. Get your ass there.'"

Of the many cast members from shows bearing the Sid & Marty Krofft Productions logo, the brothers have maintained perhaps the thinnest ties to the leads of *The Bugaloos.*

Says Sid: "We've kind of lost touch. I know that John McIndoe is still here in the States. As a matter of fact, he works with puppets. I bumped into him last year. I was in a restaurant and he saw me. I wouldn't even have recognized him, because everybody changes their look over time. But he was the one who recognized me. I don't know why everybody recognizes me. I feel like I've changed too. But there I was in the restaurant and I hear, 'It's Sid Krofft. My God.' And it was John McIndoe. It was nice to see him again.

From the Beatles to the Bugaloos

In terms of making an impact on people's lives, perhaps no one was affected more dramatically by *The Bugaloos* than one of the show's young leading men, John McIndoe.

The blond musician-turned-actor who starred as IQ says his involvement in the show virtually ruined any musical aspirations he had. Yet it also launched him in a different direction, the field in which he works to this day.

"I was typecast after *The Bugaloos*," McIndoe says. "For years, I couldn't get any work. Because in the mind of American agents in this country and all that, they thought, 'Oh, he's a Bugaloo. What else can he do?' It's just like what they had done to the Monkees.

"You see, I worked in London before I came over. I used to do part-time work at Apple, the Beatles' company, and I had my own band that John Lennon was helping us with at the time at Apple Records. So I was active in the music industry. I left that to do *The Bugaloos* and my whole music career was shot after that because people kept thinking, 'Well, this guy's going to sing a song about la-la-la.'

"And my whole music career and everything was down the drain. So I went and worked for Sid and Marty at the Factory. As a matter of fact, I worked on most of their other shows."

Refreshingly, McIndoe expresses no bitterness about losing out on a possible music career while runners-up for his role, Phil Collins and John Reed, thrived.

"Oh, I'm not mad, not at all. It was a beautiful journey. I'm just having a laugh at it. Seeing how things might have changed. Looking at how things could have been different. It's okay. I've learned that what He dealt you is what He dealt you."

Music might not have been in the cards for McIndoe. But thanks to his contact with Sid and Marty, a career in puppetry was waiting.

"I build animatronic robotic puppets now and I actually produce TV shows. I'm on my second one now. It's all kids stuff. The first show I did is out on TFI Films, an hour-long special called *A Halloween Story,* and it's all done with puppets I built. It's forty-three puppets that I built.

"I write and I create stuff too. I'm working on a movie that I created a few years ago called *The Wizards of Australia* and it's the story of a little Aboriginal boy and a little Australian girl from the bush and a little magical koala. And these three characters go through all these great adventures in dreamtime, where anything is possible. It's a musical, by the way. So far, I've got a bite from Universal. We'll see what happens."

As for this twist of fate, the fact that he is now following a trail blazed decades earlier by Sid and Marty, McIndoe says simply, "Well, everything is a journey."

He says he cherishes the time he spent working on the show—"it was the best"—and is pleased whenever people recognize him as a former Bugaloo. "Sometimes I'll bump into people and they'll say, 'Oh, you're the guy from *The Bugaloos,* aren't you? I used to watch that show all the time.' And they'll start pulling out toy lunchpails and things.

"Here in Sedona, a few people have found out who I am and it's like they've loved the show forever. They bring me these old albums and stuff and ask me to sign it. I say sure. No problemo."

As for the trippy, counter-culture nature of the show and the fact that many fans consider its weird, acid-trip-like elements to be thinly veiled references to drug use, McIndoe is reminded of when he was working in the presence of the Beatles.

Fans practically dissected Beatles songs in late 1960s, looking for any lyrical or musical passage that could be interpreted as having a second, hidden meaning.

"When I worked over at Apple, they used to make jokes about that...the Beatles themselves, I mean. Sometimes you would come in and say, 'Hey, look, they just figured out another meaning for this song.' And they'd want to know what it was. 'Let me hear it,' they'd say. 'Really?' I mean, at times, they were more amazed than the fans were."

"As for where the others are and what they're doing, I just don't know. I believe they all live in England somewhere. Caroline Ellis was so beautiful. But who knows where she is? She might be a grandmom by now."

Well, not quite a grandmother, but she does have a daughter, born in 1986, who Caroline insists "would be a wonderful Joy if ever a new *Bugaloos* series was made."

Ellis has remained close with one of her costars, Laryea, through the years. "He's still in the business, but on the other side of the camera now. Like myself, after *The Bugaloos,* he carried on in television. But he did a lot of directing for the BBC and then he opened up his own production company, which he still has got. He's merely changed the side of the camera, which he says is more secure and just as interesting."

There's also no mystery about McIndoe's whereabouts. He lives in Sedona, Arizona. He builds animatronic puppets and has even ventured into the field of producing children's programming, making him yet another example of the Krofft influence on a new generation of artists. "Sid and Marty are my heroes," McIndoe says.

As for keeping up with his former band mates, McIndoe admits, "We're old pals, but it's funny: The last three or four years, we've kind of not made too much contact. Just a brief talk now and then.

Neither McIndoe nor Ellis have any knowledge of what has become of Philpott, the fourth member of the group.

Says McIndoe: "I know that Little John had a window-cleaning business. He got out of the business."

Ellis adds, "I know he [Philpott] carried on with his musical group for a while, spending a lot of time touring in the Nordic countries, in Northern Europe. But I've lost contact with him."

Perhaps the Kroffts lost touch with these young stars because *The Bugaloos* didn't prove to have the same endurance as some of the brothers' more successful shows.

Even after *Pufnstuf* wrapped production, for example, there were more than four years of reruns, a movie follow-up and stage shows starring Jack Wild and/or *Pufnstuf* characters. But *Bugaloos* reruns played for only one more season and the *Bugaloos* movie that had been planned early on (with the idea of developing some of the concepts that went unrealized in the series) never materialized.

Like an insect that leads an oh, so short life, *The Bugaloos* came and went without much fanfare. "But you know what?" Sid says. "It made as much of an impact with the kids as *Pufnstuf* did. I'm talking about today. When you talk to people who remember it, nowadays they understand it more. Today, not when they were first watching it.

"It wasn't a successful show. We only did one season of *The Bugaloos*, but it made a hell of an impact. Because when you mention *The Bugaloos* to people today, they say, 'Oh, my God, I loved *The Bugaloos*,' and they know everything about it. They can read back the entire premise to you. Not bad for a show that wasn't what you'd call successful."

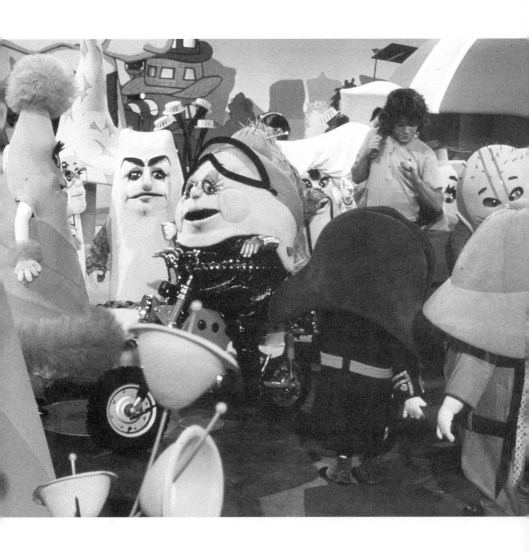

Lidsville was a land of living hats.
SID & MARTY KROFFT PICTURES.

How's That For a Topper?
...or Lidsville is the Living End

When Butch Patrick entered the lives of Sid and Marty Krofft, he found himself in a world he would hardly describe as wonderful.

"I didn't know what I was getting into when I agreed to do their show," he says. "I didn't have the slightest idea."

Patrick is the former kid actor best remembered for playing a lovable wolfboy on an endearing and enduring sitcom classic. He was Eddie Munster on *The Munsters* (1964–66). He signed on to star in the Kroffts' third television series, *Lidsville,* in 1971, during the summer of his eighteenth birthday.

The premise was like something out of a Lewis Carroll tale: After Patrick's character, a boy named Mark, had been dazzled by a magic show, he sneaked backstage hoping to learn how the magician had performed his illusions. There he found the magician's top hat, which suddenly grew to King Kong size. Still curious, Mark peered inside over the brim and fell in. And the next thing he knew ("he couldn't believe his ears or eyes," as the theme song put it), he had become a resident of a strange land populated by over-sized living hats.

It was a premise that literally cried out to use just about every hat-, head- and hair-related pun under the sun.

Patrick's assessment of the whole thing?

"I hated it, I hated it, I hated it. I hated every day I went to work. I don't know why I got myself into this thing. I was so pissed off, because I thought it was stupid. I felt like I had done some good, solid acting in previous years on *The Real McCoys* and *The Munsters* and to have it all culminate in this Saturday morning, silly-ass show, well, let's just say I had a bad attitude the whole time I was doing it."

That was then, mind you. This is now. The passage of time has changed his opinion.

"I remember when *Pee-wee's Playhouse* came out and won all these awards and was such a huge hit. Well, I looked at that and said, 'You know, *Lidsville* was better than *Pee-wee's Playhouse*.' So twenty years after the fact, twenty-five years after the fact, *Lidsville*, even though it brings back some very painful memories, I look at it for what it's worth now and the fact is it was a great little show for children."

Funny he should mention *Pee-wee's Playhouse*. That's one you can chalk up as one of Sid Krofft's biggest blunders, the fact that he let Pee-wee Herman slip through his fingers.

"Paul Reubens, I saw him at a party," Sid says, "and he always tells everybody that his show was taken from all of our shows. The talking this and talking that. Which is weird because years earlier this woman who worked for us in development brought me to the Roxy one time to see *Pee-wee's Playhouse*. It was a stage show before it went on television.

"She brought me to see it because she thought it would be a great show for television. But I didn't like it. I wasn't angry or anything like that. I didn't feel like he had ripped us off or anything. I just couldn't see it. I thought, 'Gee, we've already done that. Why

This Hat Person Was Over Their Heads

Even though the networks rarely tinkered with Krofft shows regarding their content, there were occasions when the folks from Standards and Practices—the networks' self-appointed censors—put their two cents in.

Si Rose had a long and at times adversarial relationship with censors from his prime-time days. "They have a tough job, but it sort of gets crazy at times. They say, 'Well, why don't you just change this?' And I say, 'If you change that, the whole story doesn't work and we can't do the script.' And they wouldn't realize that if you take out that one little thing, it affects everything around it."

Rose remembers one memo that came regarding *Lidsville*, however, that was more amusing than infuriating.

"One of the characters, her name was Mother Wheels, and since they were all hats, she was like a motorcycle helmet. A helmet with eyes and a mouth and all. That was what she looked like, with character added to it. And she became Mother Wheels and she was almost human.

"And we got a call from the censors, the people at Program Practices. They said, 'We've got a problem with Mother Wheels. She's on a motorcycle. She has to wear a helmet.'

"And all we could say was, 'But she *is* a helmet.'"

would we want to do it again?' And this guy, acting like a little kid—I don't know, it just didn't work for me. And of course, he went off to become a big star. So I blew it."

Well, everyone makes mistakes—and Sid's underestimating the star power of Pee-wee Herman is no different, really, than Patrick's underestimating the clever charm of *Lidsville,* a show that completed a sort of trippy trilogy with *H.R. Pufnstuf* and *The Bugaloos.*

Lidsville premiered on September 11, 1971, on ABC. *Pufnstuf* reruns had stopped playing on NBC (although they would return a year later on ABC) and *Bugaloos* reruns from the previous season were still running on NBC. And the three were beginning to have a powerful combined impact.

Simply put, the Krofft Look had begun to take over Saturday mornings. Krofft TV had become a genre unto itself.

In retrospect, Sid feels somewhat vindicated when he hears of Butch Patrick's change of heart about the show.

"He's right about one thing," Sid says. "He did have a bad attitude. He never really 'believed' in the Hat People. I don't know why. But I think it's interesting that he has realized now what a cool show it was. It still lives on. It's not like a show that went away and never came back. I mean, everybody knows *Lidsville*."

But even if Patrick still only spoke ill of the show, that would not affect Sid's fondness for it in any way.

Lidsville is just as elaborately weird as many of the Kroffts' other series, maybe moreso, but its genesis actually is one of the simplest to express: Sid Krofft loves hats. He is so wild about them, in fact, you could call him a mad hatter.

"I always loved hats," he says. "That was definitely my idea, because I just love hats. I have so many. I'm a runner. I run nine miles, not every day but as often as I can, and whenever I run down at the beach I always have all these different hats for how I feel. Because every hat has a different personality. I do a lot of my work while I run. That's when I'm able to think and create. And the hats help me create, a different hat for a different mood, a different hat to reflect a different frame of mind.

"And that's where the idea for *Lidsville* came from. I thought, well, if every hat has a personality, then a bunch of hats together have all the characteristics of a whole, well-rounded community. And the more I let that turn over in my mind, the more it intrigued me. My God, the cowboy hat, the football helmet, the party hat. They all have their own personalities. If a fedora could talk, it might talk like a character in a gangster movie. A beret would speak with a French accent. A policeman's hat would be an authority figure. And it goes on and on.

"What would it be like to live in a land of living hats? That's how I created the show, from that single idea."

Of course, in the Krofft scheme of things, depicting a world of living hats first means assembling a team of little people—a Krofft tradition by this time—to wear an assortment of hat costumes. The hats would not merely be alive, but they would be oversized as well, with legs and arms and eyes and mouths.

They literally would become "Hat People."

Creating a community of Hat People, in fact, meant hiring more little people than in any other Krofft program, with the possible exception of *Pufnstuf.* "It was really a gathering ground for little people," executive producer Si Rose recalls. "It looked like *The Wizard of Oz* set."

Adds Sid: "No one employed more little people than we did."

There also were three so-called "human" parts.

Patrick was cast as Mark because, as Sid puts it, "he was a good-looking kid and he was known." There were hopes of being able to trade on his already-established *Munsters* fame.

For the role of Mark's sidekick, perky Weenie the Genie, the Kroffts called once more on their former *Pufnstuf* pal, Billie Hayes—who turned out to be a brilliant choice, given the effervescence of her performance.

And as for Horatio J. Hoo Doo—a sinister green-skinned magician who reigned over Lidsville like a wicked witch, tooling about in his giant flying hat, a "hatamaran," and directing a rabbit sidekick and a deck of oversized playing cards to do his dirty work—the Kroffts would need an actor who could be larger than life and as broad as a barn door. For this all-important Witchiepoo/Benita Bizarre-style role,

Billy, Billie and Weenie the Genie

Was Billy Barty, not Billie Hayes, the original choice to play Weenie the Genie?

Billie Hayes has always believed that to be the case—and that's the way she told the story for more than two decades. Recently, however, she learned she was mistaken.

"I always believed that the role had been originally intended for Billy," she says. "And Billy, I don't know, he took sick. I don't know whether he had a heart spell, whatever, and then they called me and asked me if I would do it. And I said, sure. I enjoyed it, but I felt that the genie could have been a far more colorful character. I think it was originally written for a guy and then, when I came in, they changed it around a little."

It couldn't have been changed too much, though, given that Weenie is a male genie, regardless of the fact that a female played the part.

Meanwhile, Hayes believed she had been the second choice on *Lidsville* for years. Then a casual conversation with Barty began to make her wonder.

"I remember Billy and I, we did a guest thing on *Access Hollywood* or one of those shows like that. And Billy and I were in the green room and we mentioned *Lidsville*. And I said, 'Listen, Billy, I have to thank you for that role, although I'm sorry that you got sick.' And he looked at me like he didn't know what I was talking about. So I don't know now whether what somebody told me is something that wasn't so or whether it's a fact."

So we took Hayes' story to the source, Sid Krofft.

"No, no, we always wanted Billie to play Weenie the Genie," he maintains. "Maybe somebody got that idea because of it being called Weenie. Maybe somebody was thinking it was originally created for a little person to do. But we always wanted Billie."

Then we told Billy Barty. His response?

"I don't know a thing about it. She's wrong. I was never asked to do Weenie the Genie. In fact, she was the best Weenie the Genie there could have been. She was great. She put life into it and held that show together, if you ask me."

Case closed.

the Kroffts selected comic actor Charles Nelson Reilly.

Like its predecessors, *Pufnstuf* and *The Bugaloos,* only one season of seventeen episodes was made. It didn't approach *Pufnstuf* in terms of popularity, but *Lidsville* was a modest success.

"It was a cute show," Hayes says. "It was a clever show. It was a different kind of show. But *Pufnstuf* still was the superior show in every way."

It also was a highly ambitious show, perhaps too ambitious, given the ever-present budgetary constraints the Kroffts were working under.

"It was a logistical nightmare at times," Rose recalls. "We had to build every character because every character had to be a hat. And that's so crazy. Because we'd have to decide, 'How many hats can we have?' If you need a crowd of hats, it's not like hiring some extras. It becomes a very involved procedure."

Director Tony Charmoli also had one quibble: "Because of the circle of a hat, it's hard to get any interesting angles to shoot."

As was the case with all of Sid and Marty's shows, the puppets they created for *Lidsville* were visually spectacular. Yet for some reason, they never quite dominated the landscape the way they were meant to.

One reason the costumed characters never had as much character as they should have, says Joy Campbell (who usually wore the Nurse Hat and Beanie costumes), is that, unlike other Krofft shows, the puppeteers rarely seemed to be playing the same characters from one day to the next.

"It was so chaotic that I have to look at the show and sometimes I can't even tell who's who. Most of the time, I am in the beanie hat. Often I'm the nurse. Once or twice I even did the Indian, but not very many times. Sharon was the football helmet most of the time, but she wasn't all of the time, and Angelo Rossitto was usually the gangster hat, and the hillbilly hat most of the time was Buddy Douglas. But really, it was chaos. Anybody can be in any costume.

"They got a whole bunch of people called the Hermine Midgets from New York. They were like a clan. Some of them were sister and brother. Some of them were married. And they stayed to them-selves. They would talk to us and everything, but they were very, very clannish. And then there were some more little people that Sid and Marty had brought in. And because there were so many people, we did not bond the way we did on the first two shows."

Campbell believes this case of "musical costumes" limited the performers because they were unable to develop distinct personal-ities. "On *Pufnstuf,* I could develop Orson and I could develop Cling. But on *Lidsville,* for all of us, you'd never know until you'd get the script what you were going to be the next day. And it's hard when someone else has worn the costume the day before, even though they take it to the cleaners and spray it with disinfectant. You're thinking, 'This is not my costume. Somebody else was wear-ing it the day before.' And one day you were the beanie hat and the next day you were the Indian for about five minutes and then they wanted to put you back into the beanie and then they wanted you to do the nurse. It was hard to get enthused."

In retrospect, one could also argue that casting Charles Nelson Reilly was both a blessing and a curse.

On the plus side, Reilly's manic, mad-hatter performance was positively brilliant. He was a real scene-stealer and became the focal point of virtually every episode. "Charles Nelson Reilly could chew up scenery like crazy," Charmoli says. "He's a real pro."

But on the minus side, by Reilly's dominating so overwhelm-ingly, the show never fully realized its out-of-this-world potential. Hayes puts it this way: "Charlie and I are good friends and I thought Charlie was wonderful as Hoo Doo. But Charlie was a one-man show and I think that's why a lot of the Hat People never seemed to become as real to the viewer. Instead of coming alive and being real, the way that the characters in *Pufnstuf* did, the Hat People were just walking costumes."

She makes a good point. Shows starring wacky humans are commonplace, but a show in which hats lived, breathed and had personalities would have been strikingly unique.

How ironic, then, that by focusing on the magician, *Lidsville* may have lost a lot of its magic.

They Really Flipped Their Lids

"*Lidsville* was just hysterical, the whole idea of it. I mean, how much dope do you have to smoke to pitch *that* to somebody?"

So says Amy Yasbeck, an actress best known for her roles on the sitcoms *Wings* and *Alright Already*. She is a huge fan of Krofft TV. "I lived in that world," she says. One of her favorite memories from working on a film called *Dracula, Dead and Loving It,* in fact, was a bit of schtick she and costar Steven Weber would do daily about *Lidsville*.

"We did a bit about a guy doing a really, really bad pitch for *Lidsville,*" she says. "I can't do it as good as Steven because it's really, really macabre. It would be the pitch for the *Lidsville* that didn't make it. He would go, 'And we could have like a Kaiser hat. And there would be something a butcher would wear.' Really, really bad hats. 'Maybe like a tiara with eyelashes.' He would go on and on and he would do like another segment of it every day. He would do, 'Maybe I didn't explain it right last time.' He was hysterical, but so was the show."

Frankly, it doesn't take much imagination to picture Sid Krofft making a similar pitch in real life.

Incidentally, Yasbeck actually met the Bugaloos when she was a kid growing up in Cincinnati.

"Remember the black one? He made a pass at my sister. The Bugaloos were making a personal appearance in Cincinnati for something and the *Pufnstuf* characters were there too, up on stage. But the Bugaloos were there and they were wearing their wings and signing autographs. And he made a pass at my sister. Well, maybe he didn't make a pass at her, but he definitely flirted with her. I was so excited."

Sid and Marty refuse to second guess themselves about casting Reilly, though. If Sid could go back in time for a little tinkering, in fact, the actor he would more likely replace would be Patrick, who underwhelmed as much Reilly overwhelmed.

"He wasn't any Jack Wild or anyone like that," Sid says of Patrick. "And I was never really that thrilled with him, but he did his job."

Not So Quiet on the Set!

Lennie Weinrib equates the voice work on *Lidsville* with being placed in a torture chamber.

The reason? When *Lidsville* went into production, the Kroffts tried an alternative to Automatic Dialog Replacement, a costly and time-consuming procedure in which the puppet characters' voices are dubbed into the show at a time well after filming.

"It was the craziest goddamn thing we've ever done," Weinrib says. "We did it live. We did it all live. Walker Edmiston, Joanie Gerber and I sat on the soundstage from morning until night doing the scenes over and over and over again. They built a little room for us on the set. They put us at a table, gave each of us a comfortable chair, and they put like a window in front of us, so we were like in a sound studio. And we had monitors in front of us. And we were watching the goddamn action and doing all the dialog as it happened.

"I guess everybody thought this would be a more practical way of doing it because we wouldn't have to go through the enormous expense

As for Reilly's performance, Sid says, "He created Charles Nelson Reilly in that series. To this day, he still plays Hoo Doo. That *is* Charles Nelson Reilly. He created that character, that persona that we all know him for, when he was on *Lidsville*."

Si Rose believes that might be something of an overstatement, but he adds: "Hoo Doo certainly brought it out a lot. I do know that. His comedy, he really utilized it on *Lidsville*. Maybe Sid's right. If you do something every week for a whole year, maybe it locks in."

Whether that's really true, perhaps only Reilly himself can say. But if it is so, it's somewhat ironic, given how much everyone says he disliked doing the part.

"I don't think that Charlie liked doing Hoo Doo," Billie Hayes says. "I just felt that he didn't know what he was getting into when he signed to do that role. I can't speak for Charlie, of course, but I don't think he knew. Being on a children's show, you think, 'Oh,

of ADR-ing all the lines, which takes a tremendous amount of energy and a lot of money and a lot of time. This way, we would have a finished product and maybe even the energy of the voice people would transfer into the little hats and their performances."

Not a bad idea, unless you view things through the voice person's eyes.

"The only thing that they forgot is, of course, you've got to do a thousand takes," Weinrib says. "So by the end of the day, none of us could speak practically. Thank God we were young and strong and had healthy voices. We came through all the episodes without anybody dying. But Walker, Joanie and I at the end of the day were three very, very, very tired voice people. Because they'd go, 'Cut, the character fell down...Cut, the light fell over...Cut, this happened.' And all that screaming and yelling, live, five takes of this, ten takes of that. We were working eight to fourteen hours a day, nonstop, the three of us doing all the characters. Well, it takes its toll on your voice. It's amazing that none of us just said, 'I can't talk any more. Sorry.'

"And I don't know what would have happened, because we were not set up to do the show any other way. They were set up to do it live. I don't know of any other show in history that has been done exactly like that."

geez, this will be a snap.' Whereas it turns out to be the opposite. It's hard work, just like anything else.

"And that makeup, it's grueling. Charlie's makeup was grueling. So was mine—I was green too—but I didn't mind it. I was accustomed to it. But Charlie, I don't think had ever done that. And I just think that once he realized what he had gotten into, he was unhappy."

Says Sid: "Well, Charles Nelson Reilly hated the green makeup and all that stuff. He said wearing it was like being in a concentration camp or something. He hated that he had to come in at six in the morning to put that green makeup on, but he loved doing that character."

Says Rose: "He used to call me Bad Hat Si. Because I'd come around and he would have to put all this makeup on and he'd have to work so hard. But that was some of the funniest stuff that he's ever done."

Adds Sharon Baird, who played Raunchy Rabbit, Hoo Doo's dumb-bunny sidekick: "It's true. He didn't like doing it. But he was really good at it and I always enjoyed working with him."

Campbell tells a story that perhaps best sums up Reilly's some-times love-hate working relationship with the Kroffts: "It was very close to the end of *Lidsville*. We've got two weeks to go or a week to go. And even though we've had a great time, we're ready to close it all. 'Let's just wind up these shots and move on.' Early on, Sid and Marty had been very flexible about shooting around Charles. We would have days where Charles wasn't there and we would do scenes without Hoo Doo. Well, of course, when that happens, you find at the very end that all the shots they need are of you. And there was a big glut of stuff Charles still needed to do.

"So they tell him one morning, 'Charles, you've got to come in at 6:00 tomorrow and we're going to go straight through. It's going to be this and this and this and this.' And he says, 'I'm not doing that.' And they said, 'Yeah, this is what we've got scheduled.' And he said to them, 'I'm not coming in tomorrow.' And they said, yeah, right. And the next day comes and Charles doesn't show up. I know they called him and it's rumored that they even sent someone out to Charles's house. And finally, by noon when they realized they couldn't do anything about it, they sent us all home. And of course, Sid and Marty were furious. And the next day, Charles comes in, just as cocky as hell, and he says, 'How did everybody like my Hoo Doo holiday?'"

As for Patrick's dislike for doing the role, Hayes puts forth this theory: "I think he was that age, that awkward stage when certain things that you're required to do seem childish to you. It was probably like he was embarrassed to be doing this. Whereas maybe, if he had been twelve or thirteen and the whole puberty thing had not kicked in as much, maybe he would have gotten into it more."

Adds Baird: "It was just the age he was at. He wanted to be grown up and this didn't seem grown up to him."

Patrick admits it's true. "Because when you're eighteen years old," he says, "the last thing you want to do is to be in something that's really corny."

There was one significant perk, however. "Everybody should be a teen idol at least once. I became sort of a teeny-bop star. I don't know what else you call it. We had records out. Heartfelt crap. And I was in *Tiger Beat* and *16 Magazine,* all of those magazines. That kind of thing had never happened when I was playing Eddie Munster.

"It was kind of funny because it was such a hoot. There's nothing like walking through the market and seeing little twelve-year-old girls looking at your face on the cover of some real cheesy magazine."

At least no one can accuse Hayes of looking down on her material and not believing in the reality of the Hat People. If there is a major shortcoming to *Lidsville,* she says, it's because some of her costars didn't believe.

"It happens so many times, when you watch children's shows, that there's a self-consciousness when adults are dealing with children," she says. "Adults can be so self-conscious. But when you're in a costume and you're self-conscious that you're doing a children's show and that this is for children, you are dead already because the reality is not there.

"If you don't believe in the reality of what you are doing, you're only going through the motions."

As Sid puts it: "You know, working with suited characters, there has to be some kind of warmth from the live actors. That's just like when we do our lifesize puppets. Not too many stars can relate to them. It intimidates them or something. I don't know what happens."

In retrospect, maybe that lack of connection between some of the human and puppet characters, combined with the fact that the Hat People were so far removed from reality to begin with, prevented *Lidsville* from being as big as it could have and should have become.

"The Hat People, that was something that you never saw before," Sid says. "There was nothing to hook onto."

Says Charmoli: "I agree. It was difficult to associate, I think, with people who would live in a hat."

In the final analysis, Sid says, "Maybe it was *too* unique."

Billy Barty emerges from his Sigmund costume.
SID & MARTY KROFFT PICTURES.

Who Ever Heard of a Friendly Sea Monster? ...or A Creative Day at the Beach

The saying goes that creativity is ten percent inspiration, ninety percent perspiration. But where does luck fit into that equation?

There are times when a great idea strikes like lightning, an unexpected bolt from the blue, and the only input the creative genius can honestly claim is that he was standing in the line of fire. In such cases, the true measure of creativity is the ability to spot a unique idea and to run with it.

Creativity is often just an accident. Communicating what was accidentally discovered is what truly counts.

Such was the case of Sid Krofft and *Sigmund and the Sea Monsters*, one of the most successful TV series to come out of Sid & Marty Krofft Productions. Not unlike the way a falling apple knocked some sense into Isaac Newton's head, the idea for *Sigmund* literally washed in out of the ocean, right at Sid's feet. The measure of his genius was his ability to make this piece of pure chance mean something.

The premise of the show: An affable young sea monster named Sigmund is outcast by his family, the Oozes, because he lacks the mean-spiritedness it takes to be a sinister sea creature. Simply put, he doesn't want to scare people. One day on the beach, he meets two boys, Johnny and Scott Stuart, and they immediately become friends. Sigmund moves into the boys' clubhouse and comic mishaps ensue as the boys try to keep his existence under wraps.

Consider it the '70s low-tech, small-screen precursor to *E.T. The Extraterrestrial,* only this E.T. was from the sea.

"The story of *Sigmund and the Sea Monsters,* that actually happened to me," Sid says. "I went with a friend of mine down to La Jolla. There's a beautiful beach down there, a cove with a lot of caves. We were on the beach and I found—well, we both found it—we found this giant Sigmund. I immediately gave him a name. I've never seen a piece of seaweed like it. It was enormous. And it was alive.

"And so I said to my friend, 'My God, we've got to take this home.' And he said, 'You can't do that. You can't take him away from his family.' And I said, 'No one's ever going to believe this.' It was such an incredible thing. So we decided we'd try to take it back with us. We were just acting crazy. We were acting like a couple of kids. I was forty-some-odd years old at that time, but, of course, I've never really grown up.

"Well, there was this guy, this hippie sitting in one of the caves, watching us. And I said to him, 'Hey, would you watch Sigmund, because I'm going to go get my car.' I don't know what I was thinking. I had a Corvette and there was no way. We were just acting crazy. It was one of those beautiful days. And the hippie said, 'Oh, yeah, man. I'll watch it.' And I don't remember why it took us so long to get back, but we got waylaid. By the time we got back, the tide had come in and the hippie was gone and Sigmund was back in the water. And it looked like he was waving at us, you know, like, 'Come on in.' But we couldn't get to him. We tried, but it was high tide and the water was really rough. So we had to leave without him.

"And on the way back to L.A., I said, 'My God, we were like two kids.' And we started acting crazy and putting this story together: 'two kids...they meet Sigmund...they hide him out...'Oh, my God, there's Mom and Dad'...he's got these two crazy brothers and his family sends the brothers out looking for him.' And that's how we created *Sigmund and the Sea Monsters*.

"When I went in to the art department and laid it all on them, they started drawing it. And I think we sold that show possibly that same week. I mean, the networks used to just wait for me to come in and act crazy with them."

Sid Krofft, center, double-checks Sigmund on the beach while Johnny Whitaker looks on.
SID & MARTY KROFFT PICTURES.

Small Talk With Billy Barty

He has appeared in more than two hundred motion pictures and worked alongside many of the biggest stars in Hollywood. Yet as far as Billy Barty is concerned, doing kids shows with Sid and Marty Krofft was anything but kid's stuff.

"They're a great twosome, Marty and Sid," he says. "They didn't pay much, but they were always very good to me. You know, those children's shows that they put together, all of them, were just great. I mean, they're even good today.

"So many people today remark that they won't let their kids watch a lot of what's on now, but they'll let their kids watch Sid and Marty's shows because it was good, clean, intelligent fun."

Barty measures just 3'9" in height, while tipping the scales at only eighty pounds, but he literally became a giant in the entertainment industry, perhaps the most famous little person in the business.

His show business career began seven decades ago in 1927 when he was just three years old. By the time he was in his teens, he had appeared in more than 120 movies. Among other roles, he played Mickey Rooney's kid brother in the Mickey McGuire shorts of the late 1920s. When television was in its infancy in the 1950s, Barty was there as well, perhaps most memorably as a member of Spike Jones' City Slickers.

Yet even though Barty was a known commodity, his face immediately familiar to moviegoers and TV viewers, he had no reservations about climbing inside any of the Krofft brothers' full-body costumes.

"It didn't matter to him whether he was a star or not," Sid says. "He was in a lot of those shows and you never got any ego trip from Billy. I mean, a job is a job. And Billy's a professional. That's the way he looked at it."

Barty entered the lives of Sid and Marty in 1971 in the *Pufnstuf* movie, in which he played Googie the Gopher, a character that hadn't been in the TV show. Almost immediately after that, he was cast to play sidekick Sparky the Firefly in *The Bugaloos*. Later, he graduated to playing the title character in *Sigmund and the Sea Monsters* and he even shed the puppet costume altogether in *Dr. Shrinker*, in which he played Hugo, the evil doctor's wicked assistant.

"I also was in a lot of the shows that they did on the road, which were just fantastic," he says. "I remember we had a packed house in Madison Square Garden. It seemed like you had to walk maybe eight miles to get there, through the tunnel that they had underneath from the hotel. But it was worth it, the way the fans greeted us when we came out."

Although Sigmund might be the most widely remembered of his Krofft characters because the series was the most successful and the longest running, Barty says he can't single out any one of them as his favorite.

"No, I couldn't do that," he says. "I liked them all. I liked the fact that I was bringing something to life, that I was taking something and making it real. You're not a puppet. You're real."

But after another moment's reflection, he adds, "Well, maybe I do have a favorite. Yes, I liked *Dr. Shrinker* because I didn't have to wear a costume."

That Barty would say that should come as no surprise, really, because working in those costumes could be difficult and challenging work. "You know, people think that costumes can be fun. Yes, it is fun. But those outfits weigh quite a bit and it gets very, very hot inside."

It's also worth noting that being a little person does not automatically qualify someone to be a Krofft puppeteer.

"You have to be able to act. In fact, you have to emote more because of the restrictions you're faced with. You have to be able to express yourself more broadly. You have to almost overplay it. Because if you don't do that while you're inside the costume, nothing comes out on the outside."

Billy Barty.
PHOTO BY TIM NEELEY.

Sigmund and the Sea Monsters, Sid and Marty's fourth series in five years, premiered on September 8, 1973, on NBC. It became one of the brothers' biggest, most memorable hits. It also was their first series to run for more than just one season of originals.

It succeeded because, like *Pufnstuf,* every one of the elements clicked: The young lead actor (Johnny Whitaker) was talented and charismatic; the *supporting* cast members were outstanding at being just that, supporting cast members, not scene-stealers; and, perhaps most important, the sea-monster puppet characters were so brilliantly conceived that they literally became real to the viewing audience.

Central to that was Sigmund himself, a little green lump of sea-weed and tentacles with a charming childlike face and a single-tooth smile. Inside Siggy was Billy Barty, whose subtle sense of movement, combined with Sidney Miller's terrific vocal interpretation, actually made viewers forget that what they were seeing was a little person in costume.

Sid says Barty was his only choice to play Sigmund. "Because Billy was the king. Billy was a performer. Billy was an actor. He could sing. He could dance. He could do everything. And to put that kind of a little person in the suit, I mean, we were honored to have Billy. He was a star."

But had either of the other critical elements—Siggy's voice or the warmth of the sea monster costume—come up short, Sid says, "None of it would have worked."

Of course, Sigmund also got a great deal of help in the believ-ability department from his two human costars, played by Johnny Whitaker, then age thirteen, and Scott Kolden, eleven.

Whitaker, who still is perhaps most widely known for playing Jody Davis on *Family Affair* (1966–71), was hand-picked by Sid and Marty for the part—no complicated casting process involved this time—and he didn't let them down.

"It was because of *Family Affair* that we knew who he was," Sid says. "I can't remember whose idea it was, but Johnny Whitaker was an established household name at that time and we felt he was perfect for this show.

Johnny on the Spot

It should come as no surprise that John Whitaker, who achieved child super-stardom on *Family Affair* in the 1960s, still could be found working for CBS three decades later.

After all, many kid actors remain in the entertainment industry after they grow to adulthood.

But Whitaker no longer is directly involved in the production of TV series and movies. He is a computer specialist who worked at the network's west coast studios. He left the network in 1997.

"My job title at CBS was 'help desk administrator,'" he says. "We had about three hundred and fifty users here and about eight different servers, big computers that serve anywhere from thirty-five to two hundred clients. And when there were software-hardware problems, they called me."

Whitaker says the leap from child actor on such shows as *Family Affair* (which aired on CBS) and *Sigmund and the Sea Monsters* to computer specialist isn't that great.

"In the eighth grade, at the time that I was doing *Sigmund and the Sea Monsters,* my father told me to learn how to type, that computers were going to be the wave of the future. He said, 'If you know how to type, you'll never go hungry.' I probably was at the top of my career at the time. But my dad still said, 'This may not be a career that lasts forever and ever. We hope it does. But if you go and learn to type, you can always find a job.'

"It's funny. There still were a couple of people there [at CBS]—they're getting up there in age now—but they remembered me from when I was in the halls as a snot-nosed kid. And I'll come in and they'll say, 'Hey, what are you doing here?' And I'll say, 'I'm here for your computer. You were having trouble, weren't you?' Some of the people have been blown away by that."

Whitaker's costar, Scott Kolden—who had himself appeared in a prime-time sitcom before *Sigmund,* the short-lived *Me and the Chimp* (1972)—also left the business of acting. After having worked for the phone company for more than a decade, he makes his living as a sound effects technician.

"He was a star and we went after him and he accepted and we were thrilled to have him. I mean, getting Johnny Whitaker to star in our show was just incredible."

Whitaker, who now goes by the name John, was in a period of transition at that time. Puberty had begun to kick in since *Family Affair* had wrapped—with subtle yet significant changes in his appearance, his voice, even the spelling of his first name (from Johnnie to Johnny)—but he made the shift from playing a supporting costar in prime time to the young lead of a children's series with tremendous ease.

Hair Apparent

When John Whitaker reflects on his days as costar to a friendly sea monster, he offers only good things to say about cast and crew.

But there is one thing that makes him cringe whenever he sees an old episode: the sight of his hair, a mass of red curls that seemed to have a life of its own. Even Sigmund's seaweed 'do wasn't as crazy.

"Every day was a bad hair day," Whitaker says with a laugh. "And there was nothing that anyone could do with it. They certainly tried. It's a mystery to me why they didn't just cut it all off."

But Sid knows why.

"Because his hair was so wild, it gave him character," he says. "It made him *into* a character.

"Remember the Three Stooges? How a lot of who they were was all about their hair? That's a little of what we got too."

Johnny Whitaker as Johnny Stuart and his sea monster friend Sigmund, played by Billy Barty.
SID & MARTY KROFFT PICTURES.

Ever since *Pufnstuf,* the Kroffts had been looking for another young lead who could be as polished and professional as Jack Wild had been. With Whitaker, they finally had found him. Of course, that should come as no surprise, given that this thirteen-year-old had more years of experience in television than Sid or Marty.

"What he did on that show—and this isn't an easy thing to do, even for big, big adult stars—he made you believe in Sigmund," Sid says. "He made Sigmund real to the viewer. That just shows what a good little actor he was."

Barty seconds that assessment: "He really made viewers believe that Sigmund was alive. His performance allowed the viewers to suspend their belief so that Sigmund wasn't someone in a costume . . . Sigmund was a real sea monster."

Says Marty: "Johnny's a terrific guy and he just loved doing *Sigmund and the Sea Monsters.* He's a very, very good guy and he's been a friend for a long time. In fact, when we did 'Pufapalooza' at Nick at Nite, Johnny was one of the ones who came to New York to help promote it all."

Whitaker, who chose to leave the acting profession after *Sigmund* wrapped production, says he cherishes the work he did on *Sigmund* as much as *Family Affair.*

"I probably was at the top of my career at the time when I was doing *Sigmund and the Sea Monsters* and had my face plastered all over the teen magazines," he says. "I loved working with Sid and Marty. They're great people. They even let me choose my own costar.

"And it's amazing to me how people still remember the show. They come up to me and tell me how much they loved it when they were kids. Just yesterday this woman came up to me, saying, 'You were my salvation during my childhood years. I'm thirty-five and I love you and thank you.' And it's nice to be remembered in that way."

The fact that Whitaker and Kolden were friends in real life who had worked together before *Sigmund* was a plus as well. The two had costarred in *Mystery in Dracula's Castle,* a live-action Disney feature, and their closeness in real life made the task of portraying brothers a breeze.

When Whitaker sang "can't live without friends who won't let you down...you gotta have friends" in the show's opening theme song, those weren't just hollow words. In fact, Whitaker says, he and Kolden are best buddies to this day.

"He and I are best friends," he says. "I mean, literally. We were ushers at each others' weddings. We do a Christmas album every year together. We live close to each other and it isn't uncommon for one of us to just to pop in on the other at any time."

The most familiar faces in the supporting cast, meanwhile, belonged to Mary Wickes as Zelda, the Stuarts' nosy housekeeper, and Rip Taylor as Sheldon the Sea Genie.

Wickes—who died in 1995, for years one of the premiere ladies of the American theater—was a marvel in a role that was essentially the *Sigmund* counterpart to *Bewitched*'s Gladys Kravitz or *I Dream of Jeannie*'s Dr. Bellows. The boys tried to keep Zelda in the dark about Siggy's nearby existence, which wasn't easy given all the awkward situations Sigmund and his family created.

Taylor—one of comedy's most uninhibited funnymen, a love-him-or-hate-him type who never makes no impression at all—joined the cast during the show's second season when Sid and Marty covered him with green makeup, locked him in the confines of a seashell and anointed him with the powers of a genie. After Sigmund discovered Sheldon's magic seashell on the beach and freed him, Sheldon was at Siggy's beck and call, a development that led to some *Bewitched/Jeannie*-esque story lines in later episodes, such as bringing Paul Revere to modern times and making the boys invisible.

Sid and Taylor's friendship goes so far back that Sid says he can't even remember how or when they first met.

Like the Kroffts, Taylor toured for a time with Judy Garland, but the brothers weren't with Garland at that time. "Did I meet him through Debbie Reynolds?" Sid says. "I don't remember. I really don't remember. I've known him for it seems like a million years."

One thing Sid has no trouble remembering, though, is why he added Taylor to the show's cast. "Well, he's outrageous. He's great. He's like a puppet. Rip Taylor *is* a puppet."

Nevertheless, what made the show stand out were Sigmund and his sea monster family, the Oozes of Dead Man's Cove.

There were stooge-like Blurp and Slurp, Siggy's big brothers, whose meanness was matched only by their dimness. There was big Sweet Mama, a bossy broad with an ironic name. And there was Big Daddy, a tough-talking shrimp who looked like a sea monster version of Edward G. Robinson. And instead of a dog, these denizens of the deep had a pet lobster with a rather yappy bark.

"The Ooze family, we took them from *All in the Family*," Sid recalls. "They were those kind of characters, basically a loud, kind of obnoxious group of people that you would be ashamed to have to admit that they're family. They were characters you could relate to. It was a concept that anyone could easily hook on to."

Sid says that many, many mockup sketches of Ooze family members were drawn before they made their final selections, but only one version of Sigmund was required.

"In our art department, we had an entire staff of so many artists who worked on the characters until we decided on the ones that we thought were the warmest and could work the best. But Sigmund, the first time he was drawn, we decided on him. Because it was something that I already saw. So I described it to the artist. And the one who drew him, or was assigned to draw him, got him the first time because of my vision of really seeing him in person. I mean, that's what he looked like when I saw him back on that beach.

"Now as for the other guys, Blurp and Slurp and the others, they were made up from Sigmund. As soon as we got Sigmund, then we knew what they needed to look like, because they were just globs of seaweed with personalities."

Simply put, unlike the Kroffts' previous series, *Lidsville*, in which the Hat People puppet characters came up just a little short, characters introduced in *Sigmund and the Sea Monsters* were extraordinary creations—too fantastic to be believed, and yet lovably familiar at the same time.

As Barty puts it, "The way I feel is, we were all alive. We weren't animated. And we weren't weirdos. We were just different kinds of characters who were part of society, our own society. And, hey, as far as we

Fire at Dead Man's Cove

During the second season of production of *Sigmund and the Sea Monsters,* a fire broke out at Goldwyn Studios that destroyed two soundstages.

Si Rose vividly remembers the blaze for three reasons: one, because of the immediate concern for life and limb, even though no one was injured; two, because of the production complications brought on by losing sets and props to the fire; and three, because of the comical sight of Rip Taylor fleeing the scene.

"Because of the fire on the cave set, a lot of the studio burned down and everybody had to evacuate," Rose says. "And Rip Taylor, it was unbelievable. Here he was in this crazy outfit—he was green from head to toe—and he's running down Santa Monica Boulevard.

"And the people who were passing by didn't know what he was all about. They thought he was from another planet or something. Because he had all this makeup on as Sheldon. I can still picture that."

Adds Sharon Baird, who played Big Daddy: "It was quite a sight, him running down Santa Monica Boulevard in green tights and green fins. And when he got back at the hotel he was staying at, he was still dressed that way. And when he stepped up at the front desk, they asked, 'Are you coming or going?'"

were concerned, the real person, the human, he was the weird one."

Si Rose, *Sigmund's* executive producer, points to *Dinosaurs* (1991–94), the puppet-populated sitcom that Jim Henson created before his death, as evidence of how good *Sigmund* was nearly two decades earlier. "I look at that show with the dinosaurs, which was on at night, in prime time, with a budget that was much, much bigger than what we ever had to work with, and I see so much of the stuff that the Kroffts did. Some of the characters were better in some ways and equally good in others."

It is worth noting, by the way, that Sid put a woman (Sharon Baird) in his Big Daddy costume and a man (Van Snowden) inside Sweet Mama.

"I visualized Archie Bunker when I was doing Big Daddy," Baird says. "I wanted to move like Carroll O'Connor on *All in the Family.* And what I found a lot of times is that sometimes a character comes across better if the opposite sex is playing the part. Because you tend to, when you play the opposite sex, exaggerate their movement, rather than just walking your regular way."

As for Snowden, he didn't care which sex he played, because he was always up, up, up anyway. "A lot of people get in the costume and they'd be so claustrophobic or frightened that their performance would go down, down, down. But I was so interested and excited and into the character that they always had to calm me down. And I still have that problem today with everything I do. I always start it real big and then I have to bring it down."

Says Barty: "Sid and Marty knew what they wanted and they got it done by surrounding themselves with the right people. Everybody was fantastic in that cast. And they had good writers and voice people. It was fun."

Sigmund also marked a notable change in the Kroffts' style. Gone was the acid-trip surreality that their first three series—*Pufnstuf, The Bugaloos* and *Lidsville*—all shared. *Sigmund* was more purely a children's show, whereas the earlier efforts could also stimulate viewers on an adult level.

That not-so-subtle change, Sid notes, was deliberate. "We were changing with the times. How many times can you do psychedelic? And it wasn't the '60s any more and I wanted to get into a whole different area. We were in the '70s and we were going into the '80s. You can't keep repeating yourself."

Next to *Pufnstuf,* Marty says that *Sigmund* is his favorite of the shows he and his brother created.

"But *my* favorite show," Rose says, "probably was *Sigmund.* That had topicality in being real life and yet the monsters, they were so unbelievable. What a great combination."

Marty calls it their "most traditional fantasy series" and yet it clearly connected with young viewers. "The values were pretty straightforward in that one: friendship, honest and simple good times."

Ready to rumble: A couple of T-Rexes tangle
in an otherwise picturesque setting in *Land of the Lost*.
SID & MARTY KROFFT PICTURES.

Saturday Morning Dino-Mite!
...or Jurassic Park, B.C.
(Before Crichton)

Long before American pop culture transformed the mighty dinosaurs from majestic, mysterious beasts of another age into kings of kitsch—before dinos became trendy and fashionable, cute and cuddly—Sid Krofft was a diehard dinosaur buff.

"I have always loved dinosaurs," he says. "One of my favorite movies as a kid was *One Million B.C.* I'm not talking about the one Raquel Welch was in, which came out many years later. I'm talking about the one that was made like twenty-five years earlier with Victor Mature. That movie made such an impression on me as a kid and it scared me to death."

One Million B.C. made so strong an impression, in fact, that Sid remembers the very theater in which he saw it.

"It was 1940. We were living in Providence, Rhode Island, at that time. It was at the Paramount Theater. I remember because my dad knew the projectionist and he used to sneak me in through the back of the theater to see the movies there every week."

Sid remains an avid moviegoer to this day, almost certain to see the latest fantasy and science fiction films in their first week of release. Of the recent dino flicks, he rates *Jurassic Park,* the Steven Spielberg-Michael Crichton collaboration, as a classic. He considers *The Lost World,* the sequel, to be a comparative disappointment. "There wasn't much of a story, but still I loved all the dinosaurs."

Sid is fascinated by dinosaurs. So is it any wonder he wanted to make a dino movie of his very own? "I always wanted to do something set in a land of dinosaurs. I guess you could say that *One Million B.C.* inspired me."

It merely took three and a half decades for him to act on the inspiration.

Land of the Lost, Sid and Marty's fifth television series in six years, premiered September 7, 1974, on NBC and was instantly a colossal hit. It is even considered by many fans, generally those who prefer pure science fiction to *Pufnstuf*-style fantasy, to be the Kroffts' finest series.

As Wesley Eure, who starred as young Will Marshall, puts it: "I get asked about the show all the time. People come up to me all the time and I can't believe they still recognize me. Adults watched us because *Land of the Lost* was technologically ahead of its time and kids loved this program because it was the only live action Saturday morning show competing with cartoons."

And a point virtually no one will dispute is that *Land of the Lost* was one of the most intelligent and ambitious TV shows ever made for children.

"That's what made it so great," Eure says. "The fact that it was such a smart show."

Says Allan Foshko, who created the show with Sid: "It was ahead of its time. Today, I go into places and people say, 'Oh my God, you created *Land of the Lost?*' You'd think that I was Walt Disney. 'I never missed one program. I never missed a show.' It's like *Star Trek* has its mystery and history and, for kids, *Land of the Lost* was theirs. I didn't realize how powerful it was. But it's amazing how many children the Kroffts affected. And I tell you, *Land of the*

It's a Jungle in Here

When Wesley Eure was starring in *Land of the Lost* while also appearing in *Days of Our Lives,* he sometimes didn't know whether he was coming or going.

"My schedule was insane," he says. "In the mornings, I would be over at *Days of Our Lives,* crying about my girlfriend's latest illness. Then I'd rush over to *Land of the Lost* and yell, 'Run, Holly, run! There's a dinosaur!'

"It made me pretty crazy. There came a point where I almost confused the two shows. So to help keep things straight, I decorated my dressing room at *Land of the Lost* like a jungle, complete with fake birds and trees, just to get in the mood."

Lost is really like my Oscar. People's eyes light up when they hear that and I'm proud of that."

The premise: Forest ranger Rick Marshall (Spencer Milligan) and his children Will (Eure) and Holly (Kathy Coleman) are river-rafting one day when they take a tumble over a waterfall and become trapped in a strange time vortex. They then find themselves transported to another world, a self-contained universe unto itself, inhabited by dinosaurs, a tribe of monkey-like "Pakuni" people and a reptilian race of malevolent "Sleestaks." Every day in this strange world presents new challenges to the Marshalls' survival skills as well as to their commitment to family unity as they try to co-exist in a land of kill-or-be-killed until they can find a way home.

A far cry from the innocent charm of *H.R. Pufnstuf* and *Sigmund and the Sea Monsters,* isn't it?

"Well, not really," Sid gently protests. "It's a different kind of show, sure, but there's still the idea that we're making an intelligent show not only for the child but for the grownup and the whole family."

Indeed, it wasn't uncommon for kids who were devoted to *H.R. Pufnstuf* years earlier but had since outgrown their Saturday morning viewing habits to tune in to *Land of the Lost.* They were closet *Land of the Lost* fans, watching at an age when it wasn't considered cool to be watching cartoons.

The Marshall family:
Wesley Eure as Will,
Kathy Coleman as
Holly and Spencer
Milligan as Rick.
SID & MARTY KROFFT
PICTURES.

The Kroffts and Foshko saw to it that there was very little cartoony about *Land of the Lost*. Not only did they spend a small fortune to make the show look as realistic as possible, hiring some of the top special effects wizards in the business, but they also brought in talented writers with extensive backgrounds in science fiction.

"We actually had writers who wrote for *Star Trek*," Sid says. "That should say it all right there. *Star Trek* is one of the greatest science fiction shows in TV history because it had intelligent stories and interesting characters. It could have been a stupid, silly show, but it wasn't because it was well written. And that's what I wanted. I wanted this show to be as smart as *Star Trek*."

Filming dinosaur
sequences required
time-consuming
precision work with
miniatures.
SID & MARTY KROFFT
PICTURES.

Some Not So 'Special' Effects

Even though *Land of the Lost* was a show filled with elaborate special effects of all kinds, sometimes the most effective ones were decidedly low-tech in nature.

Consider, for example, the episode that opened the third season, in which Spencer Milligan's Rick Marshall left the Land of the Lost at the precise moment that Ron Harper's Jack Marshall entered.

"You will probably recall seeing the father in that episode, even though the actor didn't appear in the third year," Harper says. "I believe they wanted him to come back and do the one episode where he disappeared. But actually it was our producer with a black wig on. You only saw him from the back. Our producer put on a black wig and a khaki shirt and he went into the pylon. That was him."

Another time, Harper was involved when a special effects sequence mixed the latest in Chroma-key technology with a piece of moviemaking trickery that dates back to silents.

"I was crossing hand over hand on a rope from some gorge," he says. "I remember they had a rope strung up with the blue screen behind me. And I had a bad back from when I was doing *Planet of the Apes,* from a mechanical bucking horse that they had strapped me into. So I was to do hand over hand on this rope, but I had a hell of a time doing it, mainly because my back was so sore. And I remember it was so difficult and finally they put some boxes under me."

Accordingly, David Gerrold (who wrote three *Trek* episodes, including the classic "Trouble With Tribbles") became *Land of the Lost's* story editor and main writer. Former Trek script consultant Dorothy Fontana (who wrote eleven episodes, including the classic "Journey to Babel") also wrote for *Land of the Lost,* as did a *Star Trek* cast member, Walter (Mr. Chekov) Koenig.

The Kroffts also spared no expense when tackling the technical challenges that the show posed. Sid and Marty had become accustomed to testing themselves in their television projects, but *Land of the Lost* introduced an entirely new set of hurdles to clear. After all, how do you put dinosaurs, flying reptiles, giant lizard men and tiny ape creatures on the screen without it looking patently fake and phony?

To create their prehistoric creatures, the Kroffts turned to Gene Warren, the special effects wizard who had won Academy Awards for *The Time Machine* and *Tom Thumb*. Warren designed miniatures that were authentic in appearance and movement. Each creature contained ball-and-socket joints that permitted lifelike movement of the head, legs, tail or wings. Then came the process that transformed the models into living, breathing beings—from the frightening Tyrannosaurus Rex known as Grumpy to the baby brontosaurus named Dopey.

Eure explains the process: "They shoot a dinosaur model, expose a frame of film, move the dinosaur a fraction of an inch, expose another frame and continue until it appears that the dinosaur is moving on its own. It's a painstaking task. It took almost a day and a half just to create ten seconds of action."

This footage was then integrated with separately filmed elements of the show. So while technicians worked on two adjacent stages at the General Service Studios in Hollywood, the actors were working blocks away on life-size duplicate sets of Warren's miniatures.

And other live action segments had to be shot on an enormous Chroma-key set (the actors performing in front of a blue-screen background), which were then superimposed onto footage from the miniature sets. "We constructed the largest Chroma-key set in Hollywood," Sid says, "something like seventy-five by one hundred feet, painted all in blue. We had been using Chroma-key since 1970—any time that the Bugaloos flew, for example—but never in such an involved process as this."

Going the extra mile clearly paid off, though. This was a Saturday morning TV show and it was filmed on a Saturday morning TV show budget ("we didn't even have a tenth of the money that Spielberg had to spend on his dinosaurs," Sid notes), but the results were spectacular.

In fact, unless you compare the Krofft dinosaurs directly to Spielberg's, which were created with computers after two decades of advances in special effects technology, they still are quite convincing. Fittingly, the Kroffts were honored in October 1996 with a Lifetime Achievement Award from the SciFi Universe Awards, mostly on the strength of *Land of the Lost.*

Even though the show was Sid's idea, one would be remiss to overlook Foshko's guiding hand not only in the series' creation but in its sale to the network.

"I've known Sid and Marty for forty years," Foshko says. "They were clients of mine at one time. I knew them when they were a puppet act and I managed them from time to time. I put them on *The Merv Griffin Show* constantly with their puppets. And over the years we stayed friendly and we always had a good rapport. And Sid and I used to create projects together.

"I was the creative director at Twentieth Century-Fox when I discovered that I could make the story boards myself and not have to rely on the written word, so everybody could see what I was talking about with their own eyes. In fact, today, that's what I do. I make collage art. I call it Foshkollage.

"Sid wanted to do a show like *One Million B.C.* and Sid and Marty hired me as their vice president in charge of new programming. And I went away and first wrote down the concept of how the family gets lost in the Grand Canyon, Ranger Rick and his son, and then that opened up into a prehistoric land. They go down the falls. After all, in every good adventure, you slide down something, like in *Alice in Wonderland.* Or you go through the cave entrance in J. R. R. Tolkien. You have to pass through something to get to this other place.

"And I had researched and discovered that the Grand Canyon was as old as the dinosaurs. In fact, there are fossils in the Grand Canyon *older* than the dinosaurs. So in my fertile little mind, I put this together and gave it the title *Land of the Lost.* I helped write the music and cut out all the pictures. And I created a series of storyboards out of cut paper. I brought in actors and shot them up against the blue mat and then, after we went to shoot the thing, I could Chroma-key them into the background. And with the right music and the right pacing and some special effects that we did with the camera—in those days, it was primitive—it all worked.

The Pocket Pakuni Dictionary

If you want to talk to a Paku, you can get by with universally understood gestures, but it helps even more to know a little of the language. Here are key words from Victoria Fromkin's first Pakuni-to-English dictionary. It might be wise to keep this guide handy so you will be prepared for the unlikely event that you are trapped in the Land of the Lost. After all, you don't want to be branded *doma yuman* (an ugly human), do you?

Pronunciation key: the letter "i" sounds as in "heed"; "e" as in "hate"; "a" as in "hot"; "u" as in "hoot"; and "o" as in "boat." In each word, only one syllable receives stress and that is the next-to-last syllable, the "penult." Underlined vowels denote the stressed syllables.

PAKUNI	ENGLISH	PAKUNI	ENGLISH
Paku	Paku or person	we	he/his/him
Pakuni	Pakus or persons	wa	she/her/her
yuman	human	wu	it/its
yumani	humans	wani	they/them/their
sarisataka	Sleestak	ejiri	house
sarisatakani	Sleestaks	ejirini	houses
abu	child	ota	fire
abuni	children	osu	water
abimi	man	onam	food
abimini	men	epi	light
me	I/me/my	ayo/yooo	yes
meni	we/us/our	anu/nooo	no
ye	you/your (singular)	me saku	thank you
		nanda	sorry
yeni	you/your (plural)	ba	come

"So we had the most extraordinary giant flowers and a secret mystery caveman and a beehive that was as big as the Empire State Building. All those kinds of things. I really went far out and used pictures to show it. And it was with this that they went to ABC and sold the show."

PAKUNI	ENGLISH	PAKUNI	ENGLISH
ma	give	bimisa	mannish
dinda	eat	bimiki	manly
ku	go	oke	youth
omo	smell	kesa	young
fa	take	ofu	speed
pika	trade	fusa	quick
bake	bring	fusaki	quickly
ting	push	tum	with
ji	beg	eroka	freak
aboma	leader	erokani	freaks
amura	friend	me ji ye	I beg you/please
bu	to be able/can	bisa	big
wo	have	bisasa	very big
sa	what	tusa	tall
sa paku	who/whom	tusasa	very tall
sa pakuni	who/whom(plural)	doma	ugly
sa efi	what thing/what	gosa	fierce
efi	thing	nichi	nasty
efini	things	nichichi	very nasty
ego	place	ogansa	magic
sa ego	where	wachi	now
epa	way or manner	epini	lights
sa epa	how	ru	steal
opari	reason	ewoya	flower
sa opari	why	wesa	good
kesa	young	wesasa	very good
busa	childish	tiri	quiet
busaki	childishly	oje	noise

Foshko and the Kroffts also sweated little details, such as the prehistoric language the race of Pakuni people spoke. Sid and Marty hired Victoria Fromkin, a linguistics professor at UCLA, to create an actual working language.

Patterning the Paku tongue after Swahili, Fromkin carefully developed a vocabulary of about two hundred words as well as rules of pronunciation, syllable structure and syntax. Sharon Baird, who played Pa, a Paku, recalls that the actors playing Pakuni were tutored on the nuances of their new language before ever stepping in front of the camera.

Today, it's common for science fiction shows to develop alien languages with delicate precision, but a '70s kids show probably could have gotten away with using apelike gibberish. They could have done it that way, but they didn't, because Sid wouldn't hear of it. "Because I didn't want it to be totally stupid. Because if it was a made-up language, just garbled words, then you would have laughed at it. The Pakunis were important characters and I didn't want to make their language an unimportant part of the story."

But even with all these ambitious behind-the-scenes goings-on—from the hiring of writers with top-flight credentials to the special effects and the realistic language—everything would have been moot without a strong cast.

The Kroffts hit the jackpot in that department with Eure, Coleman, Milligan and, during the final season, Ron Harper (who played Uncle Jack and replaced Milligan as the show's paternal figure).

The first step was casting Eure as Will Marshall.

Says Sid: "I already knew Wesley. I don't remember how. And I thought that he would make the perfect boy for that part. So I sent him in as the first person to see the casting person. I said, 'I can't guarantee you anything. I'm just going to send you in and the rest is up to you.' I think he was up against two or three other kids. That was it. And he was the chosen one. He had already been on a soap before that, on *Days of Our Lives,* so I knew he had the experience."

The next step was matching the other two leads, Milligan and Coleman, with Eure. Sid says that also was an easy process, one that didn't require a massive talent search.

"We had them read individually and then the two, the boy and his sister," Sid recalls. "Then we teamed them all up, the three of them, so that they looked like a family and seemed right together."

Milligan was a particularly good choice because, in addition to having an extensive theater background, he also bore a strong physical resemblance to Eure. And even though Coleman's braided blonde locks didn't match the others' dark hair, making her not so obvious a casting choice, she impressed the producers with acting skill that belied her young age.

Sid says he considered the casting so vitally important because, unlike *The Lost World,* which had a plot that left him a little cold, there was far more to *Land of the Lost* than the idea of having humans run away from dinosaurs. In fact, if you examine the shows carefully, you realize that the dinosaurs were just gimmicks, whereas two more compelling ongoing stories were what gave the show its resonance.

The most important element, subtexturally woven into the fabric of every episode, was the examination of family and family relationships, of the pressures placed on a single parent, of the growing pains that kids deal with as they advance to young adulthood, of coping with loneliness and isolation when placed in new and unfamiliar environments.

These familiar themes provided an interesting counterpoint to the other element, the unfamiliar cultures with which the Marshalls now had to co-exist.

Mind you, this wasn't entirely the way it looked in Foshko's original presentation. For one thing, his version featured a narrator to tell the story, and didn't include a Marshall girl.

"The network test-marketed it," Foshko recalls. "They took it around to see how it was received by kids and we discovered that we needed a girl. It had only been Ranger Rick and his son up until then. But the girls wanted equal time. So we put in the little girl. She looked like Patty McCormack to me, the little girl in *The Bad Seed,* because of those pigtails. I never did cotton up to that child."

Meanwhile, there was a character of Foshko's that was left out.

"I wanted a Tarzan-type character who they would learn to relate to and who gets them in and out of danger because he is so facile at maneuvering around. He had been left in the Land of the Lost by his parents. So it had that Tarzan myth attached to it. They kind of cut that out. They didn't go all the way with that."

The Wonderful World of Wesley Eure

The perception that kid actors often grow up to lead troubled adult lives is a cliché... and it became a cliché because it seems to happen with alarming regularity.

But Wesley Eure, actor turned author, is proud to say that he is not now, nor has he ever been, a member of that beleaguered fraternity.

"I did *The Sally Jessy Raphael Show* a few years ago," he recalls, "and they stuck me on with all these ex-child stars. Jay North, the guy who was Dennis the Menace, was one of them. The only reason I was there was my publisher wanted to promote my new book. I was doing a book tour and the idea was that Sally would give it a major plug, which she did. Anyway, they called me from the show weeks before and said, 'Have you ever been on drugs or depressed or in sex therapy?' I said no and I told them, 'I'm not going to do one of these has-been shows.' And they said that's not what this is.

"So I go there to promote my book. And I'm standing backstage while all these people are talking about their drug abuse and their horrible lives and how much they hate the business. And this producer comes up to me and says, 'Wesley, make this funny! Would you please? This is too depressing!'

"So I go out there and Sally asks me to tell a little about myself and I say, 'Sally, why am I here? I can't even get arrested.' What is it with all these people who hate each other and hate the business? It makes no sense. I mean, this is the funnest business in the whole world."

Although Foshko thought of it as a variation on *The Swiss Family Robinson,* it's worth noting that *Land of the Lost* tapped into a scenario not unlike H. G. Wells's *The Time Machine:* While the two species that Wells's time traveler encountered were naive, diminutive Elois and malevolent, underground-dwelling, bug-eyed Morlocks, the Marshall family met naive, diminutive Pakunis and malevolent, cave-dwelling, bug-eyed Sleestaks.

The Kroffts' villains even ate Pakuni the way that Morlocks had feasted on Elois, although it was never shown, of course. That probably would have been entirely too disturbing for young audiences.

Eure has done enough in the business to have an informed opinion. In addition to his three seasons on *Land of the Lost,* he costarred for eight years as Michael Horton on *Days of Our Lives* (1973–81), was a regular and producer for *Totally Hidden Video* and hosted *Finders Keepers,* a kids game show on Nickelodeon.

But he also has a thriving career as an author of children's and humor books. Among his half dozen

Wesley Eure.
PHOTO BY TIM NEELEY.

titles are *The Red Wings of Christmas* (Pelican Publishing, 1992) and *Dewey the Raindrop* (Pelican, 1997). Why enter this field after so many years as an actor? "I had a story I wanted to tell and I sat down and wrote it. Unfortunately, most of the books that were published are out of publication now because those companies have gone under."

His ties to children's television didn't end when *Land of the Lost* ceased production, by the way. "I have two new series for PBS, two children's shows that are going into production. One's called *Dragontails.* It's animated. And the other is called *Show and Tell Me,* hosted by Maria [Sonia Manzano] from *Sesame Street,* a live show for preschoolers."

But the Sleestaks were plenty scary anyway and posed a constant threat to the Marshalls in a way that dinosaurs never could. After all, to avoid being eaten or stepped on by a dinosaur, one merely needed to be agile enough. Outsmarting the Sleestaks, the highly intelligent race that had built the Land of the Lost, would prove to be a great deal trickier.

As Ron Harper puts it: "The dinosaurs would just make an occasional appearance to keep you on your toes. It was the Sleestaks who presented the real danger to life and limb."

Not surprisingly, Sid says he still often meets young adults who relate stories of how Sleestaks terrified them as kids, how Sleestaks gave them nightmares. "They really scared the kids to death," Sid says.

But it's worth noting that these scaly sociopaths were all bark, so to speak, and not much bite. Consider, for example, that viewers never saw anyone killed or even badly injured at the hands of the Sleestaks.

In fact, for an action series that featured the constant threat of dinosaur attacks and Sleestak raids, this was fundamentally a non-violent show.

Harper recounts the story of his first filmed fight scene with the Sleestaks as an example of the show's pacifist point of view: "The first time in the episode when I encountered the Sleestaks, the three of them came in and we were supposed to fight, so I attacked them.

"I jumped on their backs and started pounding on their heads and kicking at them. And the director said, 'Cut.' He said, 'What are you doing, Ron?' I said, 'I'm attacking these Sleestaks.' He said, 'You can't do that. This is a children's show. You can't punch them. You can't kick them. You can't hit them.' 'I can't hit them? Well, how do I fight these creatures?' He said, 'With fire. That's the only way. You stick a torch in their faces. The light blinds them. But you can't hurt them because it's a children's show.'

"Before doing *Land of the Lost,* it had usually been my experience that when you fought with the villains, you punched them or shot them or blew them up. But not here."

And about those Sleestaks. If they could only talk, the stories they might tell.

Says Eure: "Did you know that the Sleestaks were not professional actors in costume, but UCLA basketball players? Listen, it's not that easy finding a seven-foot actor. But a seven-foot basketball player, now that's a different story. The players wore wet suits with green scales and they were mighty hot under those stage lights. They could spend only about sixty seconds in costume."

Adds Harper: "We always had three Sleestaks and never more than three in any given scene because we only had three costumes. Isn't that great?"

As for the Pakuni, a sort of missing link between monkey and human, it probably required a great deal of self restraint on the

What a Character!

Some fans might be surprised to learn that *Land of the Lost's* most widely known performer—albeit not because of his work on this series—was one of the guys in a Sleestak outfit. His name is Bill Laimbeer. That's right. The same Bill Laimbeer who became an NBA All-Star.

During the first season of *Land of the Lost,* Laimbeer was a 6'10" high school senior in Palos Verdes, California. "I was recruited by college basketball coaches and scouts in the entertainment business," he recalls. "They were looking for people who were 6'10". It was my first experience with TV. It was a lot of fun and they paid me very, very well."

After one season inside the Sleestak costume, Laimbeer left his lizard man days behind. He played college basketball at Notre Dame and ultimately went on to NBA stardom, playing most of his career for the Detroit Pistons.

Could it be that Laimbeer, notorious for his bad-boy image, a player fans loved to hate, came by his reputation quite naturally because of doing duty as a Sleestak, a TV villain that viewers loved to hate? Marty thinks so.

"He was one of my favorite players," Marty says. "I always thought that he actually took the personality of the Sleestaks when he played basketball."

Kroffts' part not to copy themselves, to stick with what had worked for them in the past, by putting little people inside walk-around monkey costumes. As a result, the Pakuni weren't as lovable and cuddly as, say, the Ewoks of *Return of the Jedi*. But they were infinitely more believable and realistic.

The lead Paku—although by no means the group's leader, given that he was the littlest one of the group—was Cha-Ka, who befriended the family in the first episode after they rescued him from a "grumpy" Tyrannosaurus Rex and mended his broken leg. The humans and Pakuni weren't instant friends, mind you, but the level of trust and respect between the two species steadily grew as the series progressed.

Unlike the Sleestaks, the Pakuni were played by professional actors. That was a must, given the larger acting demands that were placed on them.

The three most noteworthy Pakuni roles were Cha-Ka, played by Philip Paley, an eleven-year-old child actor; Pa, played by Sharon Baird, the former Mousketeer who also had portrayed costumed characters in each of the Kroffts' earlier four series; and Ta, played by Joe Giamalva during the first season and by Scutter McKay in subsequent seasons.

The Marshall family and their Paku friends.
SID & MARTY KROFFT PICTURES.

It required a couple of agonizing hours in the makeup chair to be made to look like a Paku, Marty says, and they were hardly comfortable for the actors.

"But we never teased Philip for wearing that ridiculous costume," Eure jokes. "He was a black belt in karate."

After a while, the Marshalls discovered a series of triangle-like devices that contained colored crystals. These were called pylons and they not only powered this strange place but also held the key to the only doorway leading in and out of the Land of the Lost. (Because of the delicate balance of this alternate universe, incidentally, no one could leave without someone else entering—which explained how Rick Marshall and Uncle Jack, who had been searching for his missing relatives, happened to swap places at the beginning of season three.)

Again, the part that is easily forgotten, given the many sophisticated sci-fi ideas that fueled the show, is the fact that this was a program for children.

Says Harper: "Believe it or not, people still come up to me and tell me how much they loved that show. I am constantly amazed at how many people still recognize me from *Land of the Lost* and remember the show. And they say, 'I was only five at the time, but I remember it very well.'

"And I think it is primarily because the stories were so good. I had just finished doing *Planet of the Apes*, the nighttime series, which you would expect to be better written than a children's show on Saturday mornings. But I thought the stories on *Land of the Lost* were much more interesting. We reworked so many of the old legends, the Flying Dutchman, the Medusa. I remember our producer, he said that it was the most fun that he had, writing stories that experimented with ancient myths and fables. It was ambitious.

"I have an eight-year-old daughter and she has seen them all. It's her favorite show. And I don't think it has anything to do with my being in them. It's because it's a good show."

Marty acknowledges that *Land of the Lost* isn't what might be classified as an educational show. But he quickly adds that it did have tremendous teaching potential, perhaps moreso than a straight educational show because young viewers would absorb the lesson while having fun.

The theory he put forth while the show was in production: "Besides sending the kids to the encyclopedia to look up information on dinosaurs such as the tyrannosaurus rex and the brontosaurus, we are discovering that there is another less obvious benefit to this show: that parents are also watching. Parents are discovering a world where fact and fantasy are enjoined, one in which they willingly suspend disbelief and have a good time with their kids. This, in turn, stimulates 'can it be? could it happen?' type dialog between parent and child, a situation we think is good."

Eure never lost touch with Sid and Marty after the show ceased production. When American Cinematheque paid tribute to the brothers in 1995, Eure was there. What's more, he wants to work with them again. He has developed a TV project that, if produced and if they choose to come aboard, could mean a professional reunion.

There is also the possibility of his writing a book about the making of *Land of the Lost.* "I'm going to do this thing because, over the years, I've had so many requests. I had some great times on the set of *Land of the Lost.* I was living out every kid's fantasy, playing with dinosaurs. But it wasn't just the dinosaurs. The entire cast was fun."

Yet he admits he has lost touch with his fellow actors.

"Kathy Coleman, I saw her three years ago and I haven't seen her since. She's great. We were good friends. But I've totally lost touch with her. She was looking beautiful when I saw her last. Spencer Milligan? He disappeared. I haven't talked to anybody."

Eure isn't alone in that department. Sid and Marty also have lost touch with Coleman and Milligan.

Says Marty: "She vanished. When we were going to do the second version of *Land of the Lost,* she called up saying that she'd be a perfect jungle girl. She was living in Canoga Park at the time. And then she just vanished. We kept trying to get hold of her. And there was no forwarding address and nobody knew where she was."

Says Ron Harper: "I've heard that she got married and had two children already."

Another third-party report had her living in California, working in an ultra-hip clothing store and not having done any acting for a very long time.

The last the Kroffts had heard about Milligan was that he left California for his forty-acre spread in Wisconsin.

As for Philip Paley, who played Cha-Ka, Harper says his whereabouts are no mystery. "Nice guy," Harper says. "I run into him sometimes when I'm doing commercial auditions. Except I never recognize him out of that makeup. He always has to introduce himself to me."

Eure describes *Land of the Lost* as "an amazing show that was ahead of its time."

But it wasn't ahead of its time so much as timeless in its appeal—as evidenced by the fact that years after *Land of the Lost* ended its network run on NBC in 1977, the premise was still fresh enough for a new version.

The reprise of *Land of the Lost* was produced by Sid and Marty but watched over by the brothers with more of a laissez-faire philosophy than on the original. It premiered on NBC on September 7, 1991, seventeen years to the day after the original's debut, and it, too, was a ratings success.

The new show wasn't an exact clone, but it didn't stray far into unfamiliar territory. First, some significant differences: The new family was the Porters: Tom, the father (played by Timothy Bottoms), teenage son Kevin (Robert Gavin) and younger daughter Annie (Jennifer Drugan). They entered the Land of the Lost when an earthquake swallowed up their camper. Because their truck was chock-full of supplies, the Porters were better equipped for roughing it in the wilderness. And whereas the Marshalls' no-frills dwelling was a cave they called High Bluff, the Porters' gadget-filled treehouse compound wasn't that far removed from a well-stocked wilderness cabin.

As for some common elements: The Porters' Land of the Lost was also populated by dinosaurs that ranged from scary (a T-Rex dubbed Scarface) to sweet-natured (a baby dino named Tasha), a race of talking Sleestaks (which looked less like space aliens than the originals) and, of course, the Pakuni.

Also added to the mix was Christa the jungle girl (Shannon Day), a beautiful wild girl whose presence on the original probably would have been as greatly appreciated by young Will Marshall, who was at an age of sexual awakening, as it was by Kevin Porter.

The dinosaur sequences, meanwhile, were spectacular. Advances in special-effects technology since the original had made it possible to improve the show's look exponentially.

The series ran for two seasons of thirteen episodes each, then played for a third season of network reruns and later found a new home on Nickelodeon. Yet, at the time, something was sorely missing.

Says Marty: "Anyone who knows the original doesn't like the new ones. They did well and the kids seemed to like them. But anybody who watched the original dislikes the new ones."

It's a Jungle Out There

Frequent Hollywood tales of nepotism notwithstanding, family ties don't always open doors for actors.

Take the case of Kristina Krofft, Marty's daughter, who is an actor. An inside connection didn't help her land a coveted role in one of her father's shows.

"My first experience in auditioning was when I auditioned for the jungle girl in the new *Land of the Lost* series," Kristina says. "They told me I had the part and then they told me I didn't."

Shannon Day wound up getting the part of the jungle girl, Christa (which happens to be Marty's wife's name).

"It was a big wakeup call for me as to what this business is like. I said, 'Okay, if that can happen with my own dad's show…' That prepared me well."

Perhaps this statement from Sid explains why: "We weren't involved much in the new one. I was working on some other things at the time and they didn't need me."

But maybe they did.

One obvious flaw in the remake, so much so that it makes viewers appreciate the subtlety of the original in this regard, was the ham-handedness of the writing. For example, each episode seemed to close with a cliché "and what have you learned from this experience?" segment that was artificial and wholly unnecessary.

The Marshalls of the original had learned just as many valuable lessons, but they apparently didn't feel the need to recap for viewers who had missed the point. In short, the new *Land of the Lost* was written "down" to a kid's level while the original didn't condescend.

Another shortcoming of the new *Land of the Lost* was that it didn't remain true to its own sci-fi logic. Whereas the original had established a very specific set of rules about how this strange world worked, the remake would break its own rules if it suited the story.

Sid's greatest dissatisfaction with the remake also had to do with the idea of writing down to kids. Specifically, he takes issue with what was done to his once-frightening Sleestaks. "They took all the darkness out of it," he says. "The network didn't want anything dark in it."

Thus, the Sleestaks were transformed into almost comical villains. They still had evil intentions, but they had somehow also evolved into utterly inept creatures who, at times, stumbled over one another like stooges.

"You have to have dark villains if you want them to be taken seriously," Sid maintains. "The Sleestaks are very, very important in *Land of the Lost*. But the network didn't want that. They wanted them to be like Laurel and Hardy. And when they made the Sleestaks talking and almost nice, well, I hated that. When they did that, I didn't want to have anything to do with it.

"I think the second one looked great and the kids obviously watched it. It did well for the network and then it was very popular on Nickelodeon. Kids loved it. But I didn't. I like the old. It was darker and more intelligent. The new version wasn't my cup of tea because it wasn't scary enough."

Sid isn't alone either. Harper says, "I've seen parts of the most recent one that was on. It had tremendous special effects. And our special effects were very primitive. It was so many years ago. But it didn't matter. I think ours was the better show."

Not surprisingly, when the feature film version of *Land of the Lost,* in development at Disney since 1996, finally reaches theaters, Sid and Marty insist it will be true to the original.

"The original *Land of the Lost* is the one we're doing the movie of," Marty says. "The characters are Sleestaks, Cha-Ka, Marshall, Will and Holly. Marshall, Will and Holly will not be played by the same actors, but our characters will be basically the same and I think that the adventure that we're doing in this new one is going to attract both our adult audience and automatically attract the kid audience.

"As we speak, I'm waiting for the script to be finished. It's on its third writer. We're still in good shape. I think it's going to '98 or '99 before the movie gets made. But it's very much alive."

The Space Nuts, Bob Denver as Junior and Chuck McCann as Barney,
were all thumbs.
SID & MARTY KROFFT PICTURES.

i Said 'Lunch,' Not 'Launch!' ...or Gilligan's Spaceship

Given his ties to one of the most durable sitcoms in TV history, a show that has thrived in endless reruns for more than three decades, *Gilligan's Island* star Bob Denver thought he had his place in pop culture all figured out.

Acting gigs are less frequent these days and the handful he does take on typically hark back to his days as Gilligan, the bungling first mate of the shipwrecked S.S. *Minnow.*

"All you have to do is just mention the show on any sitcom," he notes, "and you're sure to get a laugh."

Denver also makes frequent appearances at autograph shows because the supply of *Gilligan* fans never seems to diminish. "It's amazing, because it's never changed for me," he says of the show's staying power. "Ever since '64, after it went on the air, it's been the same.

"Get a crowded room of strangers and mention *Gilligan* and, all of a sudden, they all have something in common. They all can sing the song. They all can talk about the things we did that didn't make sense—like why we brought so much stuff with us for a three-hour boat trip. And all of a sudden they're friends. All these strangers and you just mention *Gilligan* and—bing!—they've got this common ground."

This place in history is what Denver had come to expect in life. Then, starting around January 1997, something changed.

"It's really amazing, because these kids, these little nine-year-olds, were coming up to me and saying, 'I really like your show.' And I'd say, 'Thank you.' And then they'd ask, 'You know the episode when the monster chased you...' And I'm thinking, 'What are they talking about?' And so I say, 'Gilligan never did that. What show are you talking about?' And they would say, 'Nuts something.' And I go, 'What?'

"As the months rolled by, I came to discover that *Far Out Space Nuts* was running in reruns on the Family Channel. And it was like every child in the country at 9:30 Sunday morning, they found it and they were sitting down and watching it.

"It's funny, because I remember after I finished doing it, I never thought I'd ever see it again. Over the years, every now and then, people would come up to me and say, 'What was the name of that show?' And I'd give them names of shows I had done and they'd say, 'No, no, not that. It had something to do with Nuts in Space.' And I'd say, 'You remember that from when it was first on?'"

But now, thanks to the show's temporary revival in the mid-1990s, when Denver sees a pre-adolescent fan coming, he's not so sure any more which show will be mentioned. "I guess you could say that's a good problem to have."

Far Out Space Nuts premiered in 1975 and ran for one season on CBS. It starred Denver and Chuck McCann, a comic actor whose show business background, incidentally, involved extensive ties to puppetry. They played reluctant astronauts.

Junior (Denver) and Barney (McCann) worked for NASA, but they were only supposed to load a NASA space probe with food for the real space travelers' long trip. The bungling twosome wound up blasting off instead, however, when Junior unwittingly pressed the *launch* button instead of one marked *lunch.* The duo, soon hopelessly lost in space, became a trio once they brought aboard a furry space alien named Honk, a perky costumed creature inhabited by Patty Maloney. The adventures that ensued involved visits to strange worlds and encounters with an array of outrageous alien creatures.

At first glance, there were some obvious *Gilligan*-esque elements to *Space Nuts*. As was the case for the Castaways of *Gilligan's Island,* for example, the Space Nuts were lost and always hoping to return home. It's also worth noting that McCann—a larger-framed fellow who specialized in playing Oliver Hardy—had definite Alan Hale/Skipper qualities when paired up comedically with Denver.

On the other hand, it was already a common Krofft device for the characters of their shows to be lost and out of their element, with little hope of returning home. And pairing a skinny actor such as Denver with a larger one like McCann is also a fairly traditional casting strategy.

"This was already developed before I ever got involved," Denver says. "If it seems there's a lot of Gilligan in the show, maybe it's more a case of there being a lot of Gilligan in me and my performance."

McCann, who created the series along with writing partner Earle Doud, confirms that the show was not conceived as a "Gilligan in Space" vehicle. "Not when I was writing originally. It was Marty and Sid who got Bob Denver. We didn't know who it was going to be. In fact, it wasn't going to be me, either. I didn't want to do it. I wanted to just write. But that was one of the deal breakers. Fred Silverman said, 'I'm not going to do this unless Chuck plays Barney.' So he saw in Bob and I an outer space version of the Skipper and Gilligan or a modern Laurel and Hardy."

But even if this wasn't originally intended to be a spaced-out *Gilligan's Island,* Sid Krofft says Denver was his first and only choice to play Junior.

"I didn't think we could get him, though. But it was bizarre. As soon as you said you wanted someone for a show for kids, they were suddenly interested because that was a new experience for them, to be on a Saturday morning show. No one ever turned us down for Saturday mornings. It was always me that got these whacked-out casting ideas."

It's worth noting, too, that some viewers erroneously inferred a connection from the fact that *Gilligan* was created and produced by Sherwood Schwartz while *Space Nuts* was produced by Al Schwartz. "It's a totally different Schwartz," Denver says. "No relation at all. Al Schwartz was a really good producer, though. He had done major things over the years. I'd say, 'So what are you doing on this little show?' And he'd laugh and say, 'Same thing you're doing, I guess.' And I said, 'Well, we're all stuck in this now.'"

Denver confirms Sid's claim that doing a kids show had a definite appeal to him as an actor. "I looked at it as basically a replacement for the cartoons on Saturday morning. And yet this was still a cartoon basically."

At the same time, Denver really had no idea what he was getting himself into. "I remember that CBS had a huge function to kick it off and everything and I had never even seen a script. All I had heard was a vague premise. And the next thing I knew I was doing it. I don't know where the plots came from or who made it up or anything like that. We had writers. I guess we had writers. I assume we did. It was like this: We got a script and we shot it. And we worked real hard and fast, which I liked. Because with that kind of comedy, if you slow down it's deadly. The pace we kept was really quick. We did a lot of things on first takes."

Says McCann: "We did two episodes a week. And there was a ton of work that we did prior to even turning on a camera. We had two stages. There had been a fire at Goldwyn that burned down the soundstages for *Sigmund and the Sea Monsters*. When they rebuilt those stages, we became the first show on that stage. We actually opened up both stages. They had a big door that opened up the stages to make one big stage, which we used to make the lunar landscape and these big cities. It was all pretty big for a kids show."

Generally speaking, *Space Nuts* was a fast-paced and funny show, albeit a bit lightweight. But that didn't mean the Kroffts merely tossed this off without much thought.

Indeed, one goal the brothers attempted with *Space Nuts* was to create a show that was in keeping with an emphasis to delete violence from the world of children's TV. The Kroffts solved the problem of creating conflict without menace by using super-costumed villains and monsters who were always bested but never destroyed. They made the danger appear real but never total, while never abandoning the comedic aspects of the show.

As story editor Ray Parker put it at the time: "We are offering the kids the best of both worlds, the sustained humor of the good cartoon genre and the reality of live action. In a sense, it's not an easy show to do, because you have to find writers who have both a sense of adventure and highly developed comedy writing skills."

Perhaps the most amazing aspect of *Space Nuts*, however, involved the business arena. After all, how brazen of the Krofft brothers to introduce another space saga, *The Lost Saucer*, which also had a "lost in space" premise, the same season on a rival network, ABC. In fact, both shows premiered on the same Saturday morning, September 6, 1975.

Yet Sid says neither network expressed any complaints. "The networks bought everything we came up with," he says, "because our shows were all so successful and so wacky and perfect for kids."

The Space Nuts and their little friend Honk have a close encounter of the furry kind.
SID & MARTY KROFFT PICTURES.

What a Character!

When Bob Denver reflects on his days doing *Far Out Space Nuts,* he freely admits he doesn't remember many details regarding the plots or the guest stars.

"It was so quick and fast," he offers as explanation. "It was just like I was in fifteen shows and then it was gone. I know it was just like two or three months in the summer in '74, '75. I don't even remember when it was. But it broke me up. It was just like this little thing to do. It didn't take much time and I was in L.A. at the time, so I did it. "

The exception, the one episode Denver says he will never forget, was made memorable because of the guest appearance by John Carradine.

"What really broke me up was when they had guest stars come in for stuff," he says. "I just couldn't believe some of the actors would put up with that kind of makeup to play the monsters. John Carradine, who was a classical actor, they said John Carradine was going to do an episode. 'I beg your pardon? Did you say John Carradine?'

"He came in and he walked on the set and they had made his face all blue and they sprinkled it with sparkle dust. They did his hands blue and they put a wig on him or something. And this wild costume. Then he has this big speech to me. He got done with it and I just stood there looking at him. And they yelled, 'Cut!' And I said, 'What's wrong?' And he said, 'Well, it's your line.'

Sid remembers that he launched this sudden space kick because he was paying attention to what kids watched. *Star Trek* (1966–69) had become huge in reruns, spawning an animated Saturday morning version (1973–75), for example. Nor was it lost on him that *Lost in Space*'s most loyal audience members were the little ones who lapped up the show's campy, colorful, comic-book feel.

"*Lost in Space,* that was a family show," he says. "If it's a family show and kids are watching it, if it's a favorite of kids, the demographics experts are going to say, 'Okay, let's do one.' Basically, it's the same thing that happens with movies. As soon as the movie is successful, they're going to do ten copies of it on television."

"He just mesmerized me with the big, grand way that he talked. I just stared at him. I mean, I just enjoyed him so much I wished he'd have kept going on. Forgot my line? I didn't just forget it. It wasn't even vaguely in my mind. I was just stunned standing in front of him. Looking at him and hearing that voice and diction come out. And I just completely forgot everything. I could have just stood there for another ten minutes. 'Give him more lines. I enjoy this.' I tried to apologize, but he took it. He wanted to do it."

Chuck McCann has a different Carradine story.

"You know these doors that open up in all space shows, the doors that zip open," he says. "Well, they don't really make that 'zip' noise. There are two-by-fours nailed to the backs of these sliding doors and two guys pull them open and closed. And generally the guy who walks into the room isn't walking in from the big room that you saw in the previous shot. It's generally against the wall and there's nothing but the wall and the doors and the set, with barely enough room to stand there. But it makes the entrance look tremendous.

"Anyway, here's John Carradine. Think of all the things he has done and here he is in our cockamamie show and he's standing behind this set with the two doors closed. And Denver and I are out front and it's take one, take two, take three, and we never get to the doors opening up. We're goofing and clowning around. And all of a sudden, this booming voice comes from the back of the set, 'For Christ's sake, McCann and Denver, get it right or throw me a magazine and put up some wallpaper back here!'"

As for Denver's costar, McCann had a leg up on many Krofft show actors who were inexperienced when it came to working alongside puppets and costumed characters. That's because McCann had a background in puppetry dating back to his pre-teens.

McCann is a third-generation show business performer whose career began at age seven. His father Val McCann was musical arranger at the Roxy Theater in New York; his grandfather Jack McCann was a unicyclist with the Buffalo Bill Cody Wild West Show. By age twelve, McCann had graduated to building puppets that were featured on his first TV pilot, *Hop, Skip and Jump*, which he made at age thirteen. In his early teens, he met puppeteer Paul

Ashley, who was doing *Rooti Kazooti* on TV, and apprenticed with him for six years.

"That was a wonderful back-door entrance for me into television," McCann says, "through the puppets and working with Paul. And I was a nightclub comic and I did impressions. By the time I had come to California, I had completed about seventeen years of New York television. I had a four-hour show on Sunday and two-hour show on Saturday and an hour every day. I had one of the most successful shows in New York called *The Chuck McCann Show: Let's Have Fun.*"

Even though McCann also performed in many films (such as *The Heart Is a Lonely Hunter* and *The Projectionist*) and TV shows, he is probably most widely remembered by a generation of TV viewers as the "Hi, Guy" guy who lived on the other side of the medicine cabinet in the Right Guard deodorant commercials. "We did those for over eleven years and, when it went off the air, it made headlines. The headline in the *Chicago Times* said, 'Medicine cabinet closes forever.' It was really amazing what a little commercial could do."

McCann's association with Sid and Marty Krofft dates back to his early years as a puppeteer. During the Kroffts' *Les Poupees de Paris* days in New York, they had often spoken to McCann about working together. Years later, while McCann was in Los Angeles working on a TV variety show called *Happy Days* (1970), they got together.

"One day I suddenly had the strongest impulse to call Marty Krofft after not having seen him for several months," McCann says. "Apparently the ESP was working both ways, because when I arrived at one of the regular meeting places for ex-New York actors, there was a message to call Marty. He said, 'Gee, I'd love for you to write for me.' So I called Earle in New York and the two of us wrote for the Kroffts. We wrote some *Sigmund and the Sea Monsters*. We were writing a bunch of shows. And then my old boss from WPIX in New York, Fred Silverman, said, 'Why don't you guys write Bob Hope and Bing Crosby in outer space.' In other words, a funny space show.

"If you think about it, it hadn't really been done before. Space shows had gotten so serious, except *Lost in Space,* and that too had its serious moments. They wanted an out-and-out wacko comedy. So I said, 'Okay.' And I sat down with Earle and I created this idea. And then we went to the Kroffts with it and Sid and Marty looked at it and changed a few things and turned it upside down and shook it out and we got this wonderful series that wrote so freely because this was a new area."

And then, of course, there was the other member of the cast, the one whose presence made this unmistakably a Krofft creation. Patty Maloney's history with Sid and Marty dates back to the Six Flags theme park shows. As she puts it, working with the Kroffts changed her life. "And for the better, I might add. I went to St. Louis and worked with them in *The Bugaloos* puppet show in Six Flags Over Mid-America. I was Benita Bizarre. I was there for six months. And that led to my coming out here to California."

Remember the sensation created in *Les Poupees de Paris* by the puppet that came alive? Maloney, who is just under four feet tall, did a variation on that. As the only human amongst a cast of marionettes, she would "come alive" before unsuspecting audiences.

"Everyone on stage was a marionette, except for me. They were like the same height as me. So I would dance with them and mix with them, as far as dialog and conversation and the skits and things. It was fun. I came out on a treadmill to the stage and then stepped off of it. And people in the audience weren't sure if I was a puppet or not."

After the park's six-month season wrapped, Maloney decided to move to California, almost on a whim, and instantly found more work with the Kroffts.

"When I arrived in Los Angeles, I went to see them. And Sid was working on something new, a television special called *Fol de Rol*. And when I walked in, he just went, 'Oh, you're going to be the star.' I didn't even have an apartment yet, but I had a job. So I got myself an apartment and I stuck around. And then with them, I went on to do the road show of *Pufnstuf*. And I would travel and do all of the live stage shows with them. And that led to *Far Out Space Nuts*."

Maloney says she enjoyed working alongside Denver and McCann, but even moreso she cherished working with Sid and

Marty. She says she knows the Kroffts' TV shows made an impact because people often know who she is because of their work—which isn't easy, given that in *Space Nuts* she was covered from head to toe in her fuzzy Honk character costume.

"It's not the same as someone recognizing Bob Denver as Gilligan," she says, "It's a little bit different. But definitely, they recognize my name from doing Sid and Marty's shows, definitely."

Unlike Denver, Maloney wasn't surprised by the show's renewed popularity with young viewers after it started running on the Family Channel. "It was a good show," she says. "All of Sid and Marty's shows were good. I can see why they would be popular again today."

Yet *Space Nuts* wasn't exactly a hit when it originally aired. Our heroes traipsed across the galaxy for only one season of fifteen episodes before wrapping production. (*The Lost Saucer* ran only one season as well and later turned up in serialized form on *The Krofft Supershow*.)

"Too bad there are only fifteen episodes," McCann says. "I've been told that it was the biggest mistake CBS ever made in children's programming, to let it go. It was at a time when a new boss came in and made a clean sweep. The sets were all bulldozed and destroyed, but the episodes were still running and the ratings went through the roof. It was like the highest-rated show at the time. I also begged Sid and Marty, 'While we still have all this stuff standing, let's get a camera in here and make a movie.' It didn't happen, of course, which I thought was a shame."

Of the Kroffts' dueling space sagas, Sid now rates *Space Nuts* as the superior show over *The Lost Saucer*. "Because I think it was a little more inventive than *Lost Saucer*."

Of course, given that the Kroffts had assembled so many talented people, McCann says, how could it *not* be inventive? "The man who did our makeup, Fred Phillips, had done all the makeup for the original *Star Trek*," McCann says. "He's the one who created the ears for Spock and everything else. And there was a fellow by the name of Herman Zimmerman who was a scenic designer. He later went on to do *Star Trek: The Next Generation* [as that series' original production designer]. We had some brilliant people working on that show."

Space Nuts didn't fare as well as some other Krofft shows imme-

A View from the Inside

It has been said before, but Patty Maloney says it bears repeating: Merely being a little person does not make someone automatically qualified to act in a Krofft puppet costume.

"I think that when you get inside one of those suits and then you're totally covered, you have to work harder to make the characterization come through," she says. "It takes a great deal of acting ability, even more so than just your own face right on camera. And I think it comes from your heart and your soul—and through the costume. If you really believe you are that character, it shows and comes through.

"I think the problem a lot of times with producers is they'll build a costume and then try to fit someone into it. They don't care who it is, just as long as the costume fits. And that's when they get an inferior performance. We always used to say, all of us, that if they would first cast the actor and *then* build the costume, they would be so much better off. Because you need to know that the person who's going to get in there can move and take direction."

What's more, there are definite hazards to the job.

"It's much harder to take direction when you're in the suits," Maloney says. "It's much harder to hit your marks, because you can't see them most of the time. I mean, you have eye holes, but your vision is still very limited. It depends on the way that the costume is built, but most of the time you see like you've got blinders on, like a horse.

"You can see straight ahead. And you can see down ahead of you, but not directly in front of you. So if you are approaching a step, for example, sometimes you don't see the step as you get close to it, because it's right under you and the head or the beak or whatever is blocking your vision."

diately in syndication, perhaps because of an unfortunate stroke of timing. In the summer after *Space Nuts'* premiere, after all, space travel special effects advanced light years thanks to the opening of *Star Wars*. By comparison, *Far Out Space Nuts*—as well as *Lost Saucer*—suffered badly.

"But I've got news for you," Denver says. "Little kids today think

Long Ago, on a Soundstage Not So Far Away

Is it remotely possible that some of the unforgettable characters, images and effects of *Star Wars*, the 1977 blockbuster, could have been inspired by *Far Out Space Nuts*?

It's a preposterous notion…unless you consider some of the evidence put forth by Chuck McCann. It's inconclusive evidence, to be sure, but interesting nonetheless.

"People think I'm crazy," McCann admits. "Every time I mention this, my wife says, 'Will you please? People are going to think you're nuts.' But I could go on and on."

Remember the classic cantina scenes of *Star Wars?* There was something similar to be seen on the set of *Space Nuts*.

"Our budget was so small that we couldn't afford prosthetics, like rubber pieces and stuff," McCann says. "So Fred Phillips, our makeup man, put all the appliances directly on everyone's faces in the morning. And we couldn't have lunch because people were sitting around in all these grotesque things, so instead we would all sit outside and sip our sodas through a straw and drink our lunches. And there was no commissary, but there was a bar area in the back and we always sat around that.

"Well, one of the assistant directors who worked on *Star Wars* told me that, at that time, George Lucas was working on the lot because Francis Ford Coppola was on the lot and he had visited the sets. And the story goes that that's where Lucas was inspired, by seeing our characters sitting around drinking their lunches through straws, for the bar scene in *Star Wars*. At least that's what I was told."

Not convinced? Well, consider Han Solo's sidekick, the massive and furry Wookie named Chewbacca.

it's great. Maybe it's a dinky little show, but little kids just think it's the best. And even the adults, I can't believe them. They say, 'I really like it. It's fun to watch.' And I look at them and I go, 'Well, thanks.' What the hell? Who can tell what will connect with people and why?"

News of the 1990s Krofft comeback, meanwhile, starts the wheels of imagination churning for McCann, the show's biggest

"Now think about the characters that we had on the show, the dogs," McCann says. "The big, tall dogs. They look so much like Chewbacca it isn't funny. They look *exactly* like Chewbacca."

Now consider the weapon of choice of a Jedi master, the light saber.

"We had the first laser sword," McCann insists. "This was an episode called 'Tower of Tagot.' Anything you touch with the sword disappears. But as long as the molecular structure was still there, then you bring him back. Now here's how that happened. CBS program practices insisted that the villains were not to be killed on our show. You could not destroy the villains. So we created this sword that comes out of a flashlight. And as long as one molecule exists, he can put it in reverse and reverse the villain back whole again. Now think about *Star Wars*. What happens to Obi Wan Kenobe? Darth Vader wiped him out with the light saber and he disappeared. There's no body. He just disappears. His molecules just disintigrated."

What's more, McCann even believes he anticipated Lucas in yet another area.

"I wanted Sid and Marty to create their own special effects company. Because what we were doing was, in the middle of filming the show, we would stop everything and go off into a corner to shoot the special effects. Now this was laborious stuff and they were giving short shrift to these special effects because they didn't have the time. We had to get these shows done. So we had tons of dialog and tons of stuff to do, but they would have to stop and go off to shoot the exterior of one of the castles or one of these models. I said, 'Look, you've got all these special effects shows running. Why don't you create a company that just does special effects and buy your special effects from that company?' Do you see what I'm getting at?"

Could it be Industrial Light and Magic?

"That's exactly what I suggested the Kroffts do."

cheerleader. "I was going to present this to Marty: 'What if it's the 1990s and everyone looks up in the sky and they think it's a meteor or a flying saucer blazing across the sky and it lands? And it's the capsule. And Denver sticks his head out and says, "We're back."' And out we step from the capsule, with two full families with us, all of us piling out of that little capsule. It would be hysterical."

No directional (or parental) guidance:
Crew and passengers of *The Lost Saucer* were Fi (Ruth Buzzi),
Jerry (Jarrod Johnson), Alice (Alice Playten) and Fum (Jim Nabors).
SID & MARTY KROFFT PICTURES.

Lost in Space, Krofft Style ...or How The Lost Saucer Found an Audience

"I wish I had fifty cents—just fifty cents, never mind a dollar—for every person who has come up to me and wanted to talk about *The Lost Saucer*."

So says Ruth Buzzi, who starred in one of Sid and Marty Krofft's least heralded shows, the 1975–76 Saturday morning series in which she and Jim Nabors costarred as a pair of star-trekking, time-tripping robots.

When fans reflect today on the most memorable shows of the Krofft TV era, *The Lost Saucer* is often overlooked—and, when it is mentioned, it usually rates also-ran/footnote status compared to such classics as *H.R. Pufnstuf, Sigmund and the Sea Monsters* and *Land of the Lost*. By most accounts, in fact, *The Lost Saucer* is regarded as an unsuccessful show. But you wouldn't know that to hear

Buzzi, the legendary *Rowan & Martin's Laugh-In* alumna who has seen firsthand the impact *The Lost Saucer* made on young viewers.

"Ever since we stopped doing that show, it still happens. To this day, it happens. I meet people who stop me and say, 'Oh, remember that show that you did?' And they never know the name of it. It's funny because they go on and on about it, just raving about how much they loved it, but then they say, 'Let's see, I was little then and I can't remember the name of it.' And I say, '*The Lost Saucer.*' And they say, 'Yeah, that's it.'

"And I have realized in the last two years or so the reason that none of them remembers the name of the show is because they couldn't read. But they'll go crazy, just going on about the show. I can't tell you how many hundreds and hundreds and hundreds of people over the years have stopped me and they rave on about that. And they don't even know *Laugh-In*. The people who were seeing *The Lost Saucer,* they barely even know about *Laugh-In* because that show was gone before they were watching TV."

Although Buzzi's kids-who-can't-read-yet theory is an interesting one, there's another reason *The Lost Saucer* doesn't roll off the tongues of fans as quickly as many of the brothers' other TV shows. The fact is that the title proved to be somewhat prophetic because, in a manner of speaking, the show itself was lost for years.

Let us count the ways: For starters, *The Lost Saucer* wasn't widely played in local syndication after its original run as many of the Kroffts' other shows were. When a variety of Krofft programs were made available on videotape in the early 1990s, *The Lost Saucer* episodes were not among them. When Nick at Nite celebrated *almost* all things Krofft in 1995 with its Pufapalooza marathon, at least two episodes each from six different series were shown, but nary a one from *The Lost Saucer*. And when the Family Channel turned over three hours of its weekend morning schedule to Krofft TV, the five series that comprised the lineup did not include *The Lost Saucer.*

It's a trend that, frankly, burns Buzzi up.

"I want you to know that that hurts me," she says. "It hurts me that they have chosen not to rerun our show. It's the only show of theirs that's *not* being rerun and it kills me. Because all those people who remember it, they would get such a kick out of seeing it again."

Although a bit overstated, she does make a valid point. For even if *The Lost Saucer* isn't classic Krofft—Sid and Marty are the first to admit that—it still was an entertaining and superbly cast series.

Buzzi and Nabors played Fi and Fum, a couple of android space explorers from the year 2369 who landed on Earth, circa 1975, after sailing through a time warp. After touching down in the middle of downtown Chicago, these friendly visitors from space invited a couple of humans, a nine-year-old boy and his fifteen-year-old babysitter, aboard for a look around.

Everything was fine until a crush of police cars and fire trucks started to gather and panicky Fum hit the launch mechanism, sending their spacecraft off in a blast of smoke and back through the time warp, leaving them helplessly lost in time.

Each week brought the inhabitants of the saucer in contact with a new and very different race of beings. There was a planet where an entire population had been miniaturized to conserve resources and fight population growth. There was the world in which people had no names, only numbers. You get the idea. Even though this was intended first and foremost as a fun and funny series for children, the Kroffts tried to slip in a provocative idea from time to time.

As for the younger members of the cast, Jarrod Johnson (as nine-year-old Jerry) and Alice Playten (as his teenage babysitter Alice) were fine but they weren't going to make anyone forget Jack Wild and Johnny Whitaker.

Johnson, an African-American, later had costarring roles in *Szysznyk* (1977–78), a prime-time sitcom starring Ned Beatty, and *Friends*—no, not *that* one. This *Friends* was a 1979 series about a trio of suburban sixth-graders.

Playten went on to have a successful career as a voice specialist. Among her credits is *Doug*, Nickelodeon's hit animated series in which she did vocals for the character named Beebe.

The Bear Facts About Teddy

Great ideas often come from unlikely sources.

Take Ken Forsse, for example. Forsse, who served as consultant on miniatures for *The Lost Saucer* and effects consultant on *Far Out Space Nuts,* was hardly the best known member of the Kroffts' creative team. But for several years in the 1980s, his work created a sensation.

Lennie Weinrib, a longtime Krofft collaborator, vividly remembers the day he met Forsse at the Factory.

"He was one of the lesser-known folks at the Krofft Factory, whom I always respected," Weinrib says. "He didn't talk a lot. He was very quiet. But he was fascinating. He built all kinds of little mechanical things and I sought him out because I thought he was such an unassuming man, almost like a little Einstein-kind of guy.

"Everybody else was very out there. 'Look at what I'm building. How do you like my puppet?' But this guy was very unassuming, quiet, brilliant. He was designing and building the most incredible auto-mechanical things for the Kroffts. So I went over and I met him and we had a cup of coffee and I think we went to lunch one time. And that guy a few years later went on to

Also along for the ride was a "dorse," a half-dog, half-horse (played by Larry Larsen) that actually was one of the Kroffts' least imaginative characters.

But the area in which the show seems most lacking when viewed today is the special effects. But remember, this was 1975, pre-*Star Wars,* a time when *Star Trek*-like technology and its almost comical arsenal of sci-fi devices were about as high-tech as television got. As was the case with the original Enterprise, the Lost Saucer was equipped with plenty of flashing colored lights and chirping sounds but little scientific substance.

Even so, executive producer Si Rose recalls how Sid stretched his budget to the limit trying to make the saucer look as convincing as possible.

form his own little-bitty, teeny-weeny company and invent Teddy Ruxpin."

If the name Teddy Ruxpin doesn't ring a bell, it's likely you didn't have small children in the mid-1980s, when the toy teddy bear with animatronic movement was very much in demand and equally hard to acquire, creating Christmas shopping madness that rivaled the Elmo craze of 1996.

"I'm sure he made zillions of dollars from that craze when they sold millions of Teddy Ruxpins that talked," Weinrib says. "It's so amazing to me that this little guy, working off in the corner of a little teeny lab in the Krofft Factory, could do that. It just goes to show you the talent of the people they brought in."

Bill Tracy, the Kroffts' longtime office assistant, remembers what might have been the genesis of Teddy Ruxpin.

"There was a guy who wanted to build a pizza parlour with characters like those in the Chuck E. Cheese places. And Ken Forsse was designing all the animatronics for this thing. And he had this idea. He came up with this bear head. It had all these electronic circuits inside and, when you put it on your head and talked, the mouth would go open and closed. It was just an idea he was kicking around. And he thought about that and pretty soon he came up with Teddy Ruxpin."

"We had to build a saucer that we could use and practically it had to be the same size as a real saucer," Rose says. "That was where the problems with economics came in. Sid and Marty would want this huge, beautiful machine that could almost fly. But go find the money for that.

"Of course, on television, you only really need half of the saucer and you make up the rest of it with the camera. The camera had to make it look like it was big. But they got great effects. They also hired very talented technical people and some of the effects were just unbelievable, particularly when you take into account the budgetary restraints that were put on a Saturday morning television show."

It's also worth noting that the Kroffts went the extra mile in another area by retaining the Institute for the Future, one of the nation's first organizations dedicated to systematic and comprehensive studies of the long-range future, to critique the material. The brothers wanted the Institute, whose other clients included NASA and the National Science Foundation, to read their writers' scripts, to comment on them, to make suggestions that might help make the far-out societies with whom our heroes came into contact at least a little more scientifically plausible.

So even though no one will ever accuse *The Lost Saucer* of being the *Contact* of the 1970s, it would be unfair to dismiss the show as offering no stimulation for the brain.

As Buzzi, a longtime performer on another children's show, *Sesame Street,* puts it: "The reason I believe *Sesame Street* has been such a success is because they write jokes for adults. The producers are offended when people say, 'Oh, *Sesame Street* is a good babysitter.' They don't want people to think like that. If you would really sit down and watch *Sesame Street* for one hour, you would find that a lot of it—the sketches and especially the songs—they're takeoffs on things that children would not have any idea about. It's for the adults that they've written the jokes and the parodies. The Kroffts were the same way. I believe they had the same idea."

The Lost Saucer premiered September 6, 1975, on ABC and its sixteen episodes ran in their half-hour format for one season.

"Jim and I did it for one season," Buzzi says. "We could have done it more. But the decision was made not to do another year. I don't know whose decision that was. I really wanted to do another year, but we didn't.

"So that's when Sid and Marty split up several shows, cut them up, made them shorter, and they ran on something they called *The Krofft Supershow.* So we ran some more. So even though Jim and I weren't on there for a whole half hour, we were on there, I think, for fifteen minutes."

Given the premise of the show, the fact that Fi and Fum constantly were trying to bring their friends Jerry and Alice back home, *The Lost Saucer* fit rather neatly among a collection of serialized adventures.

Jimmy, Pufnstuf, Cling and Clang
pile in their Rescue Racer in *H.R. Pufnstuf.*

Witchiepoo and her six-armed sidekick, Seymour, hatch another sinister scheme in *H.R. Pufnstuf.*

The Bugaloos: John Philpott as Courage, Caroline Ellis as Joy, Wayne Laryea as Harmony and John McIndoe as IQ.
SID & MARTY KROFFT PICTURES.

Benita Bizarre and her sidekick Tweeter hold Joy prisoner in *The Bugaloos*.
SID & MARTY KROFFT PICTURES.

Skull session: The Good Hat People put their heads together in *Lidsville*.

The Bad Hat People take their prisoner, Mark, to their leader, the evil Hoo Doo, in *Lidsville*.

Scott and Johnny Stuart welcomed Sigmund, their unusual friend, into their home away from home in *Sigmund and the Sea Monsters*.

Members of the Ooze family—Sigmund, Blurp, Slurp and Big Mama— in *Sigmund and the Sea Monsters*.

What interesting neighbors: The Marshall family—Holly, Rick and Will—
make a housecall to a Sleestak in *Land of the Lost.*
SID & MARTY KROFFT PICTURES.

A girl and her dinosaur: Holly puts gentle Dopey,
a baby brontosaurus, to work.
SID & MARTY KROFFT PICTURES.

A warm and fuzzy moment for reluctant astronauts Junior (Bob Denver),
Honk (Patty Maloney) and Barney (Chuck McCann) in *Far Out Space Nuts*.
SID & MARTY KROFFT PICTURES.

Jay Robinson as
Dr. Shrinker, "a
madman with
an evil mind".
**PHOTO COURTESY JAY
ROBINSON.**

The Bay City Rollers in concert.
SID & MARTY KROFFT PICTURES.

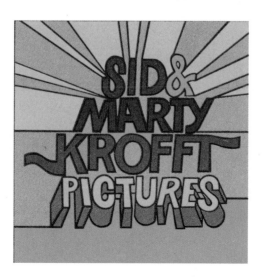

Lunch boxes from the Krofft TV shows are popular collectibles today.
From top left: *H.R. Pufnstuf, The Bugaloos, The Bugaloos* (plastic version from
Canada), *Land of the Lost* (1975), *Land of the Lost* (plastic version from 1992),
The Krofft Supershow and *Lidsville.*

Krofft memorabilia comes in all shapes and sizes.

"I loved doing the show," Buzzi says. "It was hard work because of the boxes that we had to wear that made us look like robots, the cases that we had to wear on our chests that had lights in them. It was a physically difficult costume. It was a very hot costume. And so it was not an easy shoot every day. But I loved doing it."

Well, that makes one of them.

When Nabors, the actor-singer who achieved enduring TV fame by playing Gomer Pyle on *The Andy Griffith Show* and *Gomer Pyle, U.S.M.C.,* is asked whether he liked doing *The Lost Saucer,* he offers not a moment's hesitation before saying, "No, I didn't like it at all."

Nabors and Buzzi were the best of friends when doing *The Lost Saucer,* mind you, and they remain close to this day.

To back that up, Nabors notes that he, Buzzi and her husband of twenty years got together in Indianapolis for the 1997 Indy 500. "We went together and spent the whole time together. Ruthie and I remained close personal friends as a result of working together on that show."

Says Buzzi: "Jim and I, we would have lunch together every day, just the two of us, and that was great. And then after the day's work was over, I'd always go to Jim's dressing room and we would sit and he would tell me stories about his career and everything. It was just a time to relax and it was wonderful. And we got to be very, very dear, dear friends. We were friends before that, but he shared so much with me, with his life and everything. I really gained so much respect for Jim and I was very sorry that we weren't going to do another year."

Again, Nabors loved working with Buzzi but hated doing the show, with which he had two major beefs.

Complaint No. 1, in Nabors' own words: "I felt it was not written well. Ruthie and I had to make up most of the business. I remember a paragraph [in one of the scripts], all it said was, 'Ruth and Jim are funny.' And I went, 'What?' I went ballistic from that one.

"Because I was so used to working script-wise. That was my whole conditioning, from *Andy Griffith* on. If it wasn't in the script, you didn't have to worry about it. But here, this page, this one page that says Ruth and Jim are funny. But Ruthie was just wonderful. She said, 'Oh, let's do that, come on.' And it turned out we were funny."

Complaint No. 2, as Buzzi saw it: "Jim had a hard time with the costume, because it was hard on his back. He had to take the top of his outfit off quite a bit, because it was pulling his back. It was a physically difficult costume. But he's not the type who would complain. That's why he probably never told you any juicy little stuff, any personal things that we went through. It was a physically uncomfortable show for sure."

In fairness to Sid and Marty, neither say they remember a script with stage directions as vaguely expressed as "Ruth and Jim are funny." But whether it really happened precisely that way is less important than the fact that Nabors remembers it that way. By telling that story, he expresses what he considered to be the show's greatest shortcoming.

In fact, when told of the comeback that Krofft shows have made in the mid-1990s and teased with the possibility that *The Lost Saucer* ultimately might join the wave of nostalgia, Nabors says, "Oh, my God, I hope not."

Whereas Buzzi says she can't wait for that day to come. The fact that the first episode rated inclusion in the fall of 1997 in a two-tape Columbia House video sampler of Krofft shows was a step in that direction.

"I always have been aware of the power of reaching a child," Buzzi says. "I've done lots of children's shows, guested on a lot of children's shows and Saturday mornings. Besides doing this show with Jim, I've done tons of cartoons and everything. Agents don't like you to do the shows because most of the shows don't pay top dollar like prime-time shows do and therefore it's a lot less commission for the agent. But to me, it's money in the bank. It's fans in the bank.

"When you see how the show affects the children, you all of a sudden understand what it means to be Santa Claus. When you see these children running up to you. Some of them smile, but a lot of them, they'll be serious when they come up to you and then, when they see that you're going to welcome them, they hug you and they hug your legs so tight. You know that you really reached them.

"And to this day, to see people still remember. Oh, all the time. That show, it made such an impact on their lives."

Not a bad legacy for what is widely considered to be an unsuccessful show.

Kaptain Kool & the Kongs (clockwise from left):
Louise DuArt as Nashville, Mickey McMeel as Turkey, Debby Clinger as
Superchick and Michael Lembeck as Kaptain Kool.
SID & MARTY KROFFT PICTURES.

S-A-T-U-R-D-A-Y Morning
...or The Kroffts Meet the Boys of Bay City

Can you picture Tom Hanks starring in a Saturday morning TV series? It could have happened.

But like the Boston Red Sox owner who traded Babe Ruth to the Yankees or Napoleon, who pocketed only pennies per acre with the Louisiana Purchase, Sid and Marty Krofft let Hanks, something of an unknown at the time, slip through their fingers.

"We were doing *The Krofft Supershow* and we were looking for three guys who could be like the Three Stooges for the '70s," Sid recalls. "And Tom Hanks came in to audition for us. You could tell he didn't want the job, though, and he just acted totally stupid. And my brother didn't like him.

"I said, 'Oh, I don't know about that. This guy is terrific.' But my brother said, 'I don't think so. That's not what we're looking for.' And look where Tom Hanks is today. He's like the biggest actor on the planet...and we could have had him."

It's fun to play *what if?*

How might Hanks' career have differed had he landed the part, which preceded his *Bosom Buddies* breakthrough by only two years? And would his presence have had any real impact on the fate of *The Krofft Supershow*, also known as *The Krofft Superstar Hour?*

The world will never know, of course. But one near certainty is that the Krofft credit probably would have won points for the actor on the homefront years later.

Patty Maloney tells why:

"I worked on *Tales from the Crypt* with Van Snowden, who played Pufnstuf in the road shows that we did. We were the puppeteers who worked the Cryptkeeper. And Tom Hanks was on the show, directing the episode, and we asked him if he would take a picture with the puppeteers. And when he started talking to us and he found out that Van was Pufnstuf, he went bananas. He was going, 'Can I have your autograph?'

"I mean, who would have dreamed? Tom Hanks was asking Van for his autograph for his kid. He was saying, 'Oh, *Pufnstuf* is his favorite thing in the whole wide world. My kid just loves it. He loves anything with Pufnstuf in it.'

"And he said, 'I will go home a hero in my kid's eyes if you will give me your autograph.' So you don't even have to say anything else after that."

Snowden says simply, "It was very weird."

Says Sid: "I always tell people the story of how we didn't hire Tom Hanks. Everyone makes mistakes and I guess that one's ours."

At any rate, *The Krofft Supershow*—an ambitious collection of serialized adventures for kids—can't list Hanks among its alumni. But the Kroffts can count such personalities as Deidre Hall (soap opera star), Michael Lembeck (actor turned Emmy-winning sitcom director) and Louise DuArt (one of the entertainment industry's leading impressionists) as their own.

"We put together some pretty good talent on that show," Marty says.

A Small World

There is literally no telling what Tom Hanks must think of Pufnstuf these days. When he met Puf, and the person inside the costume, while doing *The Rosie O'Donnell Show* in 1996, he was in for a huge surprise.

Kristina Krofft tells the story: "I was Pufnstuf on *Rosie O'Donnell*. They put me in a Pufnstuf costume and it was me introducing Rosie O'Donnell. I did it because I got a free trip to New York. And after I opened the show, I was walking down the hallway and I took the head off.

"Tom Hanks was a guest on the show and his dressing room door was open and he sees me and says, 'Hey, Pufnstuf, come here.' And I said, 'No, you're not supposed to see me without my head on.' It's like you can't see the Disney characters without their full costume, right? Well, it's the same with Pufnstuf. But he said, 'No, come here, come here.'

"So I did. I could barely fit through the door with this big dragon costume on and I walk in and he's looking at me and he's looking at me and he's not sure if he recognizes me. And he says, 'Wait a minute. Aren't you the belly dancer from Savern & Tony's?'"

Kristina used to perform as a belly dancer at Savern & Tony's, the popular Greek restaurant in Los Angeles. "I said, 'Yeah, remember? I gave you and your wife that little belly dance lesson once.'"

Hanks' response: "You're Pufnstuf too?"

Did they ever. And it was an eclectic collection at that. Probably better remembered by viewers for the various series within the series, *The Krofft Supershow* premiered on ABC on September 9, 1976. The show, originally ninety minutes in length, trimmed to sixty in December 1976, was hosted by Kaptain Kool and the Kongs, a quartet of oh, so-'70s rock-'n'-rollers who would in turn introduce serialized segments of smaller series.

The original lineup: *ElectraWoman and DynaGirl,* an "electrafantastic" comic book-style adventure that put a campy feminist spin on *Batman; Dr. Shrinker,* which pitted three teenagers, shrunken to the size of mice, against an evil scientist plotting world conquest; *Wonderbug,* about a dune buggy that one-upped Herbie the Love Bug, by giving the vehicle a voice; and re-edited segments of *The Lost Saucer.*

After one season, two other segments were added: *Magic Mongo* (about a bumbling beach genie) and *Bigfoot and Wildboy* (which suggested the odd but intriguing possibility that Sasquatch could be an environmental crime fighter).

So many shows, meted out in such small portions. So which was the case? Had the Kroffts created this umbrella format because they were ambitious, wanting to tell many different stories, or were they merely unable to come up with a single idea they felt most strongly about?

Sid says it definitely was the former. "It was like, remember the days of the serials? I mean, it was time to do that kind of a show. Which was another idea. The networks wanted us to keep coming up with different kinds of shows and different formats. *The Krofft Supershow* was very popular, I think, because it was different from what kids were used to seeing at that time."

Indeed, ask viewers today which segments made the biggest impression and they name a variety of favorites, although the ones Sid and Marty say they hear about most often are *ElectraWoman and DynaGirl* and *Dr. Shrinker.*

Sid says if he had to single out any one of the *Supershow* installments as his favorite, it would have to be *ElectraWoman and DynaGirl.* "I didn't know at the time that it was so bizarre. It definitely was a weird show. I didn't realize that it was so tacky. But that was the whole deal. That was the approach. It was a hysterical, stupid show because it was supposed to be. That's what's fun about it."

Also, there's just something about the show's title that makes him smile. "I always loved the crazy names they used to come up with for superheroes in the comics."

Meanwhile, Marty singles out the *Dr. Shrinker* installments. "*Dr. Shrinker,* you look at that today and it holds up pretty well. I liked that one a lot. But I liked *Wonderbug* too. You know, we did a lot of pretty far-out shows."

Of course, for other viewers, the most memorable aspect of the show came later, when the hosts, Kaptain Kool and the Kongs, were replaced by the Bay City Rollers, a group of Scottish rock-'n'-rollers who became an overnight pop music sensation in America.

Marty has gone on record as having regrets about signing the Rollers: "The biggest mistake I ever made was getting on that plane to Scotland to sign those kids. Their lead singer was impossible. I still question to this day whether they sang any of their songs themselves."

But Sid is more forgiving. "They were just kids," he says. "They didn't understand why they were even there."

Kaptain Kool and the Kongs

Consider this the human counterpart to the Banana Splits. The Splits, remember, was a fab foursome of rock-'n'-roll animals who hosted a Saturday morning cartoon variety show for Hanna-Barbera. Kaptain Kool and the Kongs did the same duties for the Kroffts. The only difference: The segments introduced by KK&K (that's K as in Krofft, of course) were like living cartoons.

The band members: Michael Lembeck as Kaptain Kool, Debra Clinger as Superchick, Mickey McMeel as Turkey and Louise DuArt as Nashville.

As was the case with the Monkees and the Partridge Family, musical ability wasn't the primary concern in assembling the members of Kaptain Kool and the Kongs. First and foremost, they had to be photogenic.

Says Sid: "Kaptain Kool and the Kongs were a group that we just put together out of actors who could sort of sing."

The band even had their own album, released in 1978 on Epic. They never made much of an impact musically, but individual members certainly made their mark.

Says Sid: "Who would have guessed that Michael Lembeck would turn out to be one of the top sitcom directors in the business? Or that Louise DuArt could be the greatest impressionist? She's still out there, playing major places. She works all the time."

Lembeck—the son of Harvey Lembeck, best-remembered for playing Corporal Rocco Barbella, sidekick to Sergeant Bilko on *The Phil Silvers Show*—went on to costar in such sitcoms as *One Day at a Time* (1979–84) and *Foley Square* (1985–86). Today, he is one of the top directors in the field of TV comedy, an Emmy winner who has directed numerous episodes of *Friends, Mad About You* and *NewsRadio*.

Kaptain Kool & the Kongs in concert.
SID & MARTY KROFFT PICTURES.

For DuArt, an amazing vocal talent who specializes in celebrity impersonators, her most recent TV project is *Cafe DuArt,* a series for Nostalgia Television that launched in the fall of 1997. But it was yet another Krofft series in which her skills were put to best use: providing the voices for celebrity puppets on *D.C. Follies.*

"You know how my career started with impressions?" DuArt says. "We were doing a show, a Kaptain Kool and the Kongs special, and the girl they had hired who was going to do a Cher lookalike canceled at the last minute. And I said, 'Oh, I can do that.' They said, 'Really?' So they put the wig on me and the costume and I did the Cher. And after that, I thought, 'Oh, gee, maybe I can do more.' And I would start listening to celebrities and before I knew it, I had quite a repertoire going.

Which is Witch, Part II

Given that Louise DuArt is one of the most gifted voiceover artists in the business, it's easy to imagine her doing a Billie Hayes/Witchiepoo impersonation.

It's particularly easy, in fact, for anyone who saw live *Pufnstuf* stage shows in the early 1970s.

"I did the stage version of *H.R. Pufnstuf*," DuArt says. "As a matter of fact, that was the first impression I ever did in my life, professionally, was of Billie Hayes as Witchiepoo. Years later, Billie and I did a series together where I played her sister [*Horror Hotel,* a segment on *The Bay City Rollers Show*].

"I was nineteen when I got my first job with Sid and Marty. I go back to the early, early '70s with them. But the man who was responsible for me working with Sid and Marty on television was Squire Rushnell. Squire was the head of ABC daytime and children's programming and he had seen me at a party that Sid and Marty had thrown for the kids at ABC where I played Witchiepoo. And Squire Rushnell saw me and thought I had some talent and said to Sid and Marty, 'I'd like you to screen-test her for this series that you're talking about.' And so I screen-tested and Squire liked me and hired me. And my relationship on television started at that point with Sid and Marty, with Kaptain Kool and the Kongs."

There's an interesting postscript to that story, one involving a reunion for DuArt and Rushnell.

"Recently I was doing a musical in New York City and Squire, who is now the head of Nostalgia Television in Washington, saw my name in the *New York Times.* I hadn't talked to him in years, but he decided to surprise me and come to my show. So I saw him at the show. We had dinner and we started talking and next thing I know we're doing a series together now, twenty-six shows on the air called *Cafe DuArt,* about a woman who runs a cabaret and has got these crazy people working with her. And one of the people who is a regular on the show is Patty Maloney. And Patty, of course, I met over twenty-five years ago working with Sid and Marty Krofft. So everything is connected. It's amazing."

"That's not why they hired me. They hired me just to do the character of Nashville. And it was funny because I didn't know I could do that. I mean, as a kid I always would do voices, but I never really considered myself an impressionist. I would do other people in school or my friends' parents. So when this Cher thing came about, I said, 'Oh, let's see what else I can do.' And I started doing more. I made a whole career out of it. I didn't know it was going to happen for me either. It just happened."

As for Clinger, who costarred with Priscilla Barnes on *The American Girls* (1978), and McMeel, the Kroffts have lost touch. "I haven't seen Debbie Clinger in anything for a long time," Sid says. "She probably got married and went to heaven or something."

Kaptain Kool and the Kongs served as hosts of *The Supershow* for two seasons, but they got the hook in 1978 when the Kroffts made what they thought would be the biggest casting coup of the decade. Sid and Marty were about to bring Rollermania to America.

Nevertheless, DuArt gets comments about her Kaptain Kool and the Kongs days to this day. "It's amazing the impact that the show had," she says. "When I go on talk shows, like radio shows, it's inevitable that somebody is going to bring up Kaptain Kool and the Kongs. That show has such a cult following."

The Bay City Rollers

They were supposed to become the *new* Beatles.

But, as Sid notes, "Instead of being the new Beatles, they were—ah, how do I say this?—they were *not*."

The freshly scrubbed, plaid-wearing quintet from Scotland—formed in 1970 while all five original members (Leslie McKeown, vocals; Eric Faulkner, guitar; Stuart Wood, guitar; Alan Longmuir, bass; and Derek Longmuir, drums) were still in their teens—didn't stack up musically to the Beatles, of course. In fact, they were more in the New Kids on the Block/Hanson bubblegum-pop league, building a rather intense teenage fan base in the United States by early 1976, thanks to a U.S. concert tour and a number one hit record ("S-A-T-U-R-D-A-Y Night!").

But given that the early-teen set was the demographic group Sid and Marty coveted as Saturday morning viewers—and given also that the Kroffts think big—they courted the Rollers, now a few years into their twenties, to host a revamped version of the *Supershow*.

Marty signed them—and regrets doing so to this day. "That was one of the worst ideas we ever came up with. They were nothing but trouble. And for rock singers, they couldn't sing worth a damn."

Says Sid: "Yeah, well, they were not professionals. They would not be in on time. Someone would oversleep. Whatever. They just didn't understand what they had gotten into. Show business has to be in your blood. They were kids who were picked up and a group made out of them from Scotland. It wasn't even like they were from London, where they would have a little background in the-ater or something. It's just they were weird kids. They were kids. They didn't understand why they were even here doing this show."

The Krofft Superstar Hour premiered on NBC on September 9, 1978, and ran for two months in a one-hour format before being pared back to thirty minutes in early November, with a title change to *The Bay City Rollers Show*. Neither version seemed to take with viewers, however, and the band and the show was off the air by January 1979. One-hit U.S. wonders turned five-month TV flops.

In retrospect, though, Sid makes no apologies for miscalculat-ing the power of Rollermania. "The Bay City Rollers were becom-ing huge in England and so we thought it would spill over. I mean, that was a coup to get the Bay City Rollers to America like that."

Patty Maloney, who became a regular on this version of the show, as herself, not as a little person in a costume, also thinks Marty is a little harsh in his assessment of the band and their abilities.

"They were wonderful," she says. "I was crazy about them. They came and went like a lot of groups do, but you can't hold that against them, the fact that they didn't stay on top for very long. In fact, it wasn't long ago I saw a commercial where you can buy these music collections that they advertise on TV and there was the Bay City Rollers. And I sort of just smiled, because they were so neat. I really liked those guys. We had a good time with them."

Bigfoot and Wildboy

For years, people have combed the forests of the Pacific Northwest for signs of Bigfoot, the enormous creature that some theorize could be a missing link between man and beast.

Bigfoot, a.k.a. Sasquatch, has become legendary for his elusiveness, which places him with such unsolved mysteries all-stars as the Loch Ness Monster and UFOs.

But for anyone who watched *The Krofft Supershow,* the mystery of Bigfoot was solved in an absurd yet ingenious manner. Not only does Bigfoot really exist, Sid and Marty Krofft would have us believe, but he and his human protege, a teenager he raised since childhood in the wild, also are superheroes, battling criminals whose sinister schemes threaten to destroy the environment.

As Sid notes, "Well, somebody has to protect our environment. Why can't it be Bigfoot?"

That was the premise of *Bigfoot and Wildboy,* easily the most action-packed segment of *The Krofft Supershow.* Starring Ray Young as Bigfoot and Joseph Butcher as Wildboy, it premiered during the second season of *The Krofft Supershow,* playing originally in fifteen-minute segments, and was expanded to a half hour the following year, when the Bay City Rollers were hosts. In fact, *Bigfoot and Wildboy* owns the distinction of being the only *Supershow* segment that later aired as its own self-contained series, running for three months in reruns on ABC during the summer of 1979.

What was the inspiration for *Bigfoot and Wildboy?*

"Well, Bigfoot was hot," Sid says. "Bigfoot was in the news. So why not? I mean, it always interested everybody, didn't it? We never saw him, but we all sort of rooted for him, I think. But at the same time, you can't just string together a bunch of random Bigfoot sightings and call it a series. Kids won't accept that. They want to see him. And since you have to have some kind of story, why not give him a career? Why not make Bigfoot a hero?"

Why not indeed.

Ray Young as Bigfoot, a.k.a. "the Foot."
SID & MARTY KROFFT PICTURES.

Joseph Butcher as Wildboy.
SID & MARTY KROFFT PICTURES.

"It was a very clever idea and very timely," says Young, the actor who went through hell in that Bigfoot getup. "It was a kids show and it was fantasy from the standpoint of what he was able to do, so why not just go all out?"

Young looks back on the show with great fondness, but he also is quick to note how physically demanding the series and the role were for him.

"It was fun. It's a lot more fun looking back on it, I think, than when we were doing it, though. It was very strenuous work. We shot at such a fast rate. We'd shoot nonstop, sometimes three shows in a week. We didn't stop moving much. We shot out in what is called Lake Sherwood, out in the Westlake area of the Valley. And it was very, very hot—middle of the summer, of course. And at the time, I was no kid. I was like thirty-seven, thirty-eight when we were doing that. And wearing that outfit, it could be grueling. It was a body stocking with hand-tied human hair on it. And it was very, very hot.

"And I remember I wouldn't be able to go in my trailer, because it was air-conditioned. Because if you go into the air conditioning, you could get pneumonia. So the crew, God bless them, fashioned this fan on a generator that was portable. So when I wasn't shooting, I could sit and this fan would be used on me. The guys in the crew were terrific. They helped keep me sane while I was doing the Foot."

The Foot?

"Yeah, that's what we called him: The Foot."

Although Young is tickled by the fact that one internet website contains an elaborate critical analysis of *Bigfoot and Wildboy* and its social ramifications, he doesn't mind that people rarely, if ever, recognize him from the show.

"There was too much makeup involved for anyone to recognize me...thank God."

"Let me tell you: Ray Young is a great guy," Sid says. "He's a real character."

Young's hair bristled, so to speak, when he heard that remark. "Sid says about somebody else that they're a character? Now that's

Hairy Situations

A bear may do it in the woods, but Bigfoot couldn't.

Ray Young reveals that portraying a creature in the wild could be problematic whenever, ahem, nature called.

"I remember when they told me that, if I wanted to, I could go out and take a look at the suit being constructed. It was Ziggy, wigmaker to the stars, who made it. And they had gotten all the way up to the chest and made no provisions in case Bigfoot had to go to the bathroom.

"Well, I got on the phone posthaste and said, 'I can handle one of them. But the other one, I don't think so.' So they had to go back and put a zipper in the front."

Suffice it to say, then, that Bigfoot wasn't anatomically correct.

"Well, to tell you the truth, he was," Young says. "I mean, all I had on underneath that thing was a jockstrap. So if the hair wore off, we were all in big trouble.

"And the hair would wear off in places where an animal that hairy would normally have hair wear off: on the knees and on the fanny. So all the little elves spent a lot of time sewing new hair on those two suits."

a hoot for you. I'm not even going to pursue that. That's funny. For Sid to call somebody else a character, that's wonderful. . . . But he's right, I guess."

Young says he barely knew Sid at the time he was cast, but he had a feeling the series would be worth his while because a mutual friend, a veteran Krofft player, had vouched for them.

"I didn't know Sid and Marty prior," he says. "I think I knew Sid maybe kind of peripherally. I had met him a few times, but it really had nothing to do with my being cast. I had seen *Les Poupees de Paris*, the puppet show, at a place down on Santa Monica and Crescent Heights, a place called P. J.'s. In fact, that may have been where I met Sid. But that was the only thing I really knew about the Kroffts.

"But a very good, personal friend of mine is Billie Hayes, who was Witchiepoo on *H.R. Pufnstuf*. I did the TV *Li'l Abner* and Billie had done Mammy Yokum on Broadway. And since Billie had been Witchiepoo—she was a wonderful character in that and she got a pretty good profile from that show—I talked to her and got her input before I did the Foot."

And even though the work wasn't easy, Young enjoyed some of the challenges the production faced.

"I remember we had a heck of a time trying to figure out how to jump in and out of shots," he says. "In the beginning, they had like a trampoline that they wanted us to jump on. But when you're wearing those feet, you can't spot yourself. It's impossible. I almost killed myself the day we were doing test shots and stuff, with me jumping in and out.

"I had a terrific double, a kid named Al Wyatt. He's not a kid any more. And we were trying to do it. And I remember saying, 'If you can figure out a way on that trampoline for it to be done, for the close shots, I'll do it.' But I said, 'If he can't do it, I'm not going to either.'

"But I had guested on *Bionic Woman* the season before, so I knew how Lindsay Wagner did it. And what I finally suggested and what we ended up doing was just slo-mo'ing it, the same way they did with Lindsay in *The Bionic Woman* and Lee Majors in *The Six Million Dollar Man*. What they did was just crouch down and jump and then they cut before you're out of frame. And I would jump out and down from a ladder to jump into a shot. And then there was stock footage of Al going through the air and doing stuff."

As for his costars—Butcher and Yvonne Regalado, who played Cindy—Young admits he has lost touch.

"I remember Joe is somewhere in the state of Washington and I heard that he was selling real estate. And the little girl, Yvonne Regalado, was a real sweetheart. But she was so much younger than I was. And essentially, in that kind of a situation, there wasn't time to form some really lasting friendships.

"I mean, one day we shot something like eighty setups. And I think in the second season, we maybe shot on a stage two or three days. There was one episode about a cave and the cave was on a special effects stage. But otherwise, it was all shot outside and you hit the ground running and you didn't stop until it was over with that evening. And Joe and I were in like ninety percent of the shots. So it wore me out.

"Let me put it this way: I was not going home crying that we weren't going to do a third season."

An interesting postscript: Young actually reprised his character, so to speak, once more after *Bigfoot and Wildboy* wrapped production in 1978.

"When I got out of that suit, when I took it off for the last time, I thought, 'Well, that's that.' I was kind of relieved because it was so rough physically.

"Well, the next thing I did the next season was a show called *Salvage One,* which starred Andy Griffith and was about a junkman in space. And I'll be damned if I didn't get a part in it of this creature. I don't remember exactly what he was. But they were going on and on about the outfit and they asked me, would I come out for a fitting?

"So I go in and they said, 'Here's what we've got. Do you think it will fit?' And I said, 'Don't worry about a thing. I wore it for two seasons.' It was my old outfit. The studio had rented it from the Kroffts.

"And I thought, 'Well, what does that say? I'm right back in it again.' The next thing I did the next season and there I was back in the old Foot suit again."

Dr. Shrinker

"As they say in *Halliwell* about me: 'Famed portrayer of eccentrics.' Well, I say thank God for eccentric roles."

So says Jay Robinson, not only about his career in general but also about Dr. Shrinker, "a madman with an evil mind" (as the theme song, performed by the Osmonds, put it).

Robinson, whose acting career on stage, screen and TV spans more than fifty years, has worked alongside legendary stars of the business. He costarred on Broadway with Katharine Hepburn and

Boris Karloff and in films with Richard Burton, Jean Simmons and Bette Davis. Davis, in fact, was so close a friend to Robinson that she insisted on writing the foreword to his autobiography, *The Comeback,* in the 1970s.

All of which makes his remarks so much more meaningful when he refers to *Dr. Shrinker* as "a treasured memory, a golden memory. That summer that we filmed it is a time I will always cherish."

One of the original and best-remembered installments of *The Krofft Supershow, Dr. Shrinker* put a Krofft spin on a durable premise that has remained fresh throughout centuries of retelling, from *Gulliver's Travels* to *Honey, I Shrunk the Kids.*

The Evil Dr. Shrinker (Jay Robinson) PHOTO COURTESY JAY ROBINSON.

The premise: After a storm forces three teenagers to land their small plane on a nameless island, they encounter Dr. Shrinker, a wild-eyed scientific genius who has created a shrinking ray only he can operate and control. Shrinker aspires to achieve fame, fortune and power with his reducing machine. But to prove the worth of his vile device, he must prove it works. So he shrinks the unsuspecting young people. But the "Shrinkies" escape his laboratory and flee into the jungle, now the vulnerable tiny prey of the notorious Dr. Shrinker, his sinister assistant Hugo and, of course, the gigantic creatures that roam the island.

"It was an absolute sensation," Robinson says of the show. "We got monstrous rating and share for Saturday morning. It was phenomenal. And why we didn't do more than the one season, I will never understand. We certainly should have. We didn't get renewed for a second year, although God knows it ran and ran and ran in reruns. I think somebody at network said it was a little 'violent' for the children watching.

"But it's amazing even today. My wife and I will go down to the beach and people who were then kids, now approaching thirty, they will come up to me and say, 'Oh, my God, aren't you Dr. Shrinker?' It has become a great cult thing. And I still get mail, not a lot, maybe half a dozen letters a week, about *Dr. Shrinker,* more than twenty years later."

The show endures not only because of the ageless gimmick, little people in a suddenly enormous world, but also because of the performances of Robinson and Billy Barty, who played Hugo. It might have eluded young viewers when they watched the show originally, but Robinson and Barty played their characters in an over-the-top style that puts one in the mind of classic horror movies of the 1930s, in which the villains were shamelessly broad in their delivery, almost as if they were still making silents.

"Yes, well, I was always larger than life," Robinson says. "They call it over the top now. Just like Bette Davis used to say, 'Every line is an Academy Award.' It was always my way. I didn't believe in letting the camera come to me. I always wanted to paint a vivid picture. When I came into the business, it was all Brando and Dean.

"And Billy, I think he had the same idea. We had such an incredible rapport and just worked off each other. I would say, 'Don't tempt me, Hugo!' And he would give it right back to me. He was a terrible scene stealer. We complemented each other very well. It was just a wonderful character to play. Marty once told me, 'Of all our things, you and Witchiepoo were our most remembered and colorful characters.'"

Barty agrees with that assessment. "Jay Robinson was such a great actor," he says. "He was fantastic to work with. But he was just a little disappointed that he didn't get more good roles. I think he was a fantastic actor who didn't get enough of a chance."

Similarly, Robinson has only high praise for Barty. "Billy and I couldn't have been closer during that summer. He would drive me home after work. The little guy in the great big car. His feet could not reach the floor boards. We did some telethons together. But somehow or another, we lost touch. Working together was the foundation on which the relationship stood."

Robinson and Barty's flamboyant styles worked on two levels: as gently spine-tingling fun for younger audiences and as high camp for adult viewers.

It also was totally in synch with the old-style horror movie feel that Sid and Marty were going for. The inspiration for the series, after all, was Sid's fondness for classic science fiction films from his childhood.

"*Dr. Shrinker* came from *Dr. Cyclops,*" he reveals. "Because I loved *Dr. Cyclops*. That movie scared me to death."

In that movie, released in 1940, Albert Dekker starred as a wild scientist who shrank humans to the size of dolls. Sound familiar?

Although he also is familiar with the movie, Robinson says he had no idea it was the inspiration for the show. But he finds it amusing, given that he chose to emulate the classic horror-movie actors, many of whom were his friends.

"My first Broadway show was with Boris Karloff and he was a lovely man. And Vincent Price or Bela Lugosi, different people who I knew over the years. And Lionel Atwood. They all had that wonderful style and they're all back there in my memory. I believe they all contributed somewhat to the Shrinker thing."

The series—sixteen episodes of fifteen-minute installments—was filmed over a span of about eight weeks, two episodes per week. "It was done at breakneck speed," Robinson recalls. "All the other shows, *Wonderbug* and *ElectraWoman and DynaGirl,* were shot there at the same studio, the same lot. We'd see Deidre Hall, who was ElectraWoman, who is now the doyenne of daytime. But we were too busy working on our show to spend much time with the others."

It's worth noting, by the way, that only Barty, who delighted in the fact that his role as Hugo allowed him to be a giant, at least to the Shrinkies, was specifically in Sid and Marty's minds from the beginning.

Even Robinson, who did not know the Kroffts, had to jump through a few hoops to get his part.

As for the Shrinkies, Sid says the casting director looked at a lot of young actors before they decided on Ted Eccles as Brad (the handsome one), Susan Lawrence as B. J. (Brad's beautiful blonde girlfriend) and Jeff MacKay as Gordie (B. J.'s bungling brother).

Of the three, MacKay probably had the most visibility after *Dr. Shrinker*. Perhaps best remembered as Mac on *Magnum, P.I.* (1980–88), he also was in *Baa Baa Black Sheep* (1976–78) and *Battlestar Galactica* (1978–79). Eccles, who appeared in more than seventy TV commercials, may be most familiar to soap opera fans as Bobby Chandler of *General Hospital*. And Lawrence, a gifted singer and musician, had roles in *Happy Days* and *Mork & Mindy* in addition to recording the theme song for the TV series *Angie* (1979–80).

"Jeff, who was the funny one, did rather well for himself," Robinson says. "I believe Ted became a PR man. Susan, I don't know whatever happened to her. It's harder for her maybe, because there's always another beautiful cute young kid coming along. My career never depended on that fact, thank God."

Among Robinson's more recent gigs: a supporting part in *Bram Stoker's Dracula,* directed by Francis Ford Coppola, and hosting duties on the Discovery Channel's *Beyond Bizarre.*

"*Dr. Shrinker* was the jewel of the crown of *The Krofft Supershow,*" Robinson says. "I think today, they could bring back *Shrinker* with somebody and make a feature film out of it. Because it was so broad and wonderful. And it's nice that people still have a warm spot for that time in their life, when they wouldn't fail to see it every Saturday morning."

ElectraWoman and DynaGirl

"I haven't worn kneeboots, spandex tights or a cape ever since."

So says Deidre Hall, the actress best known for playing Dr. Marlena Evans on *Days of Our Lives,* when asked about her ElectraBrief career as a TV crimefighter, Saturday morning's female counterpart to Batman.

What amounted to only eight half-hour episodes, featuring Hall as ElectraWoman and Judy Strangis as her perky pigtailed side-kick, DynaGirl, were made, airing during the first season of *The*

Krofft Supershow. Fans still occasionally ask Hall about the show, even though most programs with so short a lifespan rarely endure so favorably in viewers' memories.

"Actually, it was a very tough production schedule," Hall says, "and the only memories I have are surviving that summer and not being allowed to keep any of their many costumes."

But viewers remember it for different reasons.

First, there are the young women, now in their twenties and thirties, who played ElectraWoman and DynaGirl as kids. This aired at a time when TV had gotten its first wave of superheroines: Lindsay Wagner as Jaime Sommers, a.k.a *The Bionic Woman* (1976–78), Lynda Carter as *Wonder Woman* (1976–79) and JoAnna Cameron as Saturday morning's *Isis* (1975–78).

Deidre Hall and Judy Strangis as ElectraWoman and DynaGirl.
SID & MARTY KROFFT PICTURES.

ElectraGadgetry

"Have your little ElectraFun!"

So said the Sorcerer, the evil madman magician, when he was captured by crime-fighting superheroines in the first episode of *ElectraWoman and DynaGirl*. But he easily could have been referring to the mind-numbing array of ElectraGadgets at the ladies' disposal.

Here's a sampling from the first episode alone:

Headquarters was called the ElectraBase. Once they arrived in their civvies, the women donned crime-fighting costumes by activating the ElectraChange. They traveled to crime scenes in the ElectraCar and ElectraPlane. And among the ElectraPowers that their wrist ElectraComps were equipped with: an ElectraBeam and ElectraDe-gravitator.

To quote DynaGirl, "What an ElectraMess!"

Before then, with the exception of Yvonne Craig as Batgirl during the final season of *Batman* (1966–68), TV's superhero crime-fighters made splendid role models for boys. But young girls were left wanting.

"I know that lots of little girls at that time played ElectraWoman and DynaGirl," Sid says, "the same way little boys had always played Superman or Batman and Robin. So as far as making an impact, maybe that made the biggest one from *The Krofft Supershow*."

And there are young men, also in their twenties and thirties today, who have fond memories of the show for hormonal reasons. "I've heard this from guys more than once," Sid says. "They liked the show because ElectraWoman and DynaGirl looked so fine in their costumes."

But perhaps the greatest reason *ElectraWoman and DynaGirl* endures today is its camp value. Watching an episode now is simply a goofy good time.

"It really wasn't very successful for us," Sid admits. "Maybe it was before its time. In those times, the audience wasn't geared for campiness. Those weren't the times. But then when you look at it years later, you look at it and say, 'My God, that is whacked out.'

"When we show *ElectraWoman and DynaGirl* at a screening, the audience just goes crazy, just crazed, screaming, because it's so way-out, so whacked-out. It's interesting. When you say *ElectraWoman and DynaGirl,* only eight episodes, but everybody knows what you're talking about."

The show's premise basically emulated that of *Batman's:* Lori (Hall) and her protege Judy (Strangis), reporters for NewsMaker magazine, led double lives as costume-wearing crime fighters. Thanks to CrimeScope, a computerized system programmed to pinpoint criminal activity, these "voltage vixens" (as one villain called them) remained constantly plugged in to the never-ending troubles plaguing their city.

Assisting the duo from their hidden headquarters at ElectraBase was electronics expert Frank Heflin (Norman Alden), who used his technological talents to develop the ladies' powerful ElectraComps, which essentially were ElectraCounterparts to Batman's all-purpose utility belt.

ElectraWoman—decked out in a reddish-orange outfit with yellow tights, yellow boots and yellow cape, a perfect complement to her mane of flowing blonde hair—was fearless in the face of danger and resourceful when it came to thinking on her feet. DynaGirl—who stood a full six inches shorter, donned red suit, cape and boots with pink tights—often reminded viewers of Robin's "Holy Something-or-Other, Batman" catch phrase with her trademark "ElectraSupers!" and "ElectraWows!"

Even the campy celebrity guest villains—from the maniacal Sorcerer (Michael Constantine) and his shapely sidekick, Miss Dazzle, to the aptly named Empress of Evil (Claudette Nevins)—were reminiscent of what had been done on *Batman.*

In fact, just about the only elements not lifted were *Batman's* elaborately choreographed fight scenes and its obsession with littering dialog with sexual innuendo. "That's because *Batman* was made for adults," Sid notes. "*ElectraWoman and DynaGirl* was made for kids."

Sid remembers conducting a big casting search for his leading ladies. The reason the Kroffts decided on Hall (who also taped her first *Days of Our Lives* segment as Marlena in June 1976) and Strangis (who had played Helen Loomis, one the students of *Room 222*, from 1969 to 1974)? "Because they were two beautiful ladies and they were good together."

And even though it was long hours and demanding work for the ladies, Sid says they seemed to be enjoying themselves. "It was so tongue in cheek. Every one of our shows that we did, the cast always had the best time. Because it was so silly. It was a world that everybody would like to be in."

There are a handful of actors from other concurrently running Krofft shows who beg to differ: They say Hall disliked doing the show and that she didn't disguise her unhappiness. If that's true, though, she was definitely in the minority.

And even though the show might not have been hugely popular during its original play, it now rates alongside some of the Kroffts' best-known titles. During Pufapalooza, for example, two episodes of *ElectraWoman and DynaGirl* were shown, thereby rating equal play with *The Bugaloos, Lidsville* and *Sigmund and the Sea Monsters*.

"It's just so weird," Sid says. "I mean, *ElectraWoman and DynaGirl,* that's a laugh. It's like the ultimate in camp. That show was hysterical. I wish that could be a movie. You look at a show like that, it could be a movie. It would be hysterical."

It could be an ElectraGoodTime.

Magic Mongo

"Hey, no problem!"

That's what Mongo, an inept but well-meaning genie, said whenever called upon to make a little magic. The only catch was his magic usually created as many problems as it solved.

In a nutshell, that was the premise of *Magic Mongo*, a comedy that was one part *I Dream of Jeannie,* another part *Beach Blanket*

Bingo and a third part *Three's Company* (minus the sex). "That's exactly right," says Robin Dearden, one of the costars. "That's absolutely on the nose."

The story goes that a teenager named Donald (Paul Hinckley)—while hanging out on the beach with his friends Kristy (Dearden) and Loraine (Helaine Lembeck)—found an Aladdin's lamp. When he rubbed the lamp, out popped Mongo (Lennie Weinrib), a genie with a Bronx accent, a fondness for Hawaiian print shirts and rather erratic powers.

When asked to cast a spell, usually to get Donald and the girls out of a jam involving a pair of mean-spirited biker bullies (Bart Braverman and Larry Larsen), Mongo would tug at his ears and make a "bliddle-bliddle-bliddle" noise with his tongue and then survey whatever damage he had done.

'Babe-Watch'

Life was a beach for the cast of *Magic Mongo*, but the show was hardly a junior version of *Baywatch*.

So says Robin Dearden, who spent much of her days on the show in a two-piece swimsuit.

"I was like twenty-one years old at the time and I was supposed to be playing sixteen," she says. "I'm a native Californian, so living in a bathing suit was not a big deal. And also I wasn't in a bathing suit every single week. Sometimes we were up in the mountains. So my being in a bathing suit was never a big deal."

Not a big deal to her, to cast and crew or even to most of the young viewing audience. But it obviously was a huge deal to one person: Out of nearly 150 behind-the-scenes *Mongo* photos in the Krofft files, taken by a photographer who was sent to the set one day, easily more than one hundred are of bikini-clad Dearden alone.

She merely laughs when told this. "That was like twenty years ago. I probably didn't even notice. I didn't know anybody even cared."

Lennie Weinrib as Mongo
the genie, in the act of
making a little magic.
SID & MARTY KROFFT PICTURES.

The kids at the beach—
Helaine Lembeck as
Loraine, Paul Hinckley as
Donald and Robin Dearden
as Kristy—uncork Magic
Mongo's bottle.
SID & MARTY KROFFT PICTURES.

Given Weinrib's history with the Kroffts (as writer of all seventeen *H.R. Pufnstuf* episodes and voice specialist on several of their other series) as well as his years of experience as a comic actor, one might assume the show was created to showcase Weinrib's flair for comedy.

That assumption, however, would be way off the mark. In fact, Weinrib says, he practically had to twist the Kroffts' arms to get the part.

"They originally created that show with Alex Karras in mind," Weinrib says. "It was in the movie *Blazing Saddles* that Alex Karras played a big, dumb guy who punches a horse in the mouth. And the character's name was Mongo. Well, the Kroffts must have fallen in love with him in the movie and, out of that, somehow, came *Magic Mongo*.

"They told the network, 'We'll get Alex Karras.' But the deal fell apart and the next thing I knew, there was a flurry of activity around the Kroffts. I said, 'What's going on?' 'We're going to do a show called *Magic Mongo*.' I said, 'Ooh, that sounds like a wonderful character.' And the bottom line is I talked them into letting me be one of the million people they screen-tested.

"I said, 'Can I do that?' And they said, 'Well, you're very cute and funny. You do all our voices. But we have a different idea. Mongo is more of an Alex Karras. We'll get some giant famous football player.' I said, 'But I'd like to give it a try.' 'Okay, you can try.' So they tested everybody on earth and sent it all back to the network. We all did the same scene, different ways, different little schtick. I pulled my ears out and did with the tongue to do magic and I gave them a little touch of Gleason with my little crazy faces and my hat turned back. It was one of the high-ups at the network who said, 'Him.' And it was like God had spoken."

The result: sixteen delightfully silly fifteen-minute installments that ran during the second season of *The Krofft Supershow*.

Says Weinrib: "For several years after that, every so often someone would stop me and say, 'Hey, aren't you Magic Mongo?' And I'd have to do the 'bliddle-bliddle-bliddle' noise with my tongue while holding my ears. It's funny. They would recognize me, but then I would have to do that identifying thing before they'd go, 'That's it! You're him!'"

As for Weinrib's three young costars, they had very specific *Three's Company*-style character types to play. As Donald, gangly Paul Hinckley displayed a flare for John Ritter-style physical comedy. Meanwhile, his female costars, Robin Dearden (as the perpetually bikini-clad cutie) and Helaine Lembeck (as the wise-cracking one), performed their roles quite admirably.

Of the three, Lembeck—sister of Michael, a.k.a. the Kroffts' Kaptain Kool—was the most familiar face to young TV audiences, having played Judy Border on *Welcome Back, Kotter* for two seasons (1975–77).

Says Dearden, whom soap opera fans may also remember as Kate Wilson of *Generations* (1989–91): "That was my first job out of college. I had done some commercials and stuff, but I was cast in *Magic Mongo* right after graduating from college. And we had a blast. It was so much fun. It was all real new for us because we were all just starting except for Lennie, of course, and Helaine, who had done *Kotter*. And Helaine's dad, Harvey Lembeck, directed one episode, which was a blast.

"It was really a great experience. We got to shoot on the beach every day. No real difficult locations or whatever. And we all became very close because we were working long hours and stuff, but we were all kids, so it really didn't matter. And I remember at that time that kids knew who I was and what we were doing and they loved the show."

The real-life bond between Dearden and Lembeck was particularly strong.

"I've been an actor now for twenty-one years and it's the nature of what we do that you'll have friendships with people you're working with that don't last. But the one person who I have stayed in touch with for these past twenty-one years is Helaine Lembeck. She played my best friend in *Magic Mongo* and she's still a great friend today. Half of the people that I've worked with, I have no idea where they are any more. That's why it's amazing that Helaine and I are still friends."

Their other costar, Paul Hinckley, died several years ago. "Paul Hinckley was a doll," Dearden says. "It's been quite a while, actually, since he passed away, probably at least ten years."

As for the bullies, Braverman, who played Ace, a leather-clad tough guy, is perhaps best known as Binzer, Robert Urich's duplicitous side-kick on *Vega$*. Larsen, who played big dope Duncey, Ace's lackey, was something of a Krofft regular in *The Lost Saucer* and *Donny & Marie*.

Says Weinrib: "Everyone was very nice and it was just like every experience I've had with the Kroffts, one of the happiest times in my life. Those were long, long tough days, with the special effects all day long. Like standing on a magic carpet for hours in front of a big blue screen while they line up shots to get these special effects. They're very difficult and you usually have to do them many times.

"But you didn't mind working hard around those people because everybody that they hired was just so wonderful. The cast was superb and we all became friends. Sid and Marty always came down there and would give everybody a pep talk and make you feel good. I was like one of the spiritual leaders of the show and always cheering everybody on. We all cheered everybody on. It was a wonderful experience."

Says Dearden: "I'm actually surprised they didn't rerun in syndication more than they did. It was a very silly show, of course. It wasn't anything that could be taken seriously. But I think that the Kroffts did a very cute show."

As the threesome always said at the close of each episode, "That's our Mongo!"

Wonderbug

To David Levy's way of thinking, the title-character dune buggy wasn't the real star of *Wonderbug*.

"I was always much more impressed by Schlepcar," he admits. "It was a very well-constructed piece of junk."

Levy, who played Barry, one of the three human leads in *Wonderbug*, doesn't go so far as to suggest renaming the series, mind you, so that Wonderbug's rent-a-wreck alter ego can get its fair share of the credit. But he doesn't miss a chance to praise Schlepcar. "Schlepcar was the real hero."

Wonderbug and its three friends: John Anthony Bailey as C. C., Carol Anne Seflinger as Susan and David Levy as Barry.
SID & MARTY KROFFT PICTURES.

An unsung hero.

The premise of *Wonderbug:* Three teenagers—Barry, Susan (Carol Anne Seflinger) and C. C. (John Anthony Bailey)—went to the junk yard in their search for some affordable wheels and found Schlepcar, a hodgepodge of auto parts that should never have left the salvage yard. But the squeeze of a magic horn transformed the car into Wonderbug, a dazzling dune buggy that could do it all: think, talk, even fly. And together, the kids and Wonderbug fought for truth, justice and the American way...no, wait, that was Superman's gig. But it's safe to say that Schlepcar and Wonderbug were the four-wheeled counterpart to Clark Kent and Superman.

In essence, the show—an installment of *The Krofft Supershow* that ran for two seasons—was one part *The Love Bug* and one part *The Mod Squad.*

The Psychology of Krofft TV

It somehow makes sense that Barry, the self-proclaimed brains of the *Wonderbug* team, wound up with a Ph.D. in the "brains" business.

"I never thought of it that way," says David Levy, a psychologist who teaches at Pepperdine University. "That's a very good connection. I like that. In fact, the more I think about it, the more I like it."

After five or six more years in the acting field after *Wonderbug*, Levy went back to college, earned his master's and doctorate degrees, and "I've never looked back."

Given his expertise in the field, we asked him to analyze the psychology of Krofft television shows of the 1970s making a major comeback in the 1990s, including the Pufapalooza sensation on Nick at Nite in 1995.

A case of thirysomethings attempting to recapture their childhoods, right?

"Absolutely, absolutely. But it's not just their childhoods that they're trying to get back. I remember when *Wonderbug* was on and people who were in their twenties and even thirties would say, 'Hey, I recognize you. You're on *Wonderbug*, right?' And I would say yeah. And they would say, 'Oh, uh, well, I just happened to be flipping through the channels one morning.' They would try to find an excuse for explaining why they were watching a show like that in their twenties and thirties.

"They felt guilty or embarrassed. When in fact it's like many of the Warner Bros. cartoons of the '40s. They're cartoons, but they really were intended for a much broader audience. So I think partly it's adults looking

Sid says that the initial inspiration for *Wonderbug* was Herbie the Love Bug, the Volkswagen with a mind of its own and the star of a 1969 Disney movie hit and three sequels.

But Levy prefers to think of himself and his costars as the Saturday morning version of Pete, Linc and Julie.

"It was a *Mod Squad* for kids," he maintains. "Or a hybrid of *The Mod Squad* anyway, in that it had that same character composition. There was a black guy [C. C.], a white guy [Barry] and a white girl fighting crime. But we were, A) significantly younger and, B) it was

back on their childhoods, but it's partly too that many of the shows were actually quite sophisticated and easy to enjoy on an adult level."

Levy always knew the immediate impact that the show had had on young viewers, given the way that fans would mob him and his costars whenever they shot on location, but it wasn't until several years later that he saw its durability as a cherished childhood memory.

"When I started to teach, there were many students who thought they recognized me. But they couldn't place where they saw my face, because I had a beard then. Then, when I would reveal to them, typically at the end of the entire course, who I was, it was really quite something. They were, of course, seven or eight at the time *Wonderbug* was on. And here they were, twenty-three or twenty-four, taking a psychology course with Barry as the instructor."

Given his academic leanings, it's safe to say, then, that Levy was tailor-made for the part of brainy Barry.

"Well, yeah, I guess I was to some degree. I was a student at UCLA. I was in the theater arts department. I was studying to be an actor. But quite honestly, I took a lot of psychology classes back then. I enjoyed a lot of different subjects.

"I remember the auditions being so exciting, because they had several people up for each role and they would mix and match us. So I was reading and there were three or four different girls who were reading for Susan and then C. C. and then finally, that last day, they kind of matched us all up. I think they were both child actors. I know that Carol Anne Seflinger was. But for me, it was one of my first jobs. But when they put us together, I just had a feeling it was going to work out. And it did."

burlesque. It was vaudeville, in terms of the script and style of the direction. It was very campy.

"And we were doing different characterizations each week. We'd sometimes do characterizations of famous movie stars. I did a Marlon Brando-Godfather impersonation one week. We did a *Columbo* takeoff another week."

But why does Levy consider Schlepcar the real star of *Wonderbug* rather than its flashier alter ego? Let him count the ways:

"Wonderbug was sort of cool. It was okay. It was a souped-up dune buggy. But Schlepcar had all the character. A lot of it was in the special effects. In the studio, they could make Wonderbug fly. But Schlepcar they actually had rigged where, underneath the steering wheel, I had a series of levers and pins and rings and each one would pop off different parts of the car.

"So if I pulled up to a stop, I could pull a couple of these wires and the bumper would fall off or the hood would pop out. So they actually had it rigged mechanically for the thing to dismember itself. They also specifically had one tire smaller than the other three, so it always was hobbling. Even on the windshield there were two bandages in the shape of Red Cross field dressing. I was always much more impressed by Schlepcar. It was much easier to drive, much more fun to drive. Wonderbug was breaking down."

That isn't to say that Wonderbug didn't have its own far-out gadgetry as well.

"They had Wonderbug designed so that there could be a driver who would literally sit underneath and behind the passenger seat," Levy continues. "So if we were all out of the car, Wonderbug would drive by itself. They had a series of hand and foot controls, where this guy gets literally underneath the front seat and he could peer through the passenger seat and he would drive the car."

Mighty ambitious for a show targeted for kids...but then again, thinking big always was a Krofft trademark.

"They used a lot of Chroma-key technology, but some of the effects were real. They brought in a guy named Frank Welker to do the voice of Wonderbug and Schlepcar. They had hand puppets. They had models. They used all these different techniques to create the magic. And *Wonderbug* was only a twenty-minute show. It wasn't even a full half an hour. They packed a lot into that twenty minutes. We had the pace of a cartoon."

Not surprisingly, the show became hugely popular with its young TV audience.

"We wouldn't typically shoot in the studio," Levy recalls. "We'd shoot on location across Los Angeles. In Chinatown or at the beach. And the first season that we shot, well, being in Los Angeles, some people are not surprised to see TV shows or movies being shot. We'd get a few crowds. But by the time we shot our second season, the show had been on for a year and the turnouts were astonishing. There would be hundreds of kids, clamored around, because they all had been watching the show. It was really exciting."

And it wasn't only the magic of the cars that the young viewers loved. Kids also connected with the cast, a trio of early-twenties actors playing sixteen- and seventeen-year-olds.

One popular running gag: Even though Barry was the "brains" of the gang, pragmatic Susan was the one who actually came up with the brilliant plans. After which Barry would say, "I've got a better idea" and repeat Susan's idea, usually word for word. If Susan protested, Barry would counter with "There's no time for that, Susan." And then C. C. would give Barry all the credit: "One with the plan, Barry, my man!"

Says Levy: "That was our most frequently asked question when I was on the show. Whenever a kid would come up to me, the first question, almost always, was, 'Why do you always take that girl's ideas?' I mean, that notion, that bit, that running motif, really grabbed many kids' attention. I think that's what bugged them most. I should say it probably bugged the girls more than it bugged the guys. The girls would be troubled by it."

Although Levy savored his days working on *Wonderbug*—"we shot at a pace that set some incredibly astonishing standards; on several occasions, shooting an entire show in a day"—he left the acting field for a career in psychology.

As for his two costars: "I have not seen Carol Anne Seflinger, who played Susan, in many years. And I heard that John Anthony Bailey died several years ago [of cancer in 1994]. We were good friends for a while and we'd meet two or three times a year, all three of us, for several years. But you're talking about twenty years ago and we all sort of went our separate ways. But we all got along tremendously well."

As for what became of Wonderbug and Schlepcar, Levy can't even hazard a guess. Given the premise of *Wonderbug*, though, it wouldn't be unforgivable if they were parked in some junk yard somewhere.

The Kroffts scored a hit with their first variety series, *Donny & Marie*.
SID & MARTY KROFFT PICTURES.

I'm a Little Bit Country, I'm a Little Bit Rock 'N' Roll ...or Sid and Marty in Their Prime

Was it arrogance or simply the desire to add some variety to their lives? Probably a little of both.

Upon first glance, it seems as if Sid and Marty Krofft were over-reaching when the kings of kids shows tried their hand at producing prime-time variety programs.

Their earlier leap from puppet shows to children's TV, remember, made perfect sense. But isn't the chasm that separates Saturday mornings and prime time too wide a jump? What gave the Kroffts the wild idea they could just dive in and master yet another genre of television?

A lifetime of experience, Sid says. That's what.

When the Kroffts crafted a variety show to showcase the talents of Donny and Marie Osmond, premiering in January 1976, they created a hit not by accident but as the result of pure show business savvy. Moving to prime-time variety, Sid explains, was like returning to his roots.

"Because my training was live," he says. "I mean, I did an act, right? And I worked in big, big production shows as an act. And it always intrigued me. I was in the Lido. I was in the Follies-Bergere. Both were big, big epic productions. And I played Radio City Music Hall. I played Vegas. I was on *The Ed Sullivan Show*. I did my puppet act all over the world. I knew how all this stuff was done and it's always intrigued me. So I'm as qualified to do that kind of show as anybody."

Okay, so he had the know-how all along. As a matter of fact, with powerful allies at the top like Fred Silverman and Michael Eisner, the real question should be, "What kept the Kroffts out of prime time for so long?"

Silverman became president of ABC Entertainment in 1975. Eisner had been an influential programming executive at ABC for ten years until he left the network 1976. Sid credits Silverman for giving the brothers their shot at producing in prime time; Marty says it was more Eisner's doing. But what really matters is that they dove in headfirst.

"The biggest thing," Marty says, "was my business mentor always was Michael Eisner. When he was over at ABC, he gave us our first break in prime time. After we did *Pufnstuf*, he gave us a pilot called *Fol de Rol*, which didn't get on. When *Donny & Marie* came about, he gave us that break. And when he went to Paramount, he came to us again to do the *Brady Bunch Variety Hour*. Michael Eisner's always been there for us."

Sid's recollection is like this: "It was Fred Silverman, when he became president at ABC, who gave us the go-ahead. He just thought our shows were insane. He said, 'You could do a variety show. You guys are wild.' And so we did *Donny & Marie*. When he offered us *Donny & Marie*, he said, 'What kind of show would you do for them?'

Well, I was in an ice show. I was in Sonja Henie's show. So I told him we could put ice skaters on stage with Donny and Marie. And I did all the old musicals, which I loved, so I told him we could re-create that type of show. And Fred Silverman said, 'That sounds good. Go with that.' And that's how that all happened."

In addition to creating the framework for a successful *Donny & Marie* franchise (1976–79), the Kroffts also brought *Barbara Mandrell & the Mandrell Sisters* (1980–82) to TV. Not all of their prime-time forays were hits, however. The brothers also were involved in two legendary failures: *The Brady Bunch Hour* (1977) and *Pink Lady and Jeff* (1980).

The reason the Osmonds and the Mandrells succeeded while the Bradys didn't, Marty theorizes, is that the successful stars' skills were better suited for the variety show format.

"Donny and Marie were musical," Marty says. "The Mandrells were musical. That's what they did for a living. The Bradys, they had a great time doing it, but it was difficult for them. That's not where their talent lay."

As for the *Pink Lady* fiasco, well, Sid makes no apologies for trying.

Donny & Marie

"Success sometimes can really bite you in the shorts."

So says Donny Osmond, who knows whereof he speaks. Even though the *Donny & Marie* show was an instant success that out-measured even his wildest dreams, that success came with a price.

Donny was eighteen years old and his sister Marie was sixteen when their variety show premiered on ABC on January 16, 1976. "I remember Marie was the one who broke the news to me about the show," Donny says. "We were in our apartment in West L.A. and she said, 'They're thinking about doing a variety show of you and me.' My first reaction? I thought, 'Well, there goes my record career.' The theory is that as soon as you do television, if somebody can get you for free on TV, why buy a record? And that's exactly what happened. We had a hit show, but my record career was shot.

"And also, because the show was so popular, it left me with an image that was very difficult to shake. For years, particularly through my twenties, I would do anything to live down that *Donny & Marie* image. It took a very long time."

Curiously, it was a problem Marie never seemed to have.

"I think it was a lot easier for her to make that transition from that goody-goody little girl to sophisticated entertainer. Whereas it took longer for me because I had more of a teenybopper base before *Donny & Marie* hit, with songs like 'Puppy Love' and 'Go Away, Little Girl.'

Another Tale from the Krofft

"I'm a farm boy from the Ozarks," says Van Snowden, a longtime Krofft puppeteer perhaps best-known today for his Cryptkeeper puppetry on *Tales from the Crypt*. "Sometimes I wonder what am I doing here at this point in my life."

Now and again, he misses doing Krofft-style kids shows. "There aren't any shows like that any more. I mean, I've had to go to science fiction and horror movies."

So when the Osmond Family launched a musical theater in Branson, a community that has become a sort of Nashville in the Ozarks, Snowden leaped at the chance to work with them.

For Snowden, it was a voyage home, literally. "Branson is my home-town. So when I found out that they were going to open a theater there, I called Jimmy and said, 'Do you want some puppets in the show?' So I have a little company and we built them some puppets that they have in the show now.

"We're doing full-size puppets on stage. I have a three-piece puppet band, full-size, and it takes two puppeteers to work each one. And then there's some bend-over things in the show. But who would have ever dreamed, after doing this stuff all over, that I could go back home?"

"It was more difficult for people to accept me as an adult. You know what surprises me? People are still surprised by the fact that I have four children, one almost ready to graduate high school. They say, 'You're kidding? You've got children that old?' I say, 'Well, if you stop and think about it, *Donny & Marie* was on more than twenty years ago.'"

Granted, the show deserves only part of the blame for typing Donny, because he had a freshly scrubbed, wholesome persona long before TV. The part he takes issue with the most is that the series made him "the stupid one" of the duo.

"I was the fall guy. I was the one who always had to get beaten up. I was the one who Marie punched in the stomach and always looked like an idiot. Marie was portrayed as the more sophisticated one. Here's a typical example: I was the better skater, but they said, 'No, no, you look like the bad guy. You fall down and you do the pratfall.'

"And because I was on a show as Donny Osmond, not as some other character, the way it would have been if I were on a sitcom or something, people believed that was what the real Donny Osmond was like.

"Were all of those crazy stunts Sid's ideas? If they were, then I know who to blame."

Sid freely confesses to plotting the shenanigans. "Of course, they were my ideas, all those things. I used to make Donny do the craziest things."

Let Donny count the ways: "Like the time I was thrown into a 96-gallon cream pie. People still talk to me about that one. And we did bits where fire came out of my hands or I got shocked or blown up or they had me flying over the audience. That was my job, to be the weird guy."

Meanwhile, as the show progressed, Marie became more elegant and glamorous. Beginning with the second season, the producers decked her out in outfits designed by Bob Mackie, who already had given Cher her stylish look on *Sonny & Cher*.

"Marie was my favorite actually," Sid admits, "because she

always had a little devilish quality in her. I remember we did this spectacular number with her rising up out of the water like Esther Williams, like a goddess or something, with fireworks. What we did was we brought her down with fireworks and then reversed the tape. The effect was great."

"Whereas all the outfits that they had me wear," Donny adds, "the blue tuxes and stuff, were somewhat ridiculous. But it all worked, man. It all really worked."

Indeed, do you know anyone who can't identify *Donny & Marie*'s trademark "I'm a Little Bit Country, I'm a Little Bit Rock 'n' Roll" opening number? The show might have been an overblown mishmash of musical numbers, comedy skits and Vegas-style theatrics, but viewers lapped it up.

"I really didn't know much about Sid and Marty Krofft when we started," Donny recalls. "I never really watched *H.R. Pufnstuf,* so I didn't know what these guys were all about. But I guess Fred Silverman brought them in because Marie and I were very young and I had a teenybopper following and these guys knew how to get to the kids. It was a perfect tie-in."

In addition to the two young leads, brothers Alan (the oldest performing Osmond at age twenty-six), Wayne, Merrill, Jay and little Jimmy (the youngest at twelve) were regulars.

"I think if anyone hates them the most, it's Jimmy," Donny jokes. "I mean, he was the one who always had to perform with hippopotamuses and dragons and chickens, all the crazy Krofft puppet characters."

And true to Sid's wild vision, there actually was an ice rink on the stage, with a showgirls-on-ice chorus line called the Ice Vanities (in season one) and the Ice Angels (in season two) performing elaborately choreographed routines.

Sid and Marty produced the show (with Raymond Katz as executive producer) its first two seasons. After that, in late 1977, the Osmond family took over, moving production from Hollywood to Orem, Utah, where they built their own $2.5 million studio facility.

It's worth noting that the show didn't do quite as well, ratings-wise, without Sid and Marty's presence. But the foundation laid by the Kroffts helped propel the Osmonds for another two seasons. Then Marie followed with her own show, *Marie,* for one season (1980–81).

Says Marty: "When we created *Donny & Marie,* that was a big break for us. Because that wound up being a top-ten show. We went on at 8:00 on Friday with that and it was the first time that ABC ever won the nights on Friday."

The fact that Donny, Marie and their siblings are gifted musical performers was the primary element in their success. But Donny says the Kroffts deserve a lot of credit as well.

"The combination of the people is what made it work," he says. "Sure, Donny and Marie had to have some talent, because they were the ones in front of the camera. But what a lot of people don't stop and realize, particularly the stars, as it were, they think, 'Well, I'm it. I'm the one who people are buying.' But you're only as strong as the people around you. And the combination of people, including the Kroffts, created the chemistry, or embellished the chemistry, I should say, that already existed between Marie and myself."

Oh, yes, Donny adds, there also was a fair amount of luck. They merely stumbled into making "I'm a Little Bit Country, I'm a Little Bit Rock 'n' Roll" their signature tune, for example.

"We sang it because it was actually true in life. Marie had a tendency to like country music and I was more into pop. Pop music's not really considered rock 'n' roll. But they came across the song, 'I'm a Little Bit Country, I'm a Little Bit Rock 'n' Roll,' and it fit. So we sang it on the show. We had no idea it could become our signature."

Marty's assessment as to why the show worked: "First of all, they were such likable kids. But also the production values played a big part in it. It was like every week you were getting this spectacular musical-variety special."

Of the variety shows they produced, Sid quickly singles out *Donny & Marie* as his favorite: "It was great. It was so much fun."

Incidentally, when Donny speaks disparagingly about what the show did to his record career and his image, his tongue is now firmly in cheek, even though there was a time when he was bitter.

"I think that everyone goes through that, a period of where they want to be accepted for what they're doing now," says Osmond, who made a comeback doing musical theater in such productions as *Joseph and the Amazing Technicolor Dreamcoat.* "But then you become comfortable with yourself. For instance, I did a VH1 special this year and I showed *Donny & Marie* clips on it. Now we're preparing to do a *Donny & Marie* talk show/variety thing for daytime television. The only reason I would consider doing it now is that enough time has passed to where I'm comfortable with what I'm doing.

"The industry knows that that's not me any more, but it was a great part of my career. We're all a lot older now. And we can look back at it with some admiration."

The Brady Bunch Hour

It's tough to say whether this is a good thing or bad, but the '70s have made a huge comeback in the 1990s. Just ask Maureen McCormick, who played oldest girl Marcia on *The Brady Bunch* (1969–74).

"The '70s are back in fashion and they're back in the TV and music," she says. "My little girl, who I actually thought would never, ever see polyester in her lifetime, is asking to wear the platforms and all of the prints and the fabrics and the styles from the '70s."

McCormick says she didn't mind outfitting her daughter Natalie in polyester because, "She spills grape juice on it and we just send it through the washer and dryer."

But there is a limit. There is a line she would prefer that nostalgia-hungry fans not cross: *The Brady Bunch Hour,* a.k.a *The Brady Bunch Variety Hour.* Told that Krofft shows are making a comeback, McCormick literally shrieks and says, "Oh, God, please don't let them put *that* back on!"

Marcia, Marcia, Marcia

If any of the Brady kids had the tools to step into Donny and Marie's footsteps as a variety show star, it was Maureen McCormick.

McCormick, who celebrated her fortieth birthday in 1996, re-invented herself in the 1990s in large part because of her success as a country singer. She released a solo album (*When You Get a Little Lonely*) in 1995. And in the fall of 1997, she portrayed Barbara Mandrell in a CBS movie of the week (although lip-synching to Mandrell's vocals) in addition to becoming a sitcom mom in *Teen Angel,* a series airing in *The Brady Bunch's* original Friday night ABC time slot.

The coincidence that she would play Mandrell, whose variety show also was produced by the Kroffts, did not escape McCormick. "Isn't it a small world?"

Of Bradymania, she says, "I think it's really a positive thing. Like anything that you really get known for, it can be a double-edged sword. But I feel really proud to have been a part of the show. I think it's really nice the way it's in people's hearts all over still. The show lives on. It seems like it will always be a part of American culture."

The fact that *The Brady Bunch Hour* looked and felt like a *Donny & Marie* wannabe makes perfect sense once you know that a *Donny & Marie* episode actually spawned this crazed creation, a show that Barry Williams described in his 1992 memoirs, *Growing Up Brady: I Was a Teenage Greg,* as "perhaps the single worst television program in the history of the medium."

Guest appearances by Florence Henderson and several of the Brady kids on a *Donny & Marie* episode in 1976 brought in boffo ratings. So Fred Silverman, looking high and low for any show that could help bolster his third-place network, got the idea of turning the family, already huge hits in syndication, into the next Osmonds.

And bear in mind the idea isn't quite so farfetched once you consider that the six young stars toured the country in 1973, during the hiatus before the final *Brady* season, as "The Brady Kids." They even performed on *American Bandstand.*

Sid and Marty, naturally, immediately came to Silverman's mind to produce a Brady variety show—and not only because of their involvement with the *Donny & Marie* show that had started the ball rolling.

Says Marty: "We also had been involved with *The Brady Bunch* years earlier. When we did *Pufnstuf at the Hollywood Bowl,* we had 'The Brady Kids' in that show. So we had a connection with them in the early '70s. So we always had a good relationship with all the kids and their parents."

And after some negotiating with Paramount, which owned the rights to *The Brady Bunch,* and with Sherwood Schwartz, the show's creator/producer, an idea became a pilot.

The Brady Bunch Variety Hour aired on November 28, 1976, reuniting eight of the original's nine stars. (Eve Plumb, who played middle girl Jan, declined and was replaced by Geri Reischl.) This show's premise: The family moves to a beach house in southern California to star in their own variety series. And like on *Donny & Marie,* the stars were decked out in loud tuxes and glitzy gowns, sequins and fringe, and backed by a chorus line of beautiful showgirls (the Kroffette Dancers) and a pool full of Water Follies Swimmers.

"It was all very strange," remembers Susan Olsen, who was youngest girl Cindy. "It was like a freak show."

Suffice it to say that anyone who saw the Brady clan and their maid Alice (Ann B. Davis) belt out "Shake Your Bootie" probably has never been able to erase the incongruous image from their memories. Yet the pilot got a pickup, with eight episodes of the ensuing *Brady Bunch Hour* airing on a semi-regular basis (every fifth week at 7:00 Sundays in a time slot shared by *The Hardy Boys Mysteries* and *The Nancy Drew Mysteries*) from January to May 1977 before getting the hook from the network.

As Williams described the scene in his book: "Our show, even from day one, was being hastily thrown together so that it could reach the airwaves quickly.... There we were, back on stage muddling through the weirdest musical numbers imaginable."

Says Marty: "I think they had a great time doing it, but it was difficult for them and ultimately I think they weren't too happy. There's where the talent really has to come through and so it was a tough thing for them.

"Of course, Florence Henderson already was musical. The father, Robert Reed, he was not musical, not by a long shot, but he worked very hard. Maureen McCormick, she was a little less enamored by having to do it. Chris Knight, he was great. He worked hard. And so did Barry Williams. They all were cooperative. It's just that this wasn't their thing."

But it's funny. For a show that was so widely panned—named in *Bad TV,* a book by Craig Nelson, as the worst variety show in TV history and mocked even by the Bradys themselves—the show made an enormous impact on American pop culture.

Nick at Nite showcased the variety show pilot one year as the special-event finish to its annual New Year's Eve "Classic TV Countdown." And a 1997 *Simpsons* issue parodied *The Brady Bunch Hour* by doing a Simpsons variety show in which Lisa, who refused to participate, was replaced by another girl actress, aping the Eve Plumb-Geri Reischl piece of recasting. The joke wouldn't connect if no one had ever seen or heard the original.

"It's the only show in the history of television that has five different TV series come out of it," Olsen says. "Like the variety show that we did and the show called *The Brady Brides.* The show just won't die."

Says McCormick: "It's pretty amazing, isn't it? The variety show was barely on—thank God—yet people remember it. We can laugh now. I think people like it now because they love to go back there. It brings back a lot of memories. I mean, God, just the clothes alone. Whether they would watch it every week, that's another matter. But it was good for a laugh."

Says Marty: "It's a funny thing, though. If you look at *The Brady Bunch Variety Hour* and then look at *The Brady Bunch Movie,* I think you'll notice that they look an awful lot alike. Maybe we just did this at the wrong time."

Pink Lady and Jeff

"*Pink Lady and Jeff* became like a monument to bad television because it was so awful and so weird."

Those aren't the words of some brutally frank TV critic, although they certainly could have been. That critique comes from Sid Krofft himself.

Adds Marty: "It's one of those shows that's like in the time capsule. It wasn't on for very long but, boy, do people remember it."

Actually, few viewers actually saw this short-lived variety series, but it has become legendary as one of the medium's most spectacular crash-and-burn experiments. The show—starring comic Jeff Altman and two lovely Japanese rock singers, Mitsuyo (Mie) Nemoto and Keko (Kei) Masuda—lasted barely more than a month in 1980.

The girls, although very popular in their own country, were virtual unknowns on this side of the Pacific. They had only one modest hit in the States ("Kiss in the Dark"). What's more, they spoke no English.

"When they came here the first day," Sid says, "they came in and they looked absolutely beautiful, bowing and bowing, and they sat down and Marty was talking and talking and talking and they were nodding and nodding and nodding. And he went on and on and on. And then, finally, he said, 'Wait a minute. Do you understand anything I've been saying?' And they just went on nodding. They didn't understand a word. And they never did understand a word."

So right from the starting gate, this thing was a recipe for disaster. What were Sid and Marty thinking?

"It was Fred Silverman's idea," Sid says. "He had seen them. They had a record deal with RCA-Victor and they were huge, huge stars in Japan. They were like the Beatles. They played in 100,000-seat stadiums. But they never spoke any English. For the songs that they sang in English, we had a teacher who would teach them phonetically. They never knew anything that they were saying. It was hysterical."

In a manner of speaking, Sid considered it a challenge to develop something for them.

in the Pink

Although skeptics will forever question the wisdom of creating an American variety show for Japanese singing stars, Sid Krofft makes no apologies because he saw firsthand the potential of Pink Lady.

"I remember they wanted to go to Disneyland," he says. "This was before the show even went on the air. So we went to Disneyland, thinking, 'Nobody's going to know them in this country. They haven't even been on television yet.'"

Bad idea.

"There were so many Japanese there and they all instantly recognized the girls. And I have to tell you, we were mobbed. It was so bad that we had to call security. These girls were huge, absolutely huge in Japan."

"I really wanted the show to be very, very weird. Because it was very weird to have those two Japanese girls and a Jewish comedian. The whole idea was hysterical. It was funny right there, just talking about it. And when I went to Fred Silverman and presented my weird ideas, he said, 'No, that's too weird.' I said, 'Yeah, but wouldn't it be great if the next day people said, "Oh, my God, did you see that?"' And that was the whole idea. That's what I really wanted to do with that show. But he said, 'No, that's just too different. Let's just do *Donny & Marie*.'"

In effect, Sid's hands were tied. We'll never know whether his stranger vision for the show would have fared any better, of course, but Sid wishes he had gotten the chance.

"We just went back to the old variety format, singing and dancing and comedy. Of course, you need all those things, but I wanted to present it in a really odd, different way."

The series premiered on NBC on March 1, 1980, and was gone after its April 4 telecast.

As Sid sums it up, "Something just got lost in the translation."

Barbara Mandrell & the Mandrell Sisters

The saying goes that a picture is worth a thousand words. In the case of Barbara, Louise and Irlene Mandrell, Sid and Marty Krofft can confirm that the maxim is true.

When Marty was acting upon the impulse to build a variety show that would showcase the talents of Barbara, the Country Music Association's 1979 Female Artist of the Year, and her two younger sisters, one of his most valued tools was a wallet-size snapshot of the three ladies.

"It was Marty's idea totally to do that show," Sid says. "We had a commitment with NBC to do another variety pilot and so we were looking for someone. Barbara Mandrell at that time was just a country star. She was big, but nothing like the way she is now. We flew up and saw Barbara somewhere in California in a little state fair that she was playing in. And that was it. The moment we saw her perform, we knew it was a great idea.

"And then I remember Marty had this snapshot of Barbara Mandrell. It was just a pocket-size picture, with her two sisters in her back yard or someplace. And anyone who saw it, their first reaction was always, 'Oh, my God, they're so beautiful.'"

"Yes, that's exactly the way it happened," Barbara says, marveling at the simplicity of the process. "I also was told that Marty had asked, early on, 'Do the other two sisters have any musical abilities?'"

In other words, Marty had a great idea and began to act on it before actually knowing whether it was do-able.

In her autobiography, *Get to the Heart: The Barbara Mandrell Story* (Bantam, 1990), Mandrell remembered it this way: "Marty was trying to get people interested in me. At first, he didn't have much success, but then he found out I had sisters and thought that three Mandrells might be better than one. Marty inquired if there was a photograph of the three of us. We had made a photograph for our parents and Momma sent a wallet-sized copy to Marty, who started showing it to television people. Later, the three of us laughed and said we couldn't believe our gift would lead to a television career."

The result: *Barbara Mandrell & the Mandrell Sisters,* which premiered November 19, 1980, was every bit the hit that the Kroffts' previous effort, *Pink Lady,* hadn't been. It didn't hurt their cause, obviously, that the three leads were exceptionally talented.

One regularly featured segment that never failed to dazzle, for example, was "The Guitar Pull," in which the trio would play different instruments. Given that Barbara was a whiz on the banjo, steel guitar, piano and saxophone; Louise, the banjo and fiddle; and Irlene, the drums, there were plenty of intriguing combinations.

And as had been the case with the *Donny & Marie* show, each of the ladies took on a persona for their comedy bits. Irlene would play the "dumb" sexy blonde who wasn't so dumb after all; Louise was "the thinker and the dreamer"; and "bossy" Barbara was the "pie-in-the-face" butt of all jokes.

The show actually even broadened the ladies' repertoire. "We had never danced a lick in our lives," Mandrell wrote, "but Scott Salmon [the choreographer] took six left feet and taught us how to dance...or at least it looked like dancing on television."

And it all worked. In fact, it worked so well that the show has proven to be immune to the same kind of critical sniping that dogs even a hit like *Donny & Marie.*

In fact, the show actually made something of a societal impact on the viewing audience. *Barbara Mandrell & the Mandrell Sisters* literally opened doors, allowing people who never cared for country music to sample and enjoy something different.

Says Barbara: "We had an incredible amount of mail that said, 'I never liked country music before, but you've changed my mind.' And that was very important to me because country music, it's quite a passion. Yet almost every week, we had a guest who was either R&B or pop. It was important to me to have all kinds of music, not just country.

"I think Duke Ellington said it best: 'There are two kinds of music, good and bad.' Isn't that the truth? I just love music. All kinds. That just says perfectly what I think."

Another reason the show was so successful, Marty theorizes, was the show allowed the ladies to be themselves, as opposed to imposing cliché *Beverly Hillbillies*-country hick personas on them. "They were who they were," he says.

In fact, another segment of the show viewers responded quite favorably to was the way the sisters ended each show with a gospel music medley. That was Sid's idea, Marty says.

"Oh, definitely," Sid says. "That's what you call a flag-waving finale. That was always our trademark, to do a flag-waving finale. Only this time it was gospel."

It's worth noting that Barbara was the sister who resisted when Marty first broached the idea of a variety show. She subscribed to the same "well, there goes my record career" theory as Donny Osmond. She ultimately agreed, though, because she knew the show could help her younger sisters' careers and because, "Marty is a very persuasive salesman."

Says Barbara: "I said no at first. I'm glad I eventually agreed to do it. But I never wanted to do a series. In fact, when I wrote my autobiography, I remember my working title was *Never Say Never*. But that movie came out *[Never Say Never Again]* and I said, 'Well, that can't be the title.' But there were major things in my life where I said, 'No, never, absolutely not.' And then I did them. Like I said I would never do a series. And there you go. I said I'll never have a book about my life. There you go. I also said there would never be a movie about my life and now that happened."

In addition to the array of big-name guest stars (from Dolly Parton, Dottie West and Johnny Cash to Tom Jones, Gladys Knight and the Pips and the Charlie Daniels Band), the Mandrell sisters also had an unusual group of regular costars...unusual, that is, if one didn't know of the Kroffts' involvement. A group of lifesize puppets called Truck Shackley & the Texas Critters, five musicians and a dog named Dog, was the resident band.

When the show ceased production in early 1982, after two seasons and thirty-five episodes, it was not because of poor ratings but because Barbara had decided to call it quits because the demanding workload of a weekly show along with her busy concert schedule was too exhausting. Similarly, her dramatic career move in late 1997, in which she announced she was ending her music career to pursue acting full-time, was rooted in a distaste for doing things halfway.

As for her assessment of the work she had done on the variety show: "Just in the past few years, watching those old tapes, I have been able to look at the show with a sense of objectivity and say, 'Hey, I'm proud. We did a good job."

Fred Willard and the famous regulars of Washington D.C.'s hottest watering hole.
SID & MARTY KROFFT PICTURES.

'i Am Not a Muppet!'
...or The D.C. Bar Where Everyone Knows Your Name

It was a casting director's dream come true: a comedy series that assembled the biggest names from the worlds of politics, broadcast news and entertainment under one roof.

Richard Nixon and Dolly Parton. Rodney Dangerfield and Ronald Reagan. Dan Rather and Cher. Over a span of two years, these and other famous faces got together each week in a Washington D.C. pub to sip drinks and swap jokes.

"I can't think of a single TV series that had a better cast," boasts Fred Willard, who poured drinks for and chatted with the bar's famous clientele. "I never had so much fun. I mean, there I was rubbing elbows with the most famous, the most talented, the most powerful people in the world."

Oh, yes, did we mention that all of these famous personalities were puppets?

Call it the Presidential pickup.

Bill Tracy, Marty's longtime office assistant, remembers the time he briefly stopped traffic when he was called upon to chauffeur a trio of presidential puppets around town.

"It was for a photo shoot over at ABC," he says. "It was early morning and the sun was just coming up and I had the three presidents with me in the cab of my truck: Reagan, Nixon and Ford, I think. And people are walking in the crosswalk in front of me and they were all staring. And I'm thinking, 'What in the world are they looking at?'"

Tracy is around puppets all the time, so it didn't occur to him until later that people don't see a trio of presidents riding shotgun in a pickup truck every day.

Granted, the political arena always has had its share of puppets. But until Sid and Marty Krofft introduced *D.C. Follies* to the airwaves in 1987, being a political puppet never had so literal a meaning. After years of specializing in Saturday morning kids shows and prime-time variety series, the Kroffts returned to their puppeteer roots. *D.C. Follies* was as if the warped political cartoons of newspaper op-ed pages had come to life—only in this new forum, the satire often was sharper because these characters seemed so real.

In fact, after working alongside the Krofft puppets for so long, Willard often had to remind himself they weren't the genuine articles.

"I treated them like they were really there, like they were people, which wasn't hard to do because they were very realistic for puppets," he says. "They were pretty lifelike.

"I remember I came home from doing the show one night and President Reagan was on TV and I turned to my wife and I started to say, 'You know, I was talking to him today and you'll never guess what he said.' And then I realized I wasn't talking to him. I was talking to the puppet."

If Willard's disbelief could be suspended by these remarkable creations, even though he had witnessed the gifted puppeteers at work behind the scenes, imagine the effect this had on people in the viewing audience.

"We were in the Hollywood Lane parade at Christmas one year," Willard says. "I was in a big open car with the Whoopi Goldberg, the Cher and the Dolly Parton puppets. In the car, they had to have the puppeteers underneath. But there was no room for anyone doing the voices. So the puppets could turn and wave, but they couldn't talk.

"But every time we'd come to a stop, a reporter would come over with a microphone and put the mic in Dolly Parton's face and say something like, 'Dolly, what do you think about the parade?' And I'd have to say, 'Well, Dolly's very tired today and she's saving her voice.' You know, the reporters actually thought the puppets would talk."

In addition to being a funny show, occasionally even biting in its satire without getting downright mean, *D.C. Follies* was also deceptively simple in its presentation. After all, what could be more basic than filming a collection of characters as they gather around the bar?

Well, for starters, it took two people to work each puppet— one maneuvering the puppet's mouth and one hand while the second puppeteer controlled the torso and the other hand. Gestures that we take for granted, such as clapping one's hands, required tremendous coordination and teamwork from the two puppeteers, yet they worked together so seamlessly they were virtually of one mind.

Also out of sight was the team of talented voice specialists: John Roarke and Maurice LaMarche aping the voices of the famous male characters, Louise DuArt (whose previous involvement with the Kroffts, a decade earlier, was as a member of Kaptain Kool and the Kongs) doing all of the women characters.

"The people who did the voices were so talented," Willard says. "If they didn't know the voice they were supposed to be doing, they would just walk around with a tape recorder plugged into their ear and listen to the voice for a few minutes and then do it. It was really something. And none of it was pre-taped. So if, say, Tammy Faye Bakker had an argument with Dolly Parton, Louise DuArt did both parts live, right there, while we were doing it. It was just amazing."

Says DuArt: "It's not common to do it that way, to do the voices live like that, but I think it's the only way you could do that show. The only way if you wanted to have the impact and have it sound natural. I also did a series of specials for the BBC, *Spittin' Image,* and they weren't done that way. That was done ADR afterwards. And the puppets were spectacular and everything, but I think there was a certain extra charm about the Krofft puppets because we were there live doing it."

What's more, DuArt notes that, after a time, the voice people and the puppeteers worked so seamlessly together that doing ADR, or Automatic Dialog Replacement, would have been redundant. "The puppeteers just were incredible. We would have our own puppeteers and they got to know us so well that they'd know when we were going to ad-lib and, whatever we'd do, they'd just go right along with us. They were like an extension of us."

DuArt won't admit to being stumped by any of the voices she was called upon to do, but there were some tough ones here and there. "Some were better than others. I mean, I had to do everything from Vanna White to Margaret Thatcher. So that was a big range. But they ended up being okay."

There was no heavy lifting for Willard, though.

"They were the best working conditions ever," he recalls. "We only worked two days. I'd come in on Wednesday. We'd block the whole show in half a day Wednesday. And then come in Thursday and tape it. Now I know that doesn't sound like much effort was put into it, but I've found in this business if you can only work a day and a half, you can get the work done in a day and a half. And if you can work five days, the work ends up taking five days."

It never took much time, Willard jokes, because the puppets were quick studies and didn't need much time going over their lines.

"It was always kind of exciting," Willard says. "The guys who did the puppets would bring in two or three new ones every week and we'd all gather around to see who was the new puppet. I think it was the most fun I ever had. I always had a feeling that was why it was canceled. Because it was too easy for me. Someone must have been looking down and said, 'Wait a minute. Fred's getting away with murder.'"

D.C. Follies has been accused of being a ripoff of Spittin' Image, a similarly themed British puppet show that featured harsher-looking caricatures and a mean spirit. It has even been accused of being a steal from The Muppet Show. But the fact is Sid and Marty Krofft had worked with celebrity puppets for decades, the most memorable example of which was their Les Poupees de Paris show of the 1960s.

Will the Mystery Guest Please Sign In?

Despite the show's parade of wonderful guest stars, Fred Willard often was in the dark about who would be next to grace the D.C. Follies bar. What's more, it sometimes was even a mystery to Sid and Marty.

"Sometimes I really wondered about the Kroffts," Willard says. "They knew it was a fun show and every week it lent itself to a guest star. And we had wonderful guest stars, like Mike Tyson and Bo Derek. But there were times when I'd come in and say, 'Who's our guest this week?' And they'd say, 'Oh, Jeez, we forgot to get a guest.' They'd just forget or someone working for them would just forget to get a guest.

"One day I was talking to a comic I know. And Sid or Marty walked by and start talking and later they said, 'Hey, I wonder if he'd like to be our guest today?' And so they went next door to the studio and asked him if he'd like to come next door and be the guest and they quickly wrote something, put it together for him.

"I mean, it was amazing. They would come in with Bo Derek or Mike Tyson one week. And then another week, they forgot. 'Who can we get? Do you know anybody for that?'"

It's worth noting, incidentally, that the idea for the show was neither Sid nor Marty's. It was a suggestion from Marty's daughter Kristina that got them moving. The result was a series that ran for two seasons and a total of forty-five, half-hour episodes, airing in first-run syndication on an array of independent stations and network affiliates (during off-hours) throughout the country. It was a modest hit, not a huge one, but it also was victimized by misfortune.

"It was quite successful the first year," Marty recalls. "But just before we were supposed to go into production the second year, the syndicator went bankrupt and, because of that, we got a late start. We had to scrounge around to get a new syndicator. But we got a late start and got bad time slots because all the good time slots were taken. We were around the country at 2:00 in the morning. Whenever we had a good time slot, we got great ratings. When we got a bad time slot, we got the ratings that the time slot deserved."

Adds Willard: "We did another great year, but I think the problem with the lousy time slots killed us. So that meant the end of the show."

Which was a shame because it was worthy of a longer run.

"One of the things that I thought was nice about our show was the fact that, even though we poked fun at people, it was done very lovingly," Willard says. *"The Spittin' Image* show was on about the same time, but ours was more pleasant and cartoony. Theirs was very dark and mean. We treated the president and the ex-presidents with great humor.

"But I do remember they came down kind of hard on Sam Donaldson and one day I said something to them about it. I said, 'You know, we shouldn't be quite so hard on Sam Donaldson. After all, he's the guy who's sort of speaking for all of us, investigating these things.' And they said, 'Oh, no, he loves it.' They had gotten word that, in Washington, the people loved it. Sam Donaldson loved it."

The same was true for most Hollywood types who became Krofft puppets. In fact, Marty says, people literally begged the

Kroffts to be immortalized as puppets. "Oh, a lot of people," he says. "They would call up and say, 'Make a puppet of me.' Whoopi Goldberg was one."

Says Willard: "I remember when Whoopi Goldberg came on and they brought out her puppet. I thought she was just going to fall through the floor. She laughed so hard. God, she just went crazy when she saw her puppet because it looked just like her."

Adds DuArt, who does a dead-on Whoopi Goldberg voice: "When she came on as a guest star, I played Whoopi's evil twin. She hadn't seen her puppet yet and she sat down at the bar and Fred was serving her. And when I'm with the character I'm doing, I can really nail the voice. So she's sitting down there at the counter and here comes the puppet behind her and I say [in Goldberg's voice], 'Hey, Whoop. How's it goin'?' And she looked around and just screamed. She got hysterical, her talking to herself. It was just a riot. She loved that show."

Of course, not everyone considered imitation a form of flattery.

"The only feedback we got that was negative that I can remember was that Frank Sinatra and Woody Allen didn't want their puppets on," Willard says. "And you would figure that, wouldn't you? That Frank Sinatra would object?"

Says Marty: "Sinatra's lawyer, who's a friend of mine, called me. He said that Sinatra would prefer that we not use the puppet of him."

Adds DuArt: "Some people, they would feel insulted if we *didn't* make the puppet of them. I think there were only a couple of people who didn't like it, like Frank Sinatra. Another was the Pope."

Apparently concerned that thugs might show up to break some puppet kneecaps, Willard jokes, the Kroffts phased Sinatra out of the show.

"But the Pope, we didn't worry as much about him as we did Frank Sinatra," DuArt adds. "Sinatra went first. When they heard that, he was out of there. It was so funny, because the Pope can wait. We'll wait until we get another call from the Vatican. But Frank, no way."

As for Woody, they tried a different tack. Aware that Allen had a reputation for suing anyone who used his character without permission, the Kroffts merely gave their Woody Allen puppet a different name. Thus, whenever the character entered the *D.C. Follies* bar, he often could be heard saying something like, "I just don't know why people think I'm Woody Allen, because I'm not."

Says Marty: "We did that to cover our tail." What's more, it was a pretty good inside joke.

An even better inside joke was when Sid and Marty puppets—or should we say puppets of Sid and Marty?—joined the show. Bill Tracy, Marty's longtime office assistant, remembers that everyone back at the office got a real kick out of it, even if the gag was meaningless to many viewers. "I kept thinking it would be fun to just have Marty get on the phone and say, 'Hey, we'd like to have you on as a guest. Oh, you can't make it? That's okay. We'll build a puppet of you. Oh, you'll be here after all?' And then hang up and chuckle."

Given the eclectic roster of famous guest stars who visited the *D.C. Follies* bar, one might suspect that Tracy's wished-for gag was not far removed from the truth. Guest stars included Mike Tyson and Don King, Whoopi Goldberg, Bo Derek, Harry Anderson, Greg Louganis, Leslie Nielsen, Mary Hart, Dick Butkus, Mickey Gilley, Vanity and Robert Englund (as Freddy Krueger of the *Nightmare on Elm Street* movies).

Not surprisingly, Derek's visit was one that Willard remembers most vividly. "She was wonderful. She was so sweet. And she was nervous about being on the show. They had her play the fact that she and I had had a romance once. And 'How could you forget me, Fred? Remember the times we had?' It was just so cute. It was a wonderful show."

Freddy Krueger, on the other hand, wasn't quite so dreamy a guest. "Freddy Krueger came in and he took three hours in make-up. He brought his makeup man and he did this wonderful scene. I dreamed Freddy Krueger was there and then I woke up. But in other weeks, weeks later, there still were some scars on the bar from where he'd been up there. And I'd say, 'Oh, Freddy Krueger did this. That's funny. I thought that was a dream sequence.' That was a very inside joke too, but I loved it."

In fact, one inside joke that never transpired, although there had been talk of doing it, was putting a Fred Willard puppet behind the bar. "They were talking about that too at the end of the second season," Willard says. "But in a way, I'm glad they decided not to. Because if the puppet was better than me, they could get rid of me."

Just another joke? In the world of *D.C. Follies,* you can never be entirely sure.

"I remember Marty Krofft used to say to me, 'Fred, we love you. You're just a joy to work with.' And he would say, 'Fred, you were our first choice, our only choice. We immediately thought of you.' Well, one day I was in Las Vegas and I bumped into Louie Anderson and he said, 'Oh, I love you on *D.C. Follies.*' I said, 'Thanks.' And he said, 'You know, they talked to me about doing that, but I just couldn't.'"

Like Willard, Sid and Marty have warm spots in their hearts for *D.C. Follies*. After the show went off, they brought it back in the form of a stage show called *Comedy Kings* in Las Vegas, with John Byner taking over the part Willard had played. And now they even are toying around with the idea of re-inventing the show for the 1990s.

"We're trying to get it resurrected," Marty says. "But nothing's easy any more. It's hard to get a new show on."

Says Sid: "I did a whole new premise on a new *D.C. Follies*. It's called *The Hot Spot* and it's a chain of clubs, just like Planet Hollywood. There's one in New York and there's one in Nashville and there's one in Los Angeles and, of course, one in Washington D.C. And each fifteen minutes—the show would be an hour—we go to a club in a different city. And so it would have country, it would have politics, it would have Hollywood and it would have Broadway."

That's a series that DuArt and Willard would love to see come to fruition.

"Oh, it was a wonderful show," DuArt says. "I wish they'd bring it back because people still remember it and talk about how wonderful it was. The writing was very sharp. And of course, the puppets were just excellent."

Adds Willard: "You know, the more I think about it, the more I think that damn show should be back on. Can you imagine what we'd be able to do with Bill Clinton and Hillary and this administration?"

Life With Little Richard

Consider it the Kroffts' "forgotten" Saturday morning series.

When fans reflect on the body of Sid and Marty's work on Saturday mornings, *Pryor's Place* often gets omitted—separated from the others not by quality so much as time itself. Airing on CBS from September 22, 1984, to June 15, 1985, the short-lived series came along too many years after the Kroffts' other kids shows to have had the same audience.

Pryor's Place starred Richard Pryor in a live-action series. The premise: Pryor reflected on his childhood to a group of kids in an urban neighborhood. And as stories about Little Richie (played by Akili Prince) unfolded, Pryor could be found playing the parts of many eccentric neighborhood adults—as would an array of famous guest stars and Krofft puppets.

"It was a lot of fun," Sid recalls. "I did a lot of the puppetry in it. Richard Pryor really liked me a lot. When there was any kind of a problem, I always used to go in and talk to Richard.

"It was the big educational show, in a way, with morals, for CBS. That was the reason they did it. And we had some incredible guest stars, like Robin Williams and Lily Tomlin. I mean, they were unbelievable people who came on our show."

Thirteen episodes were made and then, after a one-year run, it was gone. "The ratings weren't great because the kids were watching cartoons and this was more educational."

Generation Next
...or What's Left
for the Kroffts to Do?

What does the future hold for Sid and Marty Krofft?

It's hard to predict, actually, what the next great Krofft project will be, the one that captures the public's imagination the way that *Les Poupees de Paris*, *H.R. Pufnstuf* and *Land of the Lost* did. It's even conceivable that the brothers might never create another hit on that scale.

But one thing is certain: It won't be from lack of trying or from lack of ideas.

This is Sid Krofft's philosophy on ideas: "Just throw them all out there and hope one of them sticks to the wall. It's like a Hollywood studio. They do twenty-three movies a year and they just want one of them to be a smash."

Conventional wisdom would hold that their smash could be the *Land of the Lost* movie, in development at Disney and very tentatively targeted for a 1999 release. Or it could be some other back-burner big-screen remake of a Krofft series.

The canon of '70s Krofft shows, after all, is rich material to mine.

"I think that's the good thing that we have going right now," Marty says. "With the original shows, we've got the double-edged sword: The kids can discover the shows as brand new—and I think they're timeless—and I know that the adults are going to come back."

The fact that fans flock to events like Pufapalooza in record numbers makes a retro-Krofft movie venture seem like a reasonably safe bet for success.

But that's hardly all that the Kroffts have cooking. Here is a glimpse at the menu:

A new version of *The Bugaloos* went into development at Fox a few years ago. Nothing has come of it yet, but Marty says the project isn't dead.

Sid and Marty are also passionate about reviving *D.C. Follies* in some form, with proposed names like *Rubber News* (Marty's title) and *The Hot Spot* (Sid's).

And Sid has never entirely abandoned *Mishmosh,* which his brother describes as the best Krofft series that failed to get on the air. "We sold just about everything that we created," Marty says. "But one show that my brother was real adamant about and he's still into is the one called *Mishmosh*. It was a fantasy underwater show and we never got it on."

Says Sid: "Remember when Roseanne Barr had her own cartoon on Saturdays? It was on for only one season. Well, we were picked up and then we were *not* picked up, because ABC wanted to make room for her cartoon instead. But *Mishmosh* is definitely the next *Pufnstuf*. We'll get to make it one day."

The brothers aren't limiting themselves to the worlds of film and television, either.

Marty says that if someone comes forward with the $4 million-plus startup costs, for example, it might intensify their interest in bringing back *Les Poupees de Paris* for a new generation.

Trial balloons were floated about the possibility of reviving *H.R. Pufnstuf* on Broadway. "We were offered by the Kennedy Center to do a Broadway show," Sid says. "A *Pufnstuf* musical in an environmental theater, which I think would be incredible." Given that *Pufnstuf* did sellout stage shows in Madison Square Garden and the Hollywood Bowl in the 1970s, the notion doesn't seem very farfetched.

Sid is working alongside showman Kenny Ortega on developing a Tokyo amusement park that he believes could become the crown jewel of his career.

And Sid even began work in the summer of 1997 at putting his incredible life story down on paper, tentatively titling his autobiography *World on a String*.

As for the Krofft family tradition of puppetry, will that carry over to a sixth generation? "The only way it could happen, in my opinion, is with my kids," Marty says. "But I don't see that happening right at this moment. I'm not saying it can't happen. But it doesn't look that way right now. I have three daughters and two grandchildren, but I don't know.

"One of my kids, Kristina, is an actress. My daughter Deanna works in the company. And my son-in-law, Randy Pope, who's married to Deanna, he's the head of development and production. So the family's not going to go away. But the business is definitely going to change."

Sid tends to agree on that point. "We're having a hard enough time getting by ourselves. I guess Marty's daughters could pick it up, if they're interested, but I don't know. I don't know how much further puppetry can go."

But even though their puppeteer legacy may end at generation five, the name definitely will go on. The Kroffts have made a lasting impact in terms of the talented people who worked with them and have since moved on, the artists who were influenced by their work and, of course, the legions of still-loyal fans.

In short, even if the brothers never again match the level of success and popularity they enjoyed in the 1970s during the height of the Krofft Television era, the beams that radiate from the sun of their rainbow-hued logo will shine just as brightly.

Episode Guides
and
Theme Songs

Here are episode guides to the Saturday morning TV series created and produced by Sid and Marty Krofft.

To ensure that this material is as accurate as possible, the primary source was records kept by Sid & Marty Krofft Pictures.

Series are arranged in the order in which they premiered. The sequence of episodes generally follow the order in which the individual shows were filmed, which may differ slightly from their original broadcast order.

All shows are thirty minutes unless otherwise indicated.

H.R. Pufnstuf

Seventeen episodes. Network broadcast history: September 6, 1969–September 4, 1971 (10 A.M. Saturdays, NBC); September 9, 1972–September 1, 1973 (11:30 A.M. Saturdays, ABC).

Cast: Jack Wild (as Jimmy), Billie Hayes (Witchiepoo)
Krofft puppeteers: Roberto Gamonet (H.R. Pufnstuf), Sharon Baird (Judy Frog, Lady Boyd, Shirley Pufnstuf), Joy Campbell (Orson, Cling), Angelo Rossitto (Clang, Seymour), Johnny Silver (Ludicrous Lion, Dr. Blinky), Jerry Landon, Jon Linton, Scutter McKay, Harry Monty, Andy Ratoucheff, Robin Roper, Felix Silla
Voices: Lennie Weinrib, Joan Gerber, Walker Edmiston
Created and produced by: Sid and Marty Krofft
Executive producer: Si Rose
Associate producer: Malcolm Alper
Director: Hollingsworth Morse
Writers: Lennie Weinrib, Robert Ridolfi, Paul Harrison
Music: Gene Page Jr.
Theme song and special material: Les Szarvas
Musical numbers staged by: Hal Belfer
Creative design: Nicky Nadeau

H.R. Pufnstuf—The Theme Song

H.R. Pufnstuf
Who's your friend when things get rough?
H.R. Pufnstuf
Can't do a little 'cuz he can't do enough
Once upon a summertime
Just a dream from yesterday
A boy and his magic golden flute
Heard a boat from off the bay
"Come and play with me, Jimmy,
Come and play with me,
And I will take you on a trip,

Far across the sea."
But the boat belonged to a kooky old witch
Who had in mind the flute to snitch
From her Vroom Broom in the sky
She watched her plans materialize
She waved her wand
The skies grew dark
The sea grew rough
And the boat sailed on and on and on and on and on

H.R. Pufnstuf
Who's your friend when things get rough?
H.R. Pufnstuf
Can't do a little 'cuz he can't do enough

But Pufnstuf was watching too
And knew exactly what to do
He saw the witch's boat attack
And as the boat was fighting back
He called his Rescue Racer crew
As often they'd rehearsed
And off to save the boy they flew
But who would get there first?

H.R. Pufnstuf
Who's your friend when things get rough?
H.R. Pufnstuf
Can't do a little 'cuz he can't do enough

But now the boy had washed ashore
Puf arrived to save the day
Which made the witch so mad and sore
She shook her fist and screamed away

H.R. Pufnstuf
Who's your friend when things get rough?
H.R. Pufnstuf
Can't do a little 'cuz he can't do enough

"The Magic Path"
Episode 1. On a walk through the forest, Jimmy and his magic flute Freddy are lured to Living Island and trapped there by Witchiepoo's trickery. After Jimmy meets Pufnstuf, they are captured by Witchiepoo, but they escape and discover the Magic Path that can lead Jimmy back home. Unfortunately, Witchiepoo intercepts Jimmy and makes the path disappear.

"The Wheely Bird"
Episode 2. Freddy is such a good friend, he is willing to give himself up to protect Jimmy from Witchiepoo. Freddy slips away and surrenders himself to the witch, but Jimmy and Puf hatch a plan to gain entrance to her castle by building a bird on wheels, à la Odysseus and the Trojan Horse, and recover the purloined golden flute.

"Show Biz Witch"
Episode 3. When Ludicrous Lion convinces Jimmy he has a super-duper pogo stick for sale that could bounce him home, Pufnstuf and Jimmy conduct a talent show to raise the money. Jimmy may be the star, but it's Witchiepoo who steals the show, as she and her sidekicks, Orson and Seymour, perform as the Three Oranges.

"The Mechanical Boy"
Episode 4. Jimmy tries to steal Witchiepoo's boat so he can leave Living Island, but Witchiepoo catches him. She turns him into a mechanical boy and commands him to steal Freddy for her. But Pufnstuf saves the day when he figures out how to reverse the spell.

"The Stand-In"
Episode 5. Witchiepoo captures Freddy, but Pufnstuf hatches a plot to get the flute away from her castle: Puf's sister Shirley, a movie star, is visiting the island to make a movie and he arranges for director Max Von Toadenoff to cast the witch (dressed as Lola Lollapalooza) as a stand-in in his new picture, which distracts her attention while Jimmy sneaks into the castle.

"The Golden Key"
Episode 6. Jimmy buys a map from Ludicrous Lion that shows the location

of the Golden Key, which fits the Golden Door, a secret way off Living Island. But Witchiepoo captures Pufnstuf and holds him in her dungeon, diverting Jimmy from his escape.

"The Birthday Party"
Episode 7. Witchiepoo invites herself to Jimmy's surprise birthday party. While there, she steals Freddy by rendering the partygoers helpless with laughing gas.

"The Box Kite Kaper"
Episode 8. Ludicrous Lion sponsors a kite-flying contest in his scheme to sell kites, but it gives Puf an idea: Jimmy and Freddy will attempt to fly away from Living Island during the contest in a giant box kite built by Dr. Blinky. But Witchiepoo gets wind of their scheme.

"You Can't Have Your Cake"
Episode 9. A pre-Michael Jackson "Moonwalk" dance sweeps Living Island. Witchiepoo hides in a giant cake and grabs Freddy at an opportune moment. Now for the rescue: While Judy the Frog distracts the skeleton castle guards with the moonwalk, Pufnstuf and Jimmy recover Freddy.

"Horse With the Golden Throat"
Episode 10. Horsey, a polka-dotted horse, mistakes Freddy the Flute for a carrot and swallows him. The problem is first getting the flute out of the horse (who runs away when he learns Dr. Blinky may have to operate), then keeping it away from Witchiepoo.

"Dinner for Two"
Episode 11. Jimmy and Freddy become seventy-two-year-olds when Grandfather Clock's time machine malfunctions. When Witchiepoo finds old Jimmy wandering in her forest, she decides he is her Prince Charming and makes immediate plans to marry him. Pufnstuf removes the foggy-headed old groom from the witch's castle and gets him back to twelve years of age, then turns the witch into a squalling toddler.

"Book, Flute and Candle"
Episode 12. Jimmy finds Freddy has been turned into a mushroom by the

touch of Witchiepoo's evil mushrooms. The cure can only be found in an evil book in Witchiepoo's castle. The good guys come up with a plan to get the page from the book and restore Freddy back to his "normal" state, a jewel-encrusted talking golden flute.

"Tooth for a Tooth"
Episode 13. Orson makes a dental appointment for Witchiepoo with Dr. Blinky, but he disguises her as a little girl. When the doctor extracts her bad tooth, it hurts so bad that the witch reveals her true self and flies into a rage. But before she can hurt anyone, Dr. Blinky blasts her with a love potion. This new Witchiepoo invites everyone to the castle for a party. Pufnstuf hatches a plan for Jimmy and Freddy to escape on the witch's Vroom Broom during the party.

"The Visiting Witch"
Episode 14. Witchiepoo captures Pufnstuf and plans to present him as a gift for the impending visit of Inspector Witch. But she is unaware that the visiting witch has had to postpone her stopover, which provides Jimmy with the opportunity to impersonate the inspector and get Puf back.

"The Almost Election of Witchiepoo"
Episode 15. Witchiepoo runs for mayor of Living Island, challenging Pufnstuf, the incumbent. She resorts to using a "Love Witchiepoo" potion to win votes, but Dr. Blinky undoes the spell at the last minute.

"Whaddya Mean the Horse Gets the Girl?"
Episode 16. Pufnstuf's sister Shirley stars in a movie to raise money for Living Island's anti-witch fund. The troubled production is saved when Horsey is "discovered" and stars in a western. Witchiepoo steals the director and camera operator to film her autobiography, but the horse comes to the rescue...sort of.

"Jimmy Who?"
Episode 17. A bonk on the head causes Jimmy to come down with a case of amnesia that Dr. Blinky and Witchiepoo take turns trying to cure by reminiscing about the good times they have had together. Fortunately, a second bang on the head restores Jimmy's memory.

Pufnstuf

Feature film follow-up. June 1970 (94 minutes). Witchiepoo manages to steal Freddy from Jimmy and plans to use the flute to win the Witch of the Year award at the Annual Witches' Convention. Additional cast: Martha Raye (as Boss Witch), Mama Cass Elliott (Witch Hazel) and Billy Barty (Googie the Gopher). Written by: John Fenton Murray and Si Rose.

The Bugaloos

Seventeen episodes. Network broadcast history: September 12, 1970– September 2, 1972 (9:30 A.M. Saturdays, NBC).

Cast: Martha Raye (as Benita Bizarre), Caroline Ellis (Joy), John Philpott (Courage), John McIndoe (IQ), Wayne Laryea (Harmony), Billy Barty (Sparky the Firefly), Sharon Baird (Funky Rat), Joy Campbell (Woofer), Van Snowden (Tweeter)
Voices: Joan Gerber, Walker Edmiston
Created and produced by: Sid and Marty Krofft
Executive producer: Si Rose
Associate producer: Donald A. Ramsey
Director: Tony Charmoli
Writers: John Fenton Murray, Warren S. Murray, Elon E. Packard, Jack Raymond, Maurice Richlin, Si Rose
Music: Charles Fox
Theme Song: Charles Fox (music) and Norman Gimbel (lyrics)
Musical director of the Bugaloos: Hal Voergler
Production designer: James Trittipo
Creative design: Nicky Nadeau

The Bugaloos—The Theme Song

The Bugaloos, the Bugaloos
We're in the air and everywhere
Flying high, flying loose
Flying free as a summer breeze

The Bugaloos, the Bugaloos
We're climbing high and diving low
Through the sky, 'cross the land
Straight to you with a helping hand
Ready with a helping hand

We're friends indeed
Should you need
If you ever need

The Bugaloos, the Bugaloos
We're in the air and everywhere
Flying high, flying loose
Flying free like we all could be

"Firefly, Light My Fire"
Episode 1. Because Benita's musical skills leave a lot to be desired, she kidnaps the Bugaloos, holding Joy hostage and forcing the male members to become her backup band as she attempts to record a hit single. But then Sparky the Firefly, who earlier was bailed out of a jam by the Bugaloos, returns the favor and helps them escape, becoming their new friend. Sparky writes a song for the gang that becomes a hit.

"The Great Voice Robbery"
Episode 2. Benita becomes dissatisfied with her voice, so she kidnaps Joy and uses a voice-switching machine to steal Joy's voice. And horror of horrors: Joy has Benita's voice. The rest of the Bugaloos get involved, complicating matters by scrambling everyone's voices.

"Our Home Is Our Hassle"
Episode 3. Benita wants to live in Tranquility Forest because she believes it will inspire her to write a hit song for a radio contest. So when Benita comes up with a phony land deed that guarantees her the rights to Tranquility Forest, the Bugaloos must find a way to get her to move back home.

"Courage Come Home"
Episode 4. Benita fires all of her hired help because of their incompetence. Then, when Courage takes a fall while flying and gets amnesia, Benita takes advantage of the situation by convincing him that he is her nephew and responsible for doing her housework.

"The Love Bugaloos"
Episode 5. Sparky has a crush on a lady firefly named Gina. The Bugaloos play Cupid to get them together, but bitter Benita tries every dirty trick in the book to keep them apart.

"If I Had the Wings of a Bugaloo"
Episode 6. Benita captures IQ, with the sinister intentions of surgically transplanting his wings onto her. It looks like there will be no one to save him, either, because the other Bugaloos have gone to a concert.

"Lady, You Don't Look Eighty"
Episode 7. As a prank, IQ and Courage fool Sparky into believing Joy is actually eighty years old on her birthday. When Benita overhears this and believes, she will do anything to steal the secret of Joy's youth. She kidnaps Sparky, hoping to force him to reveal the location of a Fountain of Youth.

"Benita the Beautiful"
Episode 8. Benita wants to win a beauty contest sponsored by the local disc jockey, Peter Platter, and she is willing to resort to unfair methods to achieve her goal, including kidnapping the other contestants. But the Bugaloos offer another way.

"Now You See Them, Now You Don't"
Episode 9. Thanks to a magic wand, the Bugaloos gain the ability to make themselves invisible. They use their newfound gift to rescue Sparky from Benita, who has legally adopted the firefly as her son and is forcing him to live with her.

"Help Wanted, Firefly"
Episode 10. Sparky gets a job at Peter Platter's radio station, but Benita

short-circuits everything when she pulls a power play at the station, replacing the disc jockey when he refuses to play one of her records.

"On a Clear Day"
Episode 11. The Bugaloos have a concert in Tranquility Forest at the same time Benita has another one. So Benita sabotages her rivals' concert by pumping smog into the forest, thereby forcing everyone to come to hers.

"Today I Am a Firefly"
Episode 12. Sparky grows up by learning to fly and helping rescue the Bugaloos from Benita, who has shrunken the foursome and placed them inside a music box, where they are forced to perform for her.

"The Bugaloos' Bugaboo"
Episode 13. The Bugaloos are the star attraction at Peter Platter's rock concert, but Benita passes herself off as an agent to con Sparky into writing a song for her.

"Benita's Double Trouble"
Episode 14. Benita decides to kidnap Peter Platter so she can host his radio show, a situation that gets really confusing when IQ poses as Benita.

"Circus Time at Benita's"
Episode 15. The Bugaloos forge ahead with their plans to put on a circus, even though Benita is certain to interfere.

"The Uptown 500"
Episode 16. Benita challenges the Bugaloos to an auto race in the Uptown Grand Prix and they are as determined to win the event as she is.

"The Good Old Days"
Episode 17. The Bugaloos and Benita talk over the old times as they reflect on their past adventures when the foursome faces eviction from their home and Benita gets the deed to the forest.

Lidsville

Seventeen episodes. Network broadcast history: September 11, 1971–September 1, 1973 (10:30 A.M. Saturdays, ABC); September 8, 1973–August 31, 1974 (10 A.M. Saturdays, NBC).

Cast: Butch Patrick (as Mark), Charles Nelson Reilly (Hoo Doo),
    Billie Hayes (Weenie the Genie)
Costarring: Sharon Baird (Raunchy Rabbit), Joy Campbell, Jerry Maren,
    Angelo Rossitto, Hommy Stewart, Van Snowden, Felix Silla, Buddy
    Douglas and the Hermine Midgets
Voices: Lennie Weinrib, Joan Gerber, Walker Edmiston
Created and produced by: Sid and Marty Krofft
Executive producer: Si Rose
Associate producer: Malcolm Alper
Director: Tony Charmoli
Writers: Larry Alexander, John Fenton Murray, Warren S. Murray, Mark
    Ray, Jack Raymond, Rita Sedran Rose, Si Rose, Elroy Schwartz,
    Paul Wayne
Musical director: Charles Fox
Songs by: Les Szarvas
Theme song by: Les Szarvas and Sid Krofft
"Krofft Look" by: Nicky Nadeau
Art director: William Smith

Lidsville—The Theme Song

In the middle of the summer
In the middle of a park
There began a great adventure
For a boy whose name was Mark
He had come to see the magic man
Along with all the children and
'Twas so began the day that Mark was never to forget

He performed all sorts of miracles
And Mark was so impressed
That when the time arrived to go
He lagged behind the rest
Then quietly he did return
The secret of the hat to learn
But everyone had gone away and darkness filled the set

The moment that he touched that hat, the room began to glow
And as he put it down and ran, the hat began to grow and grow and grow and
grow and grow and grow and grow and grow and grow
And grow
He was stunned and he was fascinated
Still he had to see
There was something deep inside the hat
What could that something be?
Then cautiously each step he took
He climbed up on the brim to look
And all at once the hat began to shake and rock
Look out!

Falling, falling, into the hat he fell
Spinning, turning, whirling, twirling
Down, down
And when he looked into the sky
He couldn't believe his ears or eyes

Lidsville is the kook, kook, kookiest
Lidsville is the kick, kick, kickiest
Lidsville is the groove, groove, grooviest
Lidsville is the living end, friend

If you get a chance to go-go there
You'll be glad you did
'Cause everybody who goes to Lidsville
Really flips his lid

"World in a Hat"
Episode 1. When Mark goes backstage after a magic show, he stumbles into a magic hat and falls into a strange land filled with hat people. The Bad Hats capture him and drag him to Hoo Doo, the evil magician of Lidsville. Then he is thrown into the dungeon. How is Mark going to escape? Weenie the Genie has magic up his sleeve but may not provide as much help as Mark needs.

"Show Me the Way to Go Home"
Episode 2. Colonel Poom, the British pith hat, discovers an ancient map of Lidsville that indicates the location of a golden ladder that might take Mark and Weenie the Genie up to the real world. All of the Good Hats pitch in to help Mark prepare for his journey to the ladder. But Hoo Doo gets wind of their plan and sends his mean minions to foil their efforts and retrieve Weenie.

"Fly Now, Vacuum Later"
Episode 3. After Weenie the Genie's rocket experiment goes haywire, the Hat People suggest he conjure up a magic carpet. Soon Mark is whisked off into the sky. But wait: Where did that giant vacuum cleaner come from and what is it up to?

"Weenie, Weenie, Where's Our Genie?"
Episode 4. When the Good Hats plan how to handle Hoo Doo's next attack, they ignore Weenie the Genie, a well-intentioned and good-hearted soul but a colossal bungler when it comes to anything magical. So Weenie runs away. Hoo Doo confronts the Good Hats and demands, one, the payment of their taxes, and two, the return of Weenie. To assure their good faith, the evil magician kidnaps two of the Good Hats and threatens dire consequences for the hostages if the Hats don't comply with his demands.

"Let's Hear it for Whizzo"
Episode 5. While Mark and Weenie the Genie futilely attempt to escape from Lidsville, Hoo Doo evicts the Good Hats for nonpayment of taxes and puts their homes up for sale. Mark and Weenie return to find the Good Hats gone and their homes occupied by the Bad Hats and realize something must be done. They find the Good Hats and plan to fight Hoo Doo with another magician. But where in Lidsville will they find another conjurer?

"Is There a Mayor in the House?"

Episode 6. The Hat People decide to elect a mayor to lead them in their fight against Hoo Doo and everyone enters the race. But Hoo Doo hears about the election and enters his own candidate, vowing, "This will be an honest election. I'll pick the winner." The Good Hats realize their only chance is to support only one of their own, but election day comes and something goes wrong. Could "honest" Hoo Doo be behind it?

"Take Me to Your Rabbit"

Episode 7. Hoo Doo and Raunchy Rabbit fly the Hatamaran into a thunder storm, where a bolt of lightning transfers Hoo Doo's powers to the frightened bunny. But it gradually dawns on Hoo Doo's furry henchman that he has the power and Hoo Doo must kowtow to him for a change. Will Hoo Doo get his power back? Will Lidsville survive this change of power?

"Have I Got a Girl for Hoo Doo"

Episode 8. What is wrong with Hoo Doo? He passes up a perfect chance to zap the Hat People. The answer: It's spring and he wants romance. He secretly joins a lonelyhearts club and is matched with someone named...Witchiepoo! But who is this other woman vying for Hoo Doo's attention?

"Mark and the Bean Stalk"

Episode 9. When Hoo Doo finds his treasury is empty, he blames the Hat People for not paying their taxes. Meanwhile, Weenie the Genie accidentally conjures up a magic bean that grows a beanstalk right into the sky. Mark realizes this might be the way out of Lidsville and starts to climb. But Hoo Doo spots Mark high on the beanstalk, kidnaps him and holds him for ransom to be paid by the Hat People. Hoo Doo then gets the notion that Mark's family might pay more for him than the Good Hats would, so he changes himself to look like Mark and climbs the beanstalk himself. Now Mark must escape Hoo Doo's hat house and foil Hoo Doo's sinister plans.

"Turn in Your Turban, You're Through"

Episode 10. The Bad Hats goad Hoo Doo that the Good Hats have outwitted him ever since Mark arrived. Hoo Doo, enraged, captures the boy and Weenie.

Hoo Doo then transfers Weenie's power to Mark and turns him into Marco, a new and improved genie who does his bidding without any mishaps. Hoo Doo is so pleased with his new genie that he fires all of his flunkies, then orders Marco to collect the taxes (paid in hat checks) from the Good Hats. The Hat People, stunned that their friend has turned on them, plan to recover the magic ring and change Marco the genie back into Mark the boy. Meanwhile, the Bad Hats attempt to get rid of Marco to get their jobs back.

"Alias, the Imperial Wizard"
Episode 11. The Imperial Wizard is coming to inspect Hoo Doo's habitat and the magician is in a tizzy. He realizes he needs some competent help for a change and nabs three of the Good Hats to help him entertain. Then, when the Imperial Wizard cancels his visit, Hoo Doo decides to keep the Good Hats forever. The Good Hats concoct a plan for Mark to impersonate the Imperial Wizard and make a surprise inspection on Hoo Doo to rescue their friends, but Mark is in peril when the Imperial Wizard really does show up.

"A Little Hoo Doo Goes a Long Way"
Episode 12. When Hoo Doo orders the Bad Hats to clean up their houses, they become incensed and decide to steal the Hatamaran to escape to the real world. But the Hatamaran gets away from them. Meanwhile, Weenie the Genie becomes ill and is too weak to come out of the magic ring. Nursie, the nurse hat, has a cure for the ailing genie. And with the help of Colonel Poom's shrinking potion, he is well again. The pilotless Hatamaran crash-lands near the Good Hats. Mark and Weenie think this is a perfect time to escape, but the Party Hat insists they have a farewell party before they go and, during the party, Hoo Doo appears. They convince him to join them in a toast to Mark and he unknowingly drinks the shrinking potion. But in the end, someone splashes the tiny magician with the shrinking antidote and he returns to full size.

"Oh, Brother"
Episode 13. When the Good Hats throw a birthday party for Li'l Ben, a pig, Hoo Doo believes the reason the Hat People can afford a party is because they have not paid their taxes to him. So just as the pig blows out his candle, Hoo Doo kidnaps him. This enrages the Good Hats and causes them

to revolt. But just as the Good Hats attack, Hoo Doo is summoned to the Imperial Wizard and leaves his minions to fight. Then Hoo Doo's twin brother Bruce, the white sheep of the family, comes visiting, which confuses Hoo Doo's people, who believe he is merely Hoo Doo in a white suit. When the Good Hats demand the return of the pig, Bruce kindly obliges, much to the surprise of the Baddies. Then Bruce returns all of Hoo Doo's money to the Good Hats. And when Hoo Doo returns, mayhem ensues.

"Hoo Doo Who?"
Episode 14. Hoo Doo comes down with amnesia when a lamp comes down on his head. His flunkies take advantage of the situation and turn him into their butler. Meanwhile, the Good Hats try to steal the Hatamaran. But another conk on the noggin restores Hoo Doo's memory and foils their plan.

"The Old Hat Home"
Episode 15. The Good Hats plan a show to raise money for the Old Hat Home and Hoo Doo wants to perform in it. When they tell him they already have too many performers, he angrily makes them all old and takes all of the charity money. The Bad Hats complain that having the Good Hats old is bad for a number of reasons, so Hoo Doo makes them young again. Then the Good Hats use makeup to look old to talk Hoo Doo out of the charity money. But when Hoo Doo tries to double-zap them young again, Weenie the Genie shoves a mirror in front of Hoo Doo and he becomes a baby.

"The Great Brain Robbery"
Episode 16. Hoo Doo devises a brainwash machine and lures the Good Hats into it using a magic flute, à la Pied Piper. The Good Hats are brainwashed for fighting and Hoo Doo leads them off to conquer the Imperial Wizard's palace. But Mark and Weenie the Genie, who were trying to escape on a magic carpet, are forced down by a storm and learn the fate of the Good Hats from the French Man Hole Cover, who was left behind. Mark and Weenie are able to snatch the magic flute from Hoo Doo and lure everyone back to the brainwash machine, where they make everyone, including Hoo Doo, nice.

"Mommy Hoo Doo"

Episode 17. Hoo Doo's mother comes around to see why her son is no longer rotten. So Hoo Doo's flunkies, using a flashback, try to convince her that he still is rotten. Then she goes to the Bad Hats, who try to convince her that he is still rotten, also with a flashback. Then she visits the Good Hats, who try to convince her he still is rotten, with yet another flashback. But even after all of this, she remains unconvinced. Until Hoo Doo is returning from getting his magic tuned up and tries some long distance zaps that wreck Lidsville, which does his mother's rotten little heart good.

Sigmund and the Sea Monsters

Twenty-nine episodes. Network broadcast history: September 8, 1973–October 18, 1975 (10 A.M. Saturdays, NBC).

Cast: Johnny Whitaker (as Johnny Stuart), Scott Kolden (Scott Stuart), Billy Barty (Sigmund Ooze), Rip Taylor (Sheldon the Sea Genie), Sparky Marcus (Shelby), Mary Wickes (Zelda Marshall), Fran Ryan (Gertrude), Joe Higgins (Sheriff Bevans), Bill Germaine (Blurp), Fred Spencer (Slurp), Sharon Baird (Big Daddy), Van Snowden (Sweet Mama)
Voices: Sidney Miller, Walker Edmiston
Created and produced by: Sid and Marty Krofft and Si Rose
Executive producer: Si Rose
Associate producers: Barbara Searles, Tom Swale
Directors: Dick Darley, Murray Golden, Bob Lally, Richard Dunlap
Writers: Fred Fox, Seaman Jacobs, John Fenton Murray, Warren S. Murray, Donald A. Ramsey, Jack Raymond, Rita Sedran Rose, Si Rose, Milt Rosen
Theme songs ("Sigmund and the Sea Monsters" and "Friends") by: Danny Janssen and Bobby Hart
Musical production: Wes Farrell, musical director; Michael Lloyd for Mike Curb Productions

Sigmund and the Sea Monsters—The Theme Song

You better run, you better hide
We gotta keep you out of sight
Be careful, Sigmund
Cover your tracks when you leave
'Cause you know Zelda won't believe
Your friend is Sigmund

Whoever heard of a friendly sea monster
Lovin' and laughin' his life away?

You better run, you better hide
We gotta keep you out of sight
Be careful, Sigmund

The other monsters put you down
'Cause you're not mean and now we've found
A friend in Sigmund

Whoever heard of a friendly sea monster
Lovin' and laughin' his life away?

He's all right, he's out of sight
He makes me smile, I like his style
I hope he stays a while
And he's doin' fine
He's a friend of mine

You better run, you better hide
We gotta keep you out of sight
Be careful, Sigmund
He's a friend of mine

Friends—The Other *Sigmund* Theme Song

There's nothing like a day out on the beach
When all it does it rain
You need somebody else
To make the sun come out again
When you find that special someone
You never expected to
It'll make you believe in magic
It could change your life for you

Talking 'bout friends (friends, friends)
That's what it's all about: friends (friends, friends)
Can't live without friends who won't let you down
You gotta have friends (friends, friends)

I must admit my life has changed
Since you came on the scene
And everything is twice as nice
If you know what I mean
I can't change the way I feel
And I wouldn't if I could
I never had someone before
Who made me feel so good

Talking 'bout friends (friends, friends)
That's what it's all about: friends (friends, friends)
Can't live without friends who won't let you down
You gotta have friends (friends, friends)

Talking 'bout friends (friends, friends)
Knockin' at your door: friends (friends, friends)
That's what friends are for
Friends if you're young or old
Everybody needs friends (friends, friends)

"The Monster Who Came to Dinner"

Episode 1. Sigmund gets thrown out of the sea monster cave because he doesn't want to scare people. He meets Johnny and Scott on the beach, then becomes their friend, after which he secretly moves into their club house.

"Puppy Love"

Episode 2. While hiding out in the boys' club house, Sigmund meets the neighbor girl's dog, Fluffy, and he falls madly in love. Johnny, meanwhile, has got it bad for the dog's cute owner. Guest star: Pamelyn Ferdin.

"Frankenstein Drops In"

Episode 3. When the sea monsters become angry because Sigmund has left them (they have no one to do their housework), Big Daddy, Blurp and Slurp go out to the beach looking for slaves and they capture Scott. To save his brother, Johnny disguises himself as Frankenstein's monster and makes the rescue.

"Is There a Doctor in the Cave?"

Episode 4. Sigmund gets sick and needs Big Mama's special food to cure him, so Johnny and Scott must sneak into the sea monster cave and raid the Oozes' refrigerator.

"Happy Birthdaze"

Episode 5. Sigmund secretly cleans the house for the boys on the sheriff's birthday, but Blurp and Slurp mess it up when they kidnap him to clean their cave (they want to impress Big Daddy on his birthday). To rescue Siggy, Johnny and Scott trick the brothers into believing the cave is about to be hit by a tidal wave.

"The Nasty Nephew"

Episode 6. Aunt Zelda's annoying nephew comes to visit and causes nothing but trouble for Johnny and Scott, but he isn't prepared to be terrorized by a family of sea monsters when he wanders into their cave.

"Monster Rock Festival"

Episode 7. Sigmund's family needs him back to help win a Monster Rock Concert, because he is their best singer. But Siggy doesn't want to go.

Meanwhile, the boys win a musical contest, but they can't collect the prize because Siggy can't appear in person to collect it.

"Ghoul School Days"
Episode 8. Blurp and Slurp don't want to go back to ghoul school, but they have been told that one of the Ooze boys will have to attend. So they try to trick Sigmund into taking their place. The boys, meanwhile, neglect their classwork while searching for Siggy.

"The Curfew Shall Ring Tonight"
Episode 9. Sigmund breaks Aunt Zelda's bowl and decides to go home to get money to replace it. That's when the sea monster sheriff catches Sigmund out at night and arrests him for a curfew violation.

"Sweet Mama Redecorates"
Episode 10. Sweet Mama decides to redecorate the sea monsters' cave. But to save money, she performs her cave makeover with furniture stolen from the Stuart home.

"Make Room for Big Daddy"
Episode 11. When Sweet Mama kicks Big Daddy out of the cave, he moves into the club house with Sigmund. Guest star: Margaret Hamilton.

"It's Your Move"
Episode 12. Sigmund's family evacuates the cave for a storm and Sigmund moves home to avoid Johnny and Scott's parents.

"Trick or Treat"
Episode 13. It's Halloween and Sigmund decides to go trick-or-treating with Johnny and Scott. So Siggy disguises himself as a little boy dressed as a sea monster.

"Uncle Siggy Swings"
Episode 14. When Uncle Siggy comes to visit the sea monsters, he finds that Sigmund has left the family. Uncle Siggy goes to the clubhouse after him. That's when he finds Zelda and falls head-over-tentacles in love.

"The Dinosaur Show"
Episode 15. A caveman and his pet dinosaur arrive at the Oozes' cave from the past and sets up housekeeping there, forcing the family to move out.

"The Wild Weekend"
Episode 16. Jack Wild, the movie star, vacations on the beach and meets the kids and Sigmund. Then the Oozes decide to hold him captive.

"Boy for a Day"
Episode 17. First the good news: Sigmund enters a song contest and he wins. Now the bad news: He must appear in person to accept his prize.

"A Genie for Sigmund"
Episode 18. While playing on the beach, Sigmund finds a magic sea shell and gets his very own wacky genie, Sheldon.

"Paul Revere Rides Again"
Episode 19. When everyone disagrees on an issue in history, Sheldon zaps Paul Revere into the club house to settle the issue once and for all.

"Now You See 'Em, Now You Don't"
Episode 20. Sheldon makes Johnny and Scott invisible so they can avoid an old girlfriend. But she turns out to be beautiful and the boys are out of sight. Guest star: Eve Plumb.

"Johnny-O the Great"
Episode 21. Johnny performs a great magic act for Aunt Zelda's bazaar, with the help of Sheldon's talents.

"Super Sigmund"
Episode 22. Sigmund finally gets tired of being mild-mannered and has Sheldon give him super strength that will enable him to get even with Blurp and Slurp.

"Pufnstuf Drops In"
Episode 23. Blurp and Slurp get out of hand, so Sheldon decides to use his magic to help. But he accidentally zaps H.R. Pufnstuf into the club house.

"Sheldon and the Nephew Sitters"

Episode 24. Sheldon must babysit for his young genie nephew Shelby, but he is unable to control the magic brat. He turns to Johnny and Scott for help keeping the youngster occupied.

"One Way Whammy to Tahiti"

Episode 25. Shelby sends Johnny and a girlfriend to Tahiti, but he can't bring them back.

"Cry Uncle"

Episode 26. Zelda must leave town and has a friend take over for her, but the kids and Sigmund prove to be too much to handle.

"The Haunted House"

Episode 27. While Zelda and Sheriff Bevans are at the movies, the Ooze family sneaks into the house. When Zelda and her date returns, they realize the house is haunted by sea monsters.

"Mother Makes Ten"

Episode 28. Shelby's genie mother shows up in time to take care of Blurp and Slurp, who have been kicked out of their cave for bad grades.

"You Can't Beat a Magic Carpet"

Episode 29. Shelby zaps up a magic carpet for Sigmund and they go for a ride, but they get lost.

Land of the Lost

Forty-three episodes. Network broadcast history: September 4, 1974–September 3, 1977 (10 A.M. Saturdays, NBC).

Cast: Spencer Milligan (as Rick Marshall), Wesley Eure (Will Marshall), Kathy Coleman (Holly Marshall), Philip Paley (Cha-Ka), Ron Harper (Uncle Jack Marshall)

Additional cast: Walker Edmiston (Enick), Sharon Baird (Pa), Joe Giamalva (Ta; first season), Scutter McKay (Ta; second season), Jack Tingley (Sleestak), Scott Fullerton (Sleestak), Mike Westra (Sleestak), Dave Greenwood (Sleestak), Bill Laimbeer (Sleestak), John Lambert (Sleestak)

Created by: Sid and Marty Krofft and Allan Foshko

Executive producers: Albert J. Tenzer (first and second seasons), Sid and Marty Krofft (third season)

Producers: Dennis Steinmetz (first season), Sid and Marty Krofft (first and second seasons), Jon Kubichan (third season)

Associate producers: Gene Warren (first season), Tom Swale (second season), Jim Washburn (third season)

Directors: Rick Bennewitz, Robert Lally, Joseph L. Scanlan, Dennis Steinmetz, Gordon Wiles

Story editors: David Gerrold (first season), Dick Morgan (second season), Sam Roeca (third season)

Writers: Margaret Armen, Barry E. Blitzer, Ben Bova, John Cutts, D. C. Fontana, Peter Germano, David Gerrold, Donald F. Glut, James L. Henderson, Bill Keenan, Walter Koenig, Jon Kubichan, Ian Martin, Dick Morgan, Larry Niven, Joyce Perry, Sam Roeca, Norman Spinrad, Greg Strangis, Theodore Sturgeon, Tom Swale

Music: Michael Lloyd for Mike Curb Productions

Art director: Elayne Ceder

Stop-motion animation directed by: Gene Warren

Land of the Lost—The Theme Song

Marshall, Will and Holly, on a routine expedition
Met the greatest earthquake ever known
High on the rapids, it struck their tiny raft
And plunged them down a thousand feet below
To the Land of the Lost

Land of the Lost—The Other Version

Will and Holly Marshall, as the earth beneath them trembled
Lost their father through the door of time

Uncle Jack went searching and found those kids at last
And now they're looking for a way to escape
From the Land of the Lost

"Cha-Ka"
Episode 1. The Marshalls realize this land of dinosaurs in which they have arrived is not of their world. The three moons in the sky are proof of that. While exploring, they discover a race of monkey people, Pakuni, and rescue the littlest one from the T-Rex Holly has named Grumpy. They bring the little Paku, whose name is Cha-Ka, back to their cave to set his fractured leg. Cha-Ka is dazzled by Rick's lighter and steals it, so the Marshalls set out to retrieve it, leading to a confrontation with the Pakuni. But the next morning, the Marshalls find a feast of fruit set out for them, a gift from Cha-Ka, their new friend.

"Dopey"
Episode 2. Will and Holly try to adopt Dopey, a newly hatched brontosaurus. But after several mishaps, they decide the baby dinosaur would be better off in the swamps after all.

"The Sleestak God"
Episode 3. Will and Holly embark on a trip to fill their water jugs and, while taking a shortcut back, discover the ruins of a Lost City. Inside they find a scrawling in English: "Beware the Sleestak." But the warning comes too late. Will and Holly are captured by three Sleestaks, human-like lizard creatures. Cha-Ka leads Rick to the Lost City caves where the kids are being held. The fire from his torch blinds the Sleestaks, allowing Rick enough time to cut Will and Holly free from the net that holds them and make their getaway.

"Downstream"
Episode 4. The Marshall family meets a bearded and ragged Confederate soldier who is searching for diamonds in a bejeweled cavern.

"Skylons"
Episode 5. The action turns colorful and exciting as Rick, Holly and Will find the Land of the Lost has gone insane with wild weather, a multi-colored Sky Snake and a plague of biting white bugs.

"The Stranger"
Episode 6. When a stranger appears claiming to be a forefather of the Sleestaks, the Marshall family fights him over the Majetti (a dimension mechanism) to get back to their respective times. In the end, however, Rick gives the key to escape from Land of the Lost to someone who needs it more.

"Tag Team"
Episode 7. Holly and Will are saved from an attack by a T-Rex and an allosaur through the combined efforts of Rick and the Pakuni.

"The Search"
Episode 8. Will passes up an opportunity to return to Earth, refusing to leave his injured father behind.

"The Paku Who Came to Dinner"
Episode 9. Cha-Ka follows Will and Holly home to their cave and, after smelling Rick's good cooking, he decides to stay permanently.

"Album"
Episode 10. First Will, then Holly and finally Rick fall under the spell of an "emotional vampire trap" laid by the devious Sleestaks.

"Hurricane"
Episode 11. A Texan visits the Land of the Lost, not from the state of Texas but from the new nation of Texas.

"The Hole"
Episode 12. Rick saves the life of a ferocious Sleestak named S'latch, only to have his life saved by S'latch in return.

"Stone Soup"
Episode 13. Rick averts a drought and an energy crisis brought about by the mischievous Pakunis with the gift of a blue jewel.

"The Possession"
Episode 14. A troublesome "baby" computer wreaks havoc until Rick sub-

dues it and spares its life. The Marshalls hope when it matures it will remember them and help them get out of the Land of the Lost.

"Circle"
Episode 15. To maintain the balance in the Land of the Lost, Rick recycles his family photographically through the events that got them there in the first place.

"Follow That Dinosaur"
Episode 16. Is there a hole in the Land of the Lost that leads to New England? That's what parts of a diary the Marshalls uncover may reveal.

"Elsewhen"
Episode 17. Holly's future self, a beautiful woman image who calls herself Rani, appears and gives the young girl the courage she needs to face impossible odds in saving the family from the deadly Sleestak.

"Nice Day"
Episode 18. When Holly is bitten by a toxic plant and drifts into a state of unconsciousness, the Marshalls' medicine fails to revive her and they learn about herbal magic from a medicine man.

"Split Personality"
Episode 19. When an earthquake disrupts the balance of time in the Land of the Lost, the Marshall family meets its counterpart from another dimension.

"The Longest Day"
Episode 20. When a time pylon malfunctions, Rick must consult the Library of Skulls deep in the dangerous Sleestak caves for the secret to fix it.

"Fair Trade"
Episode 21. When the Sleestaks capture Rick as food for their young, Will and Holly must find something to trade for his life.

"Zarn"
Episode 22. The Marshalls encounter a strange, alien energy-being named Zarn who is also trapped in the Land of the Lost.

"Gravity Storm"

Episode 23. In an attempt to escape from the Land of the Lost, Zarn experiments with the gravitational force of the countryside, endangering the lives of all of the creatures there when the force of gravity suddenly triples.

"One of Our Pylons Is Missing"

Episode 24. When Cha-Ka accidentally discovers the main source of power for the Land of the Lost, the pylons, Cha-Ka and the Marshalls almost become fuel for it.

"Tarpit"

Episode 25. Dopey becomes trapped in a tarpit and can only be saved by another dinosaur.

"The Baby Sitter"

Episode 26. Zarn visits Holly while she babysits Cha-Ka and helps her teach him a lesson in self defense.

"The Test"

Episode 27. Cha-Ka must steal a dinosaur egg as a test in the rites of Pakuni manhood.

"Blackout"

Episode 28. The Sleestak use a time pylon to prevent the rising of the sun so they can continue the hunting of their prized Atrusian Moths. But in doing so, they threaten the lives of all in the Land of the Lost.

"Pylon Express"

Episode 29. Rick and Will discover a pylon with a time door to their home. But when they return with Holly, they find they all missed a chance to get home.

"The Musician"

Episode 30. The kids find a new temple, open a secret door and discover a mysterious matrix table. While Holly and Will are out looking for their father, Cha-Ka plays with the matrix and accidentally causes an apparition to appear who bestows the gift of musicianship on Cha-Ka.

"The Repairman"
Episode 31. By manipulating solar-controlled crystals, the Sleestaks cause the Marshalls' water supply to dry up. But with the help of a mysterious solar repairman, ecological harmony is restored.

"After Shock"
Episode 32. A massive earthquake propels Rick back to Earth. Will and Holly are joined by their Uncle Jack, who while searching for the time tunnel on Earth has accidentally fallen into the Land of the Lost.

"Survival Kit"
Episode 33. The "magic" of Jack's flashlight batteries saves the day for the Marshalls, who are held captive by the Sleestaks.

"The Medusa"
Episode 34. Holly is lured into the land of a goddess who possesses the power to turn anything she chooses into stone.

"The Abominable Snowman"
Episode 35. Holly finds a unicorn and promptly makes it a pet, only to be confronted by the unicorn's deadly enemy, the Abominable Snowman.

"The Flying Dutchman"
Episode 36. Cha-Ka's discovery of a ship's spy glass steers the Marshalls into an adventure with a lost sea captain who is alone on his ship. Is this the way out of the Land of the Lost?

"The Hot Air Artist"
Episode 37. A balloonist from the early twentieth century drops in on the Marshalls, who hope to fly with him back to their home. But the balloonist has ideas for Cha-Ka alone.

"The Orb"
Episode 38. The Sleestaks plot to drive the Marshalls from their realm once and for all. When the light from a crystal orb is extinguished, the Marshalls will be doomed.

"The Ancient Guardian"
Episode 39. The Marshalls and Cha-Ka flee from a newly discovered monster, Kona, and come upon a statue of a Sleestak whose eyes contain an advanced form of solar equipment.

"The Medicine Man"
Episode 40. Visitors from the Indians-vs.-the-U.S. Cavalry days drop into the lives of the Marshall family.

"Cornered"
Episode 41. Will and Jack tangle with Torchy, a fire-breathing dinosaur, the most forbidding of the monsters in the Land of the Lost.

"Scarab"
Episode 42. A captured beetle bites Cha-Ka, causing a personality change in the usually gentle but mischievous Paku.

"Time Stop"
Episode 43. The Marshalls find a time plaque that just might provide the key they need to escape from the Land of the Lost. But Torchy's fiery breath welds the plates together and renders the plaque useless.

Far Out Space Nuts

Fifteen episodes. Network broadcast history: September 6, 1975–September 1976 (9 A.M. Saturdays, ABC).

Cast: Bob Denver (as Junior), Chuck McCann (Barney),
    Patty Maloney (Honk)
Executive producers: Sid and Marty Krofft
Producer: Al Schwartz
Associate Producer: Mary Jo Blue
Created by: Sid and Marty Krofft with Earle Doud and Chuck McCann
Directors: Wes Kenney, Claudio Guzman, Walter C. Miller, Al Schwartz
Writers: Buddy Atkinson, Duane Bole, Dick Conway, Earle Doud, Bruce

Howard, Sam Locke, Chuck McCann, Jack Mendelsohn, Ray Parker, Paul Roberts, Dick Robbins
Music: Michael Lloyd for Mike Curb Productions
Art director: Herman Zimmerman

Far Out Space Nuts—The Theme Song

The spaceship was ready to chart the stars
To go where no one's ever gone
Flight preparations were almost made
[Barney]: Breakfast, lunch. I said 'lunch.' Not 'launch.'
Where is the world that they used to know?
And how will they ever return?
Now they got a home where the strangest creatures roam
Honk is there to help them along

Step right up, take a look at the stars
You're leaving the world behind
Step right up, you won't believe your eyes
At what those Far Out Space Nuts find

"It's All in Your Mind"
Episode 1. Junior and Barney land on a planet that is controlled by a massive computer. The computer attempts to absorb their minds. But when it takes on Junior's brain, sparks fly and nothing seems to compute.

"Crystallitis"
Episode 2. Junior and Barney find themselves on a planet inhabited by people made of crystal. When the Crystallites decide to make Junior their new king, he is more than willing. There is a catch, though: He discovers that after one day's reign, Junior will turn into glass. Guest star: John Carradine.

"Robots of Pod"
Episode 3. Junior and Barney must help overthrow the evil ruler of a robot planet and regain the throne for a beautiful princess. To accomplish this mission, the Space Nuts must retrieve the princess' magical power belt.

"Fantastic Journey"

Episode 4. When a mad scientist takes control of a super laboratory, he recruits Junior and Barney as his "genius" assistants. Ultimately, however, all they help accomplish is bungling his nefarious plans.

"Tower of Tagot"

Episode 5. While Junior and Barney are on yet another new planet, the beautiful Queen of the Serrians becomes imprisoned high in the Tower of Tagot. The Space Nuts come to her rescue.

"Secrets of Hexagon"

Episode 6. Junior and Barney get tricked into trading their ship for a mysterious hexagon key that supposedly operates a duplicating machine. The idea is that it can make the Space Nuts a new spaceship to get home.

"Captain Torque, Space Pirate"

Episode 7. Captain Torque, the mad space pirate, seizes Junior and Barney and holds them aboard his spaceship. Then he forces the Space Nuts to rob a museum for their freedom.

"Athlete"

Episode 8. Two strange female creatures mistakenly think they see Junior lifting the space capsule. So they disguise themselves as beautiful women and lure him into challenging the galaxy's athletic champion.

"Vanishing Alien Mystery"

Episode 9. Junior and Barney are forced to land on a station in deep space. While there, they listen in on the reading of a will with several peculiar aliens. But one by one, the aliens disappear, leaving the Space Nuts to solve the mystery.

"Barney Begonia"

Episode 10. An eccentric botanical scientist sends out a mysterious ray that accidentally hits Barney. As a result, he is transformed into a half-man/half-begonia. The mad scientist, Rajac, promises to provide an antidote, but he really plans to dissect him, leaf by leaf, to learn the secret that will produce more like him.

"Three Space Keteers"
Episode 11. Junior decides to run away into the woods, where he meets some alien men who believe him to be their secret leader Junio. Junior goes along with the gag and tries to save their queen from a crystal ball prison. But matters become complicated when the real leader arrives.

"Dangerous Game"
Episode 12. Junior and Barney land on a planet where they encounter a rich lady whose obsession is hunting. She forces the Space Nuts to be her prey and, if they can get away from her, she will help them get off the planet.

"Birds of a Feather"
Episode 13. Junior and Barney arrive on the planet Vultron, inhabited by a race of bird people. The bird people, led by Falko, who anticipates the birth of an heir from the sovereign egg, capture the Space Nuts and force them to sit on the enormous egg until it hatches.

"Flight of the Pippets"
Episode 14. The tiny occupants of a three-foot flying saucer prove dangerous adversaries for Junior when they reduce him to two inches tall with a shrinking ray. The Pippets plan to exhibit their tiny hostage in a jar in their intergalactic museum as part of their menagerie of tiny creatures.

"Destination Earth"
Episode 15. Junior and Barney encounter evil scientists who possess a time machine that can take the Space Nuts back to Earth. But to do so, they must go back through time and relive all their adventures.

The Lost Saucer

Sixteen episodes. Network broadcast history: September 6, 1975–September 4, 1976 (9 A.M. Saturdays, ABC). Episodes were edited for serialized play on *The Krofft Supershow* (1976–77).

Cast: Ruth Buzzi (as Fi), Jim Nabors (Fum), Alice Playten (Alice),
     Jarrod Johnson (Jerry), Larry Larsen (the Dorse)
Created and produced by: Sid and Marty Krofft
Executive producer: Si Rose
Associate producer: Barbara Searles
Developed for television by: Sid and Marty Krofft, Dick Morgan and Si Rose
Directors: Dick Darley, Walter C. Miller, Jack Regas
Writers: Barry E. Blitzer, Fred Fox, John L. Greene, Seaman Jacobs,
     John Fenton Murray, Arthur Phillips, Si Rose
Music: Michael Lloyd

The Lost Saucer—The Theme Song

Out of the sky and out of time
Coming to see all that they can find
Nowhere to go, Fi and Fum
They've been to the moon
Now they've been to the sun

Please, please take me along
Now listen
From the future of time
They came to see
How the world used to be
But something went wrong deep inside
And they can't get off of this crazy ride

Please, please someone help us

Where are we going, in the Lost Saucer
Somebody help us in the Lost Saucer
Where are we going, in the Lost Saucer
Somebody help us in the Lost Saucer
Where are we going, in the Lost Saucer

"894X2RY713, I Love You"
Episode 1. The saucer inhabitants land on a planet that is home to a face-
less society in which everyone must be identified by number only. The

children are arrested on a 9-9-9 (facial exposure), and come to trial before a computer judge.

"The Tiny Years"

Episode 2. The saucer inhabitants land on a planet where everything, including people, has been miniaturized because the "biggies" of eras past wasted so much of the world's resources that scientists turn to molecular cell reduction to conserve energy, food and space. Guest star: Gordon Jump.

"My Fair Robot"

Episode 3. When the saucer inhabitants land in a time of simpler robots, Fi and Fum come to the aid of a clumsy robot who has fled his human masters after learning they plan to recycle him. Fi and Fum tutor him in proper robot behavior. Guest star: Richard Deacon.

"Transylvania 2300"

Episode 4. In Transylvania in the year 2300, Alice and Jerry seek aid from Dr. Frankenstein XIII, who lives in an eerie castle, when a space storm forces the saucer to land and incapacitates Fi and Fum. Dr. Frankenstein reprograms Fi and Fum to be his slaves. Guest star: Billy Barty.

"Beautiful Downtown Atlantis"

Episode 5. Jerry, Alice, Fi and Fum come down to visit the undersea city of Atlantis, where King Neptune decides to hold them and use their saucer for a big television show.

"Where Did Everybody Go?"

Episode 6. The saucer inhabitants must contend with the forces of invisibility when they arrive at a place where people, cities and even the saucer disappear at strategic moments. Fi and Fum must escape from an invisible jail in which they can't even find the unseen door.

"Get a Dorse"

Episode 7. The saucer inhabitants land in a time when the entire world is suffering from a massive power shortage and all machines are outlawed. This clearly makes the Dorse a very valuable commodity.

"Androids Come Home"

Episode 8. When Fi and Fum are unexpectedly summoned to return to their home base by their manufacturer, they are in trouble for breaking the rule that states there are to be no passengers or hitchhikers aboard their saucer. As a result, Fi and Fum are almost put out to pasture.

"Valley of the Chickaphants"

Episode 9. The saucer returns to Earth but in a time that is very different from what Alice and Jerry remember. There, the saucer inhabitants encounter cavemen and a strange creature that is part chicken, part elephant.

"Return to the Valley of the Chickaphants"

Episode 10. When the saucer inhabitants visit the prehistoric land where the hybrid chicken-elephant creature lives, the Dorse brings aboard a chickaphant egg that soon hatches. Fi finds a mother for the orphan chickaphant by pretending to be a baby chickaphant herself.

"The Laughing Years"

Episode 11. The saucer lands on Earth in the year 2180 and the inhabitants encounter a society in which everyone is always happy and giggling. It seems that every home and office is equipped with an ionator to impart positive charges that make all citizens gleeful, even when things go wrong. Trouble ensues when a malfunction prevents Fi from laughing.

"Fat Is Beautiful"

Episode 12. The saucer inhabitants run into trouble when they visit a community called Fatopolis, in which everyone is obese and where work and exercise have been outlawed. Fum gets caught doing some work and fights with an inferior robot until the power supply is cut off.

"Planet of the Lookalikes"

Episode 13. While tooling along through space, the saucer is pulled over by a space cop. Fi and Fum go to space traffic court when ticketed by the Spaceway Patrol. While there, they discover that everyone is a duplicate of the city's crazy president.

"Fi Am Woman"

Episode 14. When Fum wanders into the jungle after hitting his head and losing his memory, he finds a huge power plant operated by a beautiful modern android. He falls in love with her and decides to run away with her.

"Polka Dot Years"

Episode 15. Fi and Fum, working to earn money to buy parts for their crippled saucer, encounter prejudice in the twenty-sixth century because they do not have polka dots.

"Land of the Talking Plants"

Episode 16. While searching for food, the saucer lands on a planet inhabited by talking plants and their faithful gardener. Guest star: John Fiedler.

ElectraWoman and DynaGirl

Eight episodes (one of the serialized installments during the first season of *The Krofft Supershow*). September 11, 1976–September 1977.

Cast: Deidre Hall (as Lori/ElectraWoman), Judy Strangis (Judy/DynaGirl), Norman Alden (Frank Heflin)
Narrator: Marvin Miller
Executive producers: Sid and Marty Krofft
Producer: Walter C. Miller
Directors: Chuck Liotta, Walter C. Miller, Jack Regas
Writers: Gerry Day, Bethel Leslie, Duane Poole, Dick Robbins, Greg Strangis
Created by: Joe Ruby and Ken Spears
Developed for television by: Dick Robbins and Duane Poole

ElectraWoman and DynaGirl—The Theme Song

ElectraWoman and DynaGirl
Fighting all evil deeds
Each writes for a magazine
Hiding the life she leads

ElectraWoman and DynaGirl
Summoned to ElectraBase
By the ElectraComps they wear
Lori and Judy dare to face
Any criminal anywhere
ElectraWoman and DynaGirl

"The Sorcerer's Golden Trick"
Episode 1. After breaking out of prison, the Sorcerer, the world's notorious criminal, plots to rob Fort Knox of all its gold bars. Using a hypnotic spell caster, the Sorcerer and his sidekick, Miss Dazzle, put their scheme into action. But ElectraWoman and DynaGirl stand in the Sorcerer's way. Guest star: Michael Constantine (Judy Strangis' former *Room 222* costar).

"Glitter Rock"
Episode 2. A diabolical rock star attempts to take over the world with his mesmerizing music. But first he kidnaps a visiting prince who has a royal jewel that he needs to complete his musical satellite.

"The Empress of Evil"
Episode 3. Frank is startled when the Empress of Evil appears next to him in the ElectraBase and demands that he summon ElectraWoman and DynaGirl to make a big announcement: that she and her evil partner, the spiteful Lucretia, are going to rule the world. ElectraWoman tries to rescue DynaGirl from the Empress' clutches but finds herself caught in a trap that is being lowered into a cauldron. Guest star: Claudette Nevins.

"Ali Baba"
Episode 4. When the villainous Ali Baba captures a noted Russian scientist and his top-secret formula that alters personalities, Ali Baba uses the formula to transform DynaGirl into his slave—and ElectraWoman's enemy.

"Return of the Sorcerer"
Episode 5. Once again, the most treacherous criminal on Earth, the Sorcerer, matches brains and powers with ElectraWoman and DynaGirl, who vow to bring the master criminal to justice.

"The Pharaoh"

Episode 6. When the greedy, gruesome Pharaoh steals a powerful pyramid prism from the town museum to take over the world, ElectraWoman and DynaGirl are quick to confront the threat.

"The Spider Lady"

Episode 7. The arch criminal mistress of devious disguise, the Spider Lady, plans to steal a priceless golden icon and destroy CrimeBase in the process. But our superheroines blast their Electra X Beam to smash her wicked web of crime.

"Return of the Pharaoh"

Episode 8. The nefarious Pharaoh, an old foe of our crime-fighting heroines, robs the Coptic Eye to seize the world. He also hypnotizes ElectraWoman into fighting with DynaGirl.

Dr. Shrinker

Sixteen 15-minute episodes (one of the serialized installments during the first season of *The Krofft Supershow*). September 11, 1976–September 1977.

Cast: Jay Robinson (as Dr. Shrinker), Billy Barty (Hugo), Ted Eccles (Brad),
    Jeff MacKay (Gordie), Susan Lawrence (B. J.)
Created and produced by: Sid and Marty Krofft
Developed for television by: Si Rose
Produced by: Jack Regas
Directors: Jack Regas, William Hobin, Robert Lalley
Writers: Donald R. Boyle, Ed Jurist, Bernie Kahn, Leo Rifkin, Si Rose,
    Greg Strangis
Music: Jimmy Haskell

Dr. Shrinker—The Theme Song

Dr. Shrinker, Dr. Shrinker, he's a madman with an evil mind
Dr. Shrinker, Dr. Shrinker, he's as crazy as you'll ever find

Crashed upon the doctor's isle
Shrinkies are shrunken by laser ray
Will they always be so small?
Will they be lucky and get away?
Dr. Shrinker, Dr. Shrinker, he's a madman with an evil mind
Dr. Shrinker, Dr. Shrinker, he's as crazy as you'll ever find
Dr. Shrinker!

"Pardon Me, King Kong, But Is That You?"
Episode 1. Dr. Shrinker sends a clever chimpanzee named Boris to capture Brad, B. J. and Gordie. But after the chimp abducts B. J., the boys set out to rescue her and the doctor's plan goes awry as the monkey jumps on the shrinking ray machine and wrecks it.

"The Other Brad"
Episode 2. Dr. Shrinker and his sidekick Hugo plot to capture the elusive Shrinkies by creating a robot duplicate of Brad, but the Shrinkies turn the tables on Shrinker by having Brad impersonate the robot.

"The Shake Up"
Episode 3. Dr. Shrinker's latest concoction causes earthquakes and he uses it to shake up some tumbling trouble for Brad, B. J. and Gordie and force them back to his laboratory. But instead he triggers the eruption of a volcano and needs the help of the Shrinkies to stop it and save the island from certain destruction.

"The Shrinkie Sale"
Episode 4. Tiny Brad, B. J. and Gordie must stop Benny Bandini, the notorious millionaire magician, from buying Dr. Shrinker's infamous Shrinking Ray and taking away their only hope of returning to normal size.

"The Sands Document"
Episodes 5&6 (two parts). When a U.S. government undercover agent carrying a top-secret document crash lands on Dr. Shrinker's island, he joins the Shrinkies in a struggle against the doctor to keep the confidential paper out of enemy hands.

"Dr. Shrinker Shrinks"
Episode 7. After failing to capture the Shrinkies once again, Dr. Shrinker instructs Hugo to shrink him in an attempt to lure the kids into a trap. But the doctor's plan goes awry when Hugo, who likes being the biggest person on the island for a change, deviates from the plan, giving Dr. Shrinker a taste of his own medicine.

"Don't Hold Your Breath"
Episode 8. After the tricky Dr. Shrinker invents a raspberry containing a homing device to nab the Shrinkies, Brad, B. J. and Gordie thwart his plans with the aid of a jungle berry that makes them invisible.

"Slowly I Turn"
Episode 9. When the deranged doctor desperately concludes the only way he will catch a Shrinkie is to unshrink one, klutzy "unshrunken" Gordie suffers amnesia and is tricked by Hugo to help grab Brad and B. J.

"Gordie's Bird"
Episode 10. Gordie is spirited away by a huge bird to its nest at the top of a tree. Dr. Shrinker captures B. J. and Brad as they attempt to rescue Gordie. Their second rescue attempt involves a small helium balloon and a chainsaw.

"The Sacred Idol"
Episode 11. While Dr. Shrinker pretends to be the Wise One and turns island natives against the chief, the Shrinkies embark to prove the doctor is a phony and also to return a stolen emerald to Mahari, the sacred idol.

"Brain Storm"
Episode 12. Brad, B. J. and Gordie scheme to boobytrap the island's main booby, Dr. Shrinker. But the scientist's newest creation, the Solar Energizer, stands in the way.

"The Wild Boy"
Episode 13. When Dr. Shrinker captures a wild boy raised by jungle animals and plans to make him a circus attraction, the Shrinkies show the scientist who is the real clown.

"Treasure of the Deep"
Episode 14. Treasure-thirsty thieves, stolen gold doubloons, kidnapped Shrinkies and a monstrous monsoon weave Dr. Shrinker and the little folks in a sticky web of intrigue.

"The Splotcharia Epidemic"
Episode 15. Always a double-dose of trouble, Dr. Shrinker tricks the Shrinkies into helping him wipe out a dreaded tropical disease plaguing the island.

"The Little Prince"
Episode 16. Kind Prince Tim from a neighboring island struggles to force Dr. Shrinker to restore mini-Brad, B. J. and Gordie to normal size. But a power-hungry prime minister has other plans for them.

Wonderbug

Twenty-two 15-minute episodes (one of the serialized installments of *The Krofft Supershow*). September 11, 1976–September 2, 1978.

Cast: David Levy (as Barry Buntrock), Carol Anne Seflinger (Susan), John Anthony Bailey (C. C.), Frank Welker (voice of Wonderbug)
Executive producers: Sid and Marty Krofft
Produced by: Al Schwartz
Created by: Joe Ruby, Ken Spears
Directors: Art Fisher, Bob LaHendro, Rick Locke, Jack Regas, Al Schwartz
Writers: Jim Brochu, Earle Doud, Mark Fink, Fred Fox, Seaman Jacobs, Lee Maddux, Chuck McCann, Jack Mendelsohn, Duane Poole, Dick Robbins

Wonderbug—The Theme Song

Sittin' in a junkyard
Waitin' to be ground up is a pile of cars

Lookin' for an old car
Found a funny Schlepcar
Let's make him ours
Found a magic horn
A new car was born
The toughest of the toughest, super car

Wonderbug
Wonderbug
Wonderbug
Wonderbug
Faster than fast, smarter than smart, Wonderbug

When you hear the horn, help is on the way
So clap your hands, hip hip hooray!
For the Wonderbug, the wonderful Wonderbug!

"Go West, Young Schlepcar"
Episode 1. The kids become stranded in a western ghost town apparently haunted by a gunfighter's ghost. Undaunted, they investigate and find car thieves in one of the buildings preparing a stolen car for sale. Using Wonderbug's magic powers, they detain the bad guys for the authorities.

"Schlepnapped"
Episode 2. When the kids stumble upon a man who is being mugged, they corral the crooks with the help of their special car. But it is a ruse: The bad guys follow the kids to a hamburger stand and steal Schlepcar, then use hypnosis to get the car to commit crimes. Guest star: Avery Schreiber.

"I Kidd You Not"
Episode 3. An old woman prospector at the beach finds a treasure map to Captain Kidd's buried treasure. But when she stumbles and drops it, the wind carries it off to Susan, who also drops it, losing it to bad guys dressed in scuba gear. The kids and Wonderbug rescue the lady prospector, who has fallen part way down a cliff, and then help her recover her treasure map. Guest star: Billie Hayes.

"Keep on Schleppin'"
Episode 4. Barry, Susan and C. C. stumble upon fur thieves, but they are caught and locked in a deserted gas station. But once free, the tenacious teens set a trap at a roadside diner, hoping to capture the thieves and their boss with the stolen furs.

"Maltese Gooneybird"
Episode 5. Susan collides with a sinister-looking patron as she leaves the post office and accidentally picks up the wrong package. The kids discover the switch and find a microfilm canister inside the Maltese Gooneybird statue. C. C. hides the microfilm in Schlepcar's magic horn, but the crooks see this and steal the horn and head for the airport. But the kids recover the horn so Wonderbug can save the day.

"Anderson Android"
Episode 6. A crazed inventor, living in an abandoned amusement park, schemes to learn Wonderbug's secret so he can fine-tune his android creations.

"The Wonderbug Express"
Episode 7. By trying to help some down-and-out hobos at a deserted railroad station, the Wonderbug bunch becomes entangled in a counterfeiting scheme.

"Schlepfoot"
Episode 8. When trouble is afoot for Schlepcar, Wonderbug keeps Barry, Susan and C. C. on their toes after some nasty criminals.

"Schlep O'Clock Rock"
Episode 9. A mean motorcycle gang, the Red Vultures, tricks the lonely son of a factory owner into heisting his father's platinum. But the Wonderbug gang, disguised as '50s rock-'n'-rollers, comes to the rescue.

"The Big Bink Bank Bungle"
Episode 10. When devious criminals plot to rob a bank, Barry, Susan and C. C. drive onto the scene with Wonderbug to shatter their evil scheme.

"14-Karat Wonderbug"
Episode 11. Shaky Schlepcar is mistaken for another heap being used to smuggle gold into the country. So Wonderbug charges into high hear to put the crooks behind prison bars.

"Horse Switched"
Episode 12. When a couple of crooked cowboys set out to rig a horse show, the Wonderbug gang are hot on their trail to lasso the bad guys and put them in the pokey.

"Schleppenstein"
Episode 13. When worn-out Schlepcar runs head on into some ghoulish trouble, Wonderbug and the gang—disguised as monsters (Barry as Frankenstein, Susan as a vampire and C. C. as a wolfman)—race to end the monstrous mischief.

"No Foe Like a UFO"
Episode 14. Flying saucers and sneaky hoodlums entwine Barry, Susan and C. C. in a frightening fiasco until Wonderbug lands to smooth things out.

"The Not So Great Race"
Episode 15. Some shrewd thugs ruin a girl's car entered in a cross-country race, but Wonderbug fills in to win the race and collect enough cash to save a bankrupt orphanage.

"Lights, Camera, Wonderbug!"
Episode 16. Pretending to be movie producers, bunco artists con starstruck Barry, Susan and C. C. into stealing an actress's diamonds. But the kids quickly learn of their mistake and steer Wonderbug straight to the crooks and the stolen jewels.

"The Big Game"
Episode 17. As two tight-fisted gangsters plan to disrupt a benefit baseball game by kidnapping an All-Star, Wonderbug and the gang pitch in to strike out the crooks and save a penny-pinched orphanage. Guest stars: Casey Kasem, Don Sutton.

"The Case of the Misfortune Cookie"

Episode 18. When dastardly Duke Miller escapes from prison, he plots to steal the solid-gold Peking Duck. But the Wonderbug crew uses disguise and cunning to cook this turkey's goose.

"Dirty Larry, Crazy Barry"

Episode 19. Greedy criminals pursue Barry's lookalike cousin, an ESP genius, to force him to pick all the winning horses at the track. But Barry and the gang intervene, seeing to it that the culprits finish last.

"Fish Story"

Episode 20. After two thieves rip off a Dolphin Decoder, Barry, Susan and C. C. soon smell something fishy. The trio wind up caught in a den of jewel thieves until Wonderbug fishes them out.

"Oil or Nothing"

Episode 21. When a slick banker gone bad attempts to swindle an unsuspecting inheritor of an oil well, Wonderbug and his comrades step in to slip up his vicious plans.

"The Incredible Shrinking Wonderbug"

Episode 22. Soon after a group of car thieves uses a shrinking device to rip off autos, Barry, Susan and C. C. spin into action behind the wheel of Wonderbug to keep the robbers out of action.

Magic Mongo

Sixteen 15-minute episodes (one of the serialized installments during the second season of *The Krofft Supershow*). September 1977–September 2, 1978.

Cast: Lennie Weinrib (as Magic Mongo), Helaine Lembeck (Loraine), Robin Dearden (Kristy), Paul Hinckley (Donald), Bart Braverman (Ace), Larry Larsen (Duncey), Sab Shimondo (Huli)

Executive producers: Sid and Marty Krofft
Produced by: Jack Regas
Associate producer: Jim Washburn
Created by: Joe Ruby, Ken Spears
Directors: Bill Foster, Harvey Lembeck, Jack Regas
Writers: Fred Fox, Seaman Jacobs, Barbara Tibbles, Doug Tibbles,
    Yvette Weinberger

Magic Mongo —The Theme Song

Walkin' on the beach, having a real good time
Found an old bottle, didn't seem much of a find
What a surprise
In front of our eyes
Who conjures up?

That's our Magic Mongo
You're a genie indeed
Magic Mongo
The only friend that we'll ever need

Magic Mongo
You're a genie indeed
Magic Mongo
The only friend that we'll ever need

"Zap, You're in Love"
Episode 1. Donald asks Mongo to help him in his quest for romance with
a pretty girl who won't give him the time of day. But when Mongo casts a
love spell to make her fall in love with the first person she sees, his spell
hits Loraine instead, who falls hopelessly in love with Ace.

"The Surfing Contest"
Episodes 2&3. When Kristy is chosen to be Queen of the Surf and will get
a date with the winner of a surfing contest, Donald is determined to win
the contest.

"Teenage Werewolf"

Episode 4. Donald and the girls have to rough it on a wilderness weekend so they can pass a class at school. But Ace and Duncey insist on sabotaging their efforts, ultimately hatching a scheme to scare them by making them believe a werewolf is on the loose. Mongo turns the tables on Ace and Duncey, however, by turning Donald into a werewolf.

"Who's Got the Mongo?"

Episode 5. When Ace's sidekick Duncey witnesses Mongo's magical power, he tells Ace, who decides he should have the genie. Then Donald and the girls figure out a way to get Mongo back.

"Hermie the Frog"

Episode 6. When Donald volunteers for babysitting duty for his teacher, Mongo turns the kid into a frog. To make matters worse, the frog promptly hops away.

"You Gotta Be a Football Hero"

Episode 7. When a prank sidelines the high school team's star wide receiver, the coach names Donald the team's secret weapon. The real secret weapon, of course, is Mongo.

"Huli's Vacation"

Episode 8. Donald, Kristy and Loraine watch Huli's hotdog hut while he goes on vacation. Ace and Duncey pose as armored truck guards and rob the hut. Enlisting the help of Mongo, they track down the bad guys.

"The Kissing Bandit"

Episode 9. A case of some stolen kisses and a little misdirected Mongo magic mean trouble for Donald and the girls.

"You've Come a Long Way, Baby"

Episode 10. Mongo zaps Donald out of the way of Ace's fist, only to find that the teens and the genie are not so safe a million years in the past...and about to be trampled by a dinosaur.

"The Big Switch"

Episode 11. Mongo manages to swap Ace's personality with mild-mannered Donald's. Donald beats up Ace and even challenges Ace to a boxing match.

"The Cluck Star"

Episode 12. When the kids visit a school friend who has become a rock star, they find unscrupulous promoters want him to perform even though he has laryngitis. Mongo's help only makes matters worse.

"Two Faces of Donald"

Episode 13. When Donald finds himself going out with Lola, the girlfriend of muscleman Rocky, he turns to Mongo for help. His genie gives him the power to change from boy to girl at a snap of his fingers. The result: Donald is now dating Lola and Rocky.

"Musical Magic"

Episode 14. Nashville, from the rock band Kaptain Kool and the Kongs, blows a tire and soon is sorry she ever met the gang on the beach when Mongo's magical powers end up in Nashville. Guest star: Louise DuArt.

"The Heist"

Episode 15. When Donald's van runs out of gas, Mongo accidentally swaps the gas can for a briefcase full of stolen money. The robbers hold Kristy hostage until the gang brings the crooks all of the gold in the Santa Monica Mint.

"That Old Mongo Magic"

Episode 16. Ace and Duncey have entered the same talent show Donald and the girls are in. Ace plans to cheat to win the final audition. As usual, Mongo's magic creates more problems for the kids than it solves.

Bigfoot and Wildboy

Twenty episodes (one of the serialized installments during the second season of *The Krofft Supershow*). September 1977–September 2, 1978; also: June 2, 1979–August 18, 1979 (ABC).

Cast: Ray Young (as Bigfoot), Joseph Butcher (Wildboy),
    Monika Ramirez (Suzie), Yvonne Regalado (Cindy)
Executive producers: Sid and Marty Krofft
Producer: Arthur McLaird
Created by: Joe Ruby, Ken Spears
Directors: Leslie H. Martinson, Irving J. Moore, Charles Rondeau, Gordon
    Wiles
Writers: Donald R. Boyle, Joe Ruby, Ken Spears

Bigfoot and Wildboy—The Opening Narration

Out of the Great Northwest comes the legendary Bigfoot
who, eight years ago, saved a young child lost in the vast wilderness
and raised that child until he grew up to be Wildboy...

"Sonic Projector"
Episode 1. The U.S. Army uses the forest to test its latest military defense weapon, a sonic projector that can make other weapons disappear. The test proves a rousing success and the military officials are overjoyed until a Bigfoot impostor absconds with the valuable hardware. Bigfoot and Wildboy attempt to capture the real bandits and recover the defense system while avoiding arrest by the Army personnel who believe they are the thieves.

"Black Box"
Episode 2. When the Army tests a new weapon, bad guys steal it by using a scheme that involves impersonating Bigfoot. But the real Bigfoot comes to the rescue to return the weapon to the rightful owner.

"Abominable Snowman"
Episode 3. Bigfoot and Wildboy must battle and defeat a robotic simulation of the legendary Abominable Snowman before they can stop the evil Dr. Pathos from gaining dominion over the Earth's weather.

"UFO"
Episode 4. Evil aliens in a flying saucer land on Earth to mine crystals that will help them conquer the galaxy, but they need human slaves to retrieve the needed material from the bottom of a lake. They capture many humans, including the forest ranger and Wildboy. But Suzie and Bigfoot free their friends and send the aliens packing with sacks of rocks.

"The White Wolf"
Episode 5. A scientist develops a formula that changes an old tame wolf into a snarling monster—and a human attacked by the wolf is transformed into a super powerful match for Bigfoot. Guest star: Christopher Knight.

"Amazon Contest"
Episode 6. An evil queen from the future comes to the present to fight for possession of a royal scepter. Bigfoot is chosen as her foe's champion.

"Secret Monolith"
Episode 7. When a plane crashes nearby, Bigfoot and Wildboy find a young woman who is searching for her missing father. Mysterious things happen to them when they help her in her search.

"The Trappers"
Episode 8. Poachers have a device that makes animals vanish and transports endangered species to unscrupulous clients. They leave a rare lion behind and try to catch the one and only Wildboy.

"The Space Prisoner"
Episode 9. When two scientists try to become the first humans to make contact with an authentic UFO, they encounter an alien being, Lotar-4, with the power to dominate and control humans. A criminal newly released from prison on the planet Liberon, Lotar-4 schemes to make Earth

the base for his empire. Bigfoot and Wildboy must recapture the cosmic criminal before he regenerates his forces at the nearby power plant and becomes an invincible interplanetary monster.

"The Secret Invasion"
Episode 10. Bigfoot meets his arch-enemies, the treacherous Lohr-Khan tribe, as they prepare to use their powers to conquer all humans. Hidden and thriving in the dark, deserted tunnels of a forgotten mine, the Lohr-Khan soon trap Cindy and her archaeology professor. Wildboy and Bigfoot battle against ugly odds to save them and also to stop the deadly Lohr-Khan creatures from contaminating the community water supply with Lohr-Khan enzymes. Guest star: Richard Moll.

"The Outlaw Bigfoot"
Episode 11. A diabolic professor and his demonic assistant concoct a deadly laser projector. But they need a vital plutonium power element before the laser becomes effective. To obtain the plutonium, the cunning pair kidnap Wildboy and Cindy through clever trickery and force an outraged Bigfoot to do their wicked bidding: robbing an armored truck of the priceless plutonium.

"The Eye of the Mummy"
Episode 12. After a petty thug and an outrageous scientist hijack some priceless museum artifacts, the scientist schemes to hold the city hostage by bringing an ancient Egyptian mummy back to life to terrorize the town. But to fulfill his dark desires, the evil Dr. Zorkin must have control of a magic ruby. His greedy partner in crime has other plans for the giant gem. When trouble flares up, Bigfoot and Wildboy are soon hot on the crooks' trail and run face to face into a living, monstrous mummy.

"Birth of the Titan"
Episode 13. In an attempt to prove the dangers of power plants to the government, two college students plot to steal plutonium and build an atomic bomb. But when one of them actually touches the plutonium, he is transformed into a vicious, fiendish Titan of uncontrollable rage and power. When one of the students captures Wildboy, it's Bigfoot and Cindy to the rescue in a battle of wits and powers.

"Spy from the Sky"

Episode 14. After a huge, mysterious satellite crash-lands on Earth, a couple of foreign agents disguised as backpackers in the mountains are fast on the site. It seems the film hidden inside the satellite will prove their country was spying on the missile defenses of the United States. Bigfoot, Wildboy and Cindy must reach the film before the enemy agents and before the leaking nuclear material inside the satellite explodes and destroys the entire area.

"The Other Bigfoot"

Episode 15. When a hairy, monstrous beast resembling Bigfoot launches a campaign of terror and havoc inside the community, the police mistake the real Bigfoot as the giant attacking local farms and citizens. The other Bigfoot soon captures Cindy while Wildboy and the real Bigfoot step into action to save her and drive the unwelcome beast out of their territory.

"Earthquake"

Episode 16. While Bigfoot and Wildboy help Cindy search for lost Indian relics among the rugged mountains, the trio uncovers more than expected: two criminals plot to extort millions of dollars from the government. Using electronics and ultrapowerful generators, the ruthless pair have developed the means to cause devastating earthquakes. And they vow to destroy the country if Uncle Sam doesn't pay up.

"Return of the Vampire"

Episode 17. When treasure hunters use explosives to unearth golden treasures, they dig up more than they bargained for: the Countess, a beautiful, fierce female vampire. She makes the prospectors her slaves and plots to recruit others into her hateful coven of evil. The Countess sets out to destroy Bigfoot and makes Cindy one of her slaves. Wildboy must survive the attempts to destroy him and rescue his friends.

"Bigfoot vs. Wildboy"

Episode 18. Confusion, chaos and crime invade the calm existence of Bigfoot and Wildboy when a notorious professor of electronics creates a super-powerful robot that is an exact duplicate of Wildboy. When the evil scientist uses his robot to rob a goldmining and refining company, Bigfoot, Cindy and the police struggle to find the real Wildboy and to destroy the mighty robot double's reign of crime and terror.

"The Wildgirl"
Episode 19. When enemy spies set out to destroy a defensive missile base, they intend to leave the city completely defenseless against a fast-approaching attack rocket programmed to destroy. Bigfoot and Wildboy leap into action to upset their wicked plans. But the arrival of an unknown "wildgirl" and the kidnapping of their friend Cindy makes Bigfoot and Wildboy's struggle a grueling battle of forces. Guest star: Lana Wood.

"The Meteor Menace"
Episode 20. A gigantic meteor aimed at the western part of the United States crashes into the mountainous wilderness. Embodied in the meteor is an evil, alien presence—a force from outer space with the power to control humans—and a plot to conquer the plant. But to achieve its goal, the meteor monster needs the Tiranium Petroxide in the nearby mines. When Bigfoot and Wildboy step into the picture, they struggle to foul up the alien's foul plans. Guest star: Robin Dearden.

Pryor's Place

Thirteen episodes. September 22, 1984–June 15, 1985.

Cast: Richard Pryor (as Richard Pryor and various characters),
    Akili Prince (Little Richard Pryor), Cliffy Magee (Wally), Danny Nucci
    (Freddy), Tony Cox (Allen), Keland Love (Meatrack)
Created and produced by: Sid and Marty Krofft

"High Noon at 5:30 p.m."
Episode 1. A bully challenges young Richard Pryor to a fight. As Richie tries to come to terms with his fate, his friends offer him advice. He ultimately finds his own course to be a winner.

"To Catch a Little Thief"
Episodes 2. Little Richard Pryor sees a beautiful brand new basketball in a store window. He does not have the money for it, so he steals it. He finds things do not work out the way he expects, including being recruited into the world of "thiefdom" by Smooth Sam. Guest star: Sammy Davis Jr.

"Love Means Never Being Sorry You Didn't Say It"
Episodes 3. Richie is in love for the first time, but he can't bring himself to tell the girl. He gets advice for the love-lorn from the strangest people. He finally musters enough courage to tell her. But where is she?

"Voyage to the Planet of the Dumb"
Episode 4. Who needs school? Some cool kids play hooky and take Rich with them. But a special game at the arcade gives them food for thought. Guest stars: Pat Morita, Pat McCormick.

"Close Encounters of the Ralph Kind"
Episode 5. Under the influence of a horror movie, Richard believes he found a space creature in an alley. But no one believes him. So he learns to recognize the difference between imagination and reality.

"Sax Education"
Episode 6. Chills, the street musician, asks Richie to take good care of his prized saxophone. But he loses it. Richie spots a saxophone in a pawn shop and, believing it to be Chills's, attempts to raise enough money to recover it. Guest stars: Robin Williams, Shirley Hemphill, Rip Taylor, Ron Cey.

"Readers of the Lost Art"
Episode 7. Richie's class is assigned to read Mark Twain's *Tom Sawyer,* but Richie and his friend Wally find better things to do. Then, with the book report due in two days, the two are desperate to complete the assignment, yet they still do not feel they have the time or the inclination to read the book.

"Divorce, Children's Style"
Episode 8. Wally finds out his parents are getting divorced and he is so

upset he runs away from home that very night. Richie sticks by his best friend and goes with him and the talk to Chills, who is playing sax on the street corner. Can Chills talk some sense into the boys? Guest star: California Supreme Court Chief Justice Rose Bird.

"Kimosabe Blues"
Episode 9. Richie and Wally swear to be friends forever, but something comes between them. It comes to a head during their science report. Will they be able to patch things up?

"The Show Off"
Episode 10. When Richie is caught cutting up in class, he is sentenced to three weeks' detention or playing Romeo in the school play. It's a toss-up, but Shakespeare wins out. Then Richie seeks help dealing with the terror of stage fright. Guest stars: Willie Nelson, John Ritter, Ray Parker Jr.

"Cousin Rita"
Episode 11. Wally, age ten, develops a crush on Richie's seventeen-year-old cousin Rita. Once again, Richie makes the rounds of the colorful characters who make up his neighborhood looking for advice. In the meantime, Wally imagines he is driving his girlfriend around in a car. Guest stars: Lily Tomlin, Kim Fields.

"Home Free"
Episode 12. While Henry Winkler teaches the neighborhood kids to say "no" to bad strangers, one of the girls runs off, leaving a doll behind. Richie finds her so he can return the doll. But she doesn't want it and won't say why until he is sworn to secrecy.

"Too Old Too Soon, Too Smart Too Late"
Episode 13. Richie grumbles at having to spend his Saturdays with old Uncle Mose. But he learns to respect his uncle when Mose beats basketball great Kareem Abdul-Jabbar in a game of one-on-one. Guest star: Scatman Crothers.

Land of the Lost (the new series)

Twenty-six episodes. September 7, 1991–September 3, 1994.

Cast: Timothy Bottoms (as Tom Porter), Jennifer Drugan (Annie Mary Porter),
    Robert Gavin (Kevin Porter), Shannon Day (Christa, the jungle girl),
    Ed Gale (Tasha), Bobby Porter (Stink), Danny Mann (voice of Tasha),
    Tom Allard (Shung)
Created by: Sid and Marty Krofft
Directors: John Carl Buechler, Anthony Bona, Jeff Burr, Len Janson,
    Frank De Palma, Ernest Farino, John Strysik, Gabe Torres
Writers: Phil Combest, Jules Dennis, Janis Diamond, Len Janson,
    Chuck Menville, Richard Mueller, Gary Perconte, Michele Rifkin,
    Marianne Sellek, Reed Shelly
Music: Kevin Kiner

"Tasha"
Episode 1. Kevin and Annie find an abandoned dinosaur egg, which Annie
brings home. A tyrannosaurus rex terrorizes the tree house compound and
almost eats Tom. When the egg hatches, Annie names the baby dino
Tasha. It is little Tasha that inspires Kevin on how to chase away the T-Rex.

"Something's Watching"
Episode 2. Tom believes there might be other people in the Land of the
Lost, so the Porters search for them. In the process, Tom is bitten by a poi-
sonous lizard. Christa, the jungle girl, and Stink, the Pakuni monkey boy,
emerge from the foliage to help find an antidote to save Tom.

"Jungle Girl"
Episode 3. Tom is obsessed with finding the elusive jungle girl. The Porters
locate her cave, but Christa is very wary. Matters are complicated by a rare
confluence of the triple moons, which causes all the animals, including
Tasha, to become dangerous. The Porters ultimately learn that Christa also
comes from twentieth-century America.

"Shung, the Terrible"
Episode 4. The Porters embark on a scouting expedition in the truck to find a way out of the Land of the Lost. But the truck, with Tasha asleep in the back, is stolen by Sleestaks, taken to their cave and presented to their leader, Shung.

"The Crystal"
Episode 5. When Shung loses his power crystal, Annie comes into possession of it. The crystal gives her powers she never dreamed of. But its evil nature is slowly changing her for the worse. Annie ultimately realizes her family loves her just as she is, without the aid of the crystal and, after defeating Shung, she throws it away.

"Wild Thing"
Episode 6. Tom decides Tasha belongs in the jungle, so Annie reluctantly leads Tasha away. Things don't go easily for the little dino and she has several close calls. But when the Porters change their minds and go looking for her, they find she has learned how to cope and are relieved to know she will do fine when it does come time for her to leave.

"Kevin vs. the Volcano"
Episode 7. When a volcano erupts, Tom assigns duties to everyone, then leaves in the truck with Christa to create a lava dam. Kevin, who resents being stuck near home with a menial task, deserts Annie, Stink and Tasha and goes off with his camcorder. While videotaping the volcano, he gets trapped in a quicksand bog.

"Day for Knight"
Episode 8. A twelfth-century knight stumbles into the Land of the Lost and rescues Christa from Sleestaks. Kevin, who has a crush on Christa, is jealous of the attention the knight receives. Later, the knight commits several blunders and confesses to Kevin he has lied: He is not a knight, just a lowly squire.

"Flight to Freedom"
Episode 9. A series of earthquakes convinces Tom a new dimensional gate will materialize. So the Porters head for where Tom thinks the portal will appear. The family reaches the site. But Tasha and Stink have followed

them and are now cornered by a hungry T-Rex. The Porters must abort their escape or leave their their friends in danger.

"Mind Games"
Episode 10. Annie resents being the junior member of a male-dominated family and envies Christa's supposedly happy-go-lucky life. She spends a few days with Christa and is surprised to find that her way of life requires skill and hard work. Meanwhile, Shung finds one of Christa's keepsakes and uses it to establish a hypnotic mind control over her.

"Heatwave"
Episode 11. A hot spell dries up the local water hole, forcing Tom and Kevin to venture to the distant lake to refill the water gourds. But the drought also has driven the Sleestaks there. The Porters must have water, but if the Sleestaks spot them and locate their tree house, it will spell disaster for the family's survival.

"The Thief"
Episode 12. When things start disappearing from the tree house, Kevin is convinced that Stink is the culprit. Tom and Annie defend Stink. But as the robberies increase, even they soon have their doubts. Kevin storms off to nab "the little thief" and gets nabbed by the real thief.

"Power Play"
Episode 13. The last of the Porters' batteries finally dies, leaving them without flashlights, music or any other links to the twentieth century. Tom sets out alone, determined to find a replacement energy source in the form of crystals. This means venturing into Sleestak territory, where he winds up trapped in a cave with Shung.

"The Sorceress"
Episode 14. Annie befriends Keela, a sorceress banished to the Land of the Lost by an evil king. Keela uses her magic to entertain the Porters and turn Tasha into a talking dinosaur. But trouble follows: Keela is being pursued by Magas, a one-eyed beast who had been an evil sorcerer until Keela turned him into a monster.

"Dreammaker"

Episode 15. The Porters come upon a suburban street, right in the middle of the jungle, complete with their house. But the house turns sinister. Tasha is attacked by the refrigerator, the furniture menaces the kids and Tom's leg is pinned by the garage door. They ultimately discover an old Sleestak machine is responsible for creating the illusions.

"The Gladiators"

Episode 16. Shung uses his crystal on Christa to place her under his control and uses her to summon the Porters. When the family arrives, the Sleestaks capture them and lead them to an amphitheater where they are forced to fight each other for Shung's entertainment.

"Opah"

Episode 17. Kevin and Tasha find Opah, an old Paku who is Stink's grandfather. Stink is embarrassed by his grandfather's ways, especially his "musica," a wooden flute that has a hypnotic effect on the dinosaurs. But Stink changes his tune when Scarface threatens the family and Stink must use Opah's flute to save the day.

"Life's a Beach"

Episode 18. Stink shows the Porters, Tasha and Christa a beautiful beach, but the place makes Christa uncomfortable. While there, Annie befriends a "fish-man" creature named Namaki, who helps Christa recall the night she was separated from her family and left in the Land of the Lost.

"Future Boy"

Episode 19. After an argument with her father, Annie heads for the jungle, where she meets Simon Cardenas, who has just arrived from the future. Simon has borrowed his father's time belt to take a joy ride, only to collide with another time traveler, a dangerous alien cyborg. The collision dumped them both in the Land of the Lost.

"Siren's Song"

Episode 20. The Porters, Stink, Tasha and Christa spend the day on the beach with Namaki. But one by one, the Porters vanish without a trace as hypnotic music plays. Namaki, Tasha and Stink search for them and find that the Porters are being held by a shape-shifting siren (imprisoned by a serpent) and she wants them to become her family.

"In Dinos We Trust"
Episode 21. Kevin visits the Valley of Death to find bones to make tools out of, but an encounter with a spit-viper leaves him blind. He is forced to rely on Tasha to lead him home. They make it as far as the lake before they are set upon by Scarface. Tasha faces down the T-Rex, giving Tom and Christa a chance to drive him off.

"Annie in Charge"
Episode 22. When Tom discovers the tree house support poles have been damaged by termites, he leaves Annie in charge while he and Kevin go to cut new logs. Annie bosses Stink and Tasha around, while Tom and Kevin run afoul of the cyborg, who gasses them. When they awake, Tom's watch and their memories are gone.

"Go Ahead, Make My Day"
Episode 23. Stink explores some Sleestak ruins, where he finds a light-gun. With this weapon, Kevin is transformed into a macho tough guy, who goes looking to take on Scarface. Kevin fells the T-Rex but breaks the light-gun in the process. Then Shung shows up and grabs Tasha, demanding the weapon.

"Cheers"
Episode 24. Kevin tries to ask Christa out on a date, but he ends up tongue-tied. Meanwhile, Stink has discovered a bush of fermented fruit and gotten drunk. He shows it to Kevin, who also gets plastered. Tanked up on liquid courage, Kevin manages to ask Christa out, but his reliance on the demon drink creates more problems than it solves.

"Sorceress's Apprentice"
Episode 25. Keela asks Annie to guard her spell book without opening it. Annie finds a safe hiding place, but the temptation proves too much for her. Back at the tree house, Annie and Kevin argue, ending when Annie puts a spell on her brother. She goes back for the book so she can break the spell, only to find it taken by the Sleestaks.

"Misery Loves Company"
Episode 26. After an accident in which Stink falls off the tree house roof and hurts his ankle, Kevin carries Stink inside, tends his injuries and gives him a bicycle horn to honk when he needs something. Stink loves the attention and loves having Kevin at his beck and call. He calls often, until Tasha discovers that Stink is faking the injury.

Pufapalooza

Here are the episodes aired on September 16, 1995, during Nick at Nite's original Pufapalooza marathon:

1. *H.R. Pufnstuf:* "The Magic Path."

2. *Land of the Lost:* "The Stranger."

3. *Sigmund and the Sea Monsters:* "Puppy Love."

4. *H.R. Pufnstuf:* "The Stand-In."

5. *Live at the Hollywood Bowl.*

6. *ElectraWoman and DynaGirl:* "The Return of the Sorcerer."

7. *The Bugaloos:* "Firefly, Light My Fire."

8. *Lidsville:* "World in a Hat."

9. *H.R. Pufnstuf:* "The Mechanical Boy."

10. *Land of the Lost:* "Skylons."

11. *Sigmund and the Sea Monsters:* "Trick or Treat."

12. *ElectraWoman and DynaGirl:* "The Pharaoh."

13. *H.R. Pufnstuf:* "The Wheely Bird."

14. *The Bugaloos:* "Courage, Come Home."

15. *Lidsville:* "Show Me the Way to Go Home."

16. *Land of the Lost:* "Dopey."

Sid Gets the Last Word

The ultimate accomplishment in life is to love what you do for a living. To get paid for having this much fun makes it all the more incredible. Yet none of the wild and crazy ideas which I've been allowed to share with the world would have been possible without the contributions of hundreds of the most creative people who helped make my showbiz life a blast! I have searched through the English dictionary and my heart, and there isn't a word big enough to express my thanks to them.

My thanks as well to the fans of the Krofft insanity, who have enjoyed my madness for all these years. You're the best.

My deepest gratitude, however, I save for my loving brother and partner, Marty, who for the last thirty-eight years has made all my incredible dreams come true. You've earned my respect, you've had my love. What a trip it's been so far, and I promise you there's more to come.

SID KROFFT

Sources

Author Interviews

Jean Anderson (September 16, 1997).

Sharon Baird (August 10, 1997).

Joseph Barbera (April 14, 1994).

Billy Barty (June 26, 1997; July 11, 1997).

Michael Blodgett (October 8, 1997).

Ruth Buzzi (May 7, 1997).

Joy Campbell McKenzie (October 31, 1997).

Tony Charmoli (September 13, 1997).

Robin Dearden (September 26, 1997).

Bob Denver (April 1, 1997).

Louise DuArt (September 5, 1997).

Caroline Ellis (January 13, 1998).

Wesley Eure (September 3, 1997).

Allan Foshko (January 12, 1998).

Ron Harper (September 6, 1997).

Billie Hayes (April 30, 1997).

Deanna Krofft Pope (September 22, 1997).

Kendra Krofft (January 2, 1998).

Kristina Krofft (September 27, 1997).

Marty Krofft (September 4, 1996; May 15, 1997; June 20, 1997; August 12, 1997; September 3, 1997; September 23, 1997; September 29, 1997).

Sid Krofft (November 12, 1996; March 19, 1997; May 1, 1997; June 12, 1997; July 1, 1997; July 28, 1997; August 14, 1997; September 5, 1997; September 24, 1997).

Bill Laimbeer (October 3, 1997).

David Levy (September 26, 1997).

Patty Maloney (July 11, 1997).

Barbara Mandrell (December 5, 1997).

Chuck McCann (November 21, 1997).

Maureen McCormick (August 7, 1996; August 14, 1997).

John McIndoe (August 16, 1997).

Bill Morgan (July 17, 1997).

Jim Nabors (July 10, 1997).

Susan Olsen (January 27, 1995).

Donny Osmond (April 11, 1997).

Butch Patrick (October 14, 1996).

Cassandra Peterson (June 5, 1997).

Alan Rachins (September 8, 1997).

Jay Robinson (September 10, 1997).

Si Rose (June 13, 1997).

Van Snowden (July 11, 1997).

Lennie Weinrib (August 20, 1997).

John Whitaker (May 29, 1996).

Jack Wild (November 6, 1996).

Fred Willard (August 20, 1997).

Amy Yasbeck (November 19, 1997).

Ray Young (September 25, 1997).

Magazines and Newspapers

After Dark, Viola Hegyl Swisher, "About Those Midgets: Inside a Showbusiness Factory," September 1969.

Coast, Stephen M. Silverman, "Atlanta's High-Story Fantasy: The World of Krofft," September 1976.

Hollywood Reporter, "Kroffts Switch—Not Fight—To Family Entertainment," October 20, 1970.

Los Angeles Times, John L. Scott, "The Krofft 'Poupees': They've Got the World on a String," June 2, 1965.

USA Today, Jefferson Graham, "Krofft puppets get a hand back in TV," November 18, 1996.

Books

The Complete Directory to Science Fiction, Fantasy and Horror Television Series, Alan Morton, Other Worlds Books, 1997.

Get to the Heart: The Barbara Mandrell Story, Barbara Mandrell with George Vecsey, Bantam, 1990.

Growing Up Brady: I Was a Teenage Greg, Barry Williams with Chris Kreski, Harper, 1992.

Other Sources

Wesley Eure, Sci-Fi Channel interview.

Deidre Hall, on-line chats (May 14, 1996; September 23, 1996).

index

David Martindale.
PHOTO BY BRAD VAZQUEZ.

About the Author

It has been said that children of the 1960s and '70s frittered away their educations by watching far too many hours of television. David Martindale, a syndicated columnist whose weekly "Reruns" feature examines what's "old" on TV, made his love of television part of his education.

Born in 1960, Martindale was nine years old when *H.R. Pufnstuf* premiered. Twenty-seven years later, at age thirty-six, he met Sid and Marty Krofft. Less than a year later, he began his collaboration with the Kroffts on this book.

A former newspaper copy editor who worked at the *Houston Post,* the *Dallas Times-Herald* and the *Sporting News,* Martindale quit newspapering to become a full-time writer in 1990. His "Reruns" column launched in February 1993 in the *Houston Chronicle.* He also is a contributing editor to *Biography* magazine, writing a monthly "Where Are They Now?" column that is among the magazine's most popular features.

He lives in San Antonio, Texas, with Celeste Williams, his companion of seventeen years, and Shanney, a four-year-old Chihuahua.